£4

SUFFOLK AIRFIELDS IN THE SECOND WORLD WAR

Graham Smith

D1344040

COUNTRYSIDE BOOKS

NEWBURY, BERKSHIRE

First published 1995
© Graham Smith 1995
Reprinted 1997, 1999, 2001, 2004, 2008

All rights reserved. No reproduction
permitted without the prior permission
of the publishers:

COUNTRYSIDE BOOKS
3 Catherine Road
Newbury, Berkshire

To view our complete range of books,
please visit us at
www.countrysidebooks.co.uk

ISBN 978 1 85306 342 8

The cover painting shows a B-17 taxiing at Great Ashfield
and is reproduced from an original
by Colin Doggett

Designed by Mon Mohan

Produced through MRM Associates Ltd., Reading
Typeset by Paragon Typesetters, Clwyd
Printed by Cambridge University Press

*All material for the manufacture of this book
was sourced from sustainable forests.*

CONTENTS

SUFFOLK AIRFIELDS IN THE SECOND WORLD WAR

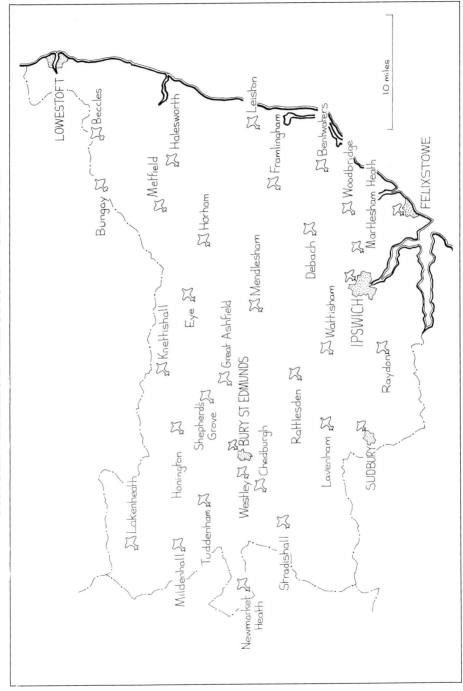

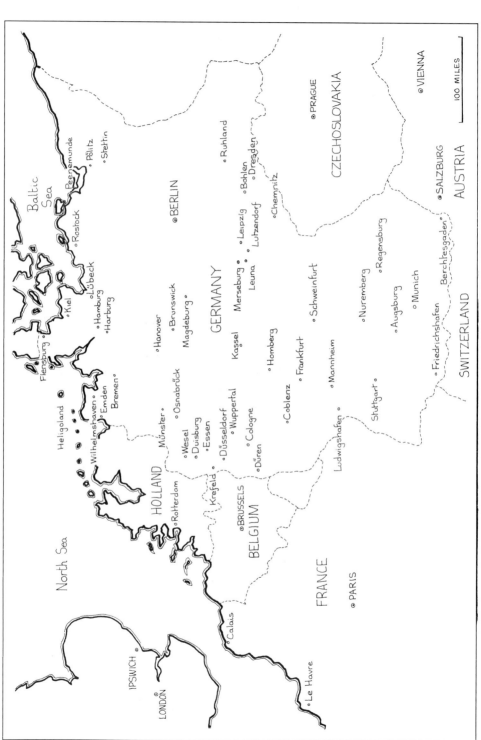

TARGETS OF RAF BOMBER COMMAND AND THE EIGHTH AIR FORCE

1

SETTING
THE SCENE

'The day war broke out' became a popular catch-phrase immortalised by the radio comedian Rob Wilton, and most people would afterwards clearly recall where they were and what they were doing on that historic day. The majority, of course, were at home anxiously awaiting the radio broadcast by the Prime Minister. At precisely 11.15 am on 3rd September 1939 Neville Chamberlain informed the nation that '... this country is now at war with Germany.'

Perhaps no RAF station more eagerly awaited the expected war signal than Wyton, which was situated near Peterborough. This airfield also housed the headquarters of No 2 Group, Bomber Command, where its Air Officer Commanding, Air Vice-Marshal C. Maclean, set in motion the first operational sortie of the war. Just one Bristol Blenheim of No 139 squadron took off shortly after mid-day on that Sunday. Within two hours the crew had managed to sight and photograph a strong force of German warships in the Schillig Roads outside the port of Wilhelmshaven. However, as they tried to pass this vital information back to Wyton they found that the aircraft's wireless equipment was not functioning properly due to the extreme cold encountered at 24,000 feet! It was therefore not until the aircraft arrived safely back at Wyton late in the afternoon that any further action could be mounted.

Considering that within three hours of war being declared a RAF aircraft had passed over the German frontier would suggest that the Service was not only at a high state of readiness but also very eager to take the attack to the enemy – as indeed the operations conducted

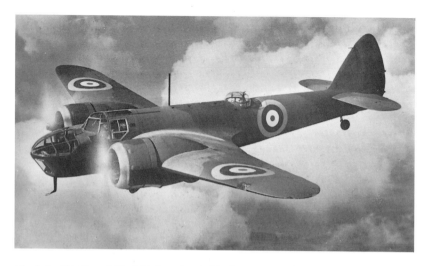

Blenheim IV: One of No 139 Squadron's Mark IVs made the first sortie of the war.

in the early months of the war fully attested. Nevertheless the big question was really how prepared and equipped was the RAF to face what would prove to be its sternest challenge?

In 1939 the RAF was still in its infancy having been formed on 1st April 1918 from the Royal Flying Corps and the Royal Naval Air Service. Although a year later it was, without doubt, the strongest air force in the world with over 380 squadrons, within three years nearly 90% of the Service had been virtually swept away. The saviour of the nascent Service proved to be its first Chief of Air Staff Sir Hugh Trenchard, who served in the post from 1919 to 1929. During this period not only did he fight doggedly for its very survival in the face of severe opposition from the other two Services, but he managed to build a Service which although small, was very professional, well trained and highly motivated. Trenchard thoroughly deserved the title of 'The Father of the RAF'.

It was Trenchard who established the Officer Cadet College at Cranwell as well as the Staff College for senior officers at Andover. Another brain-child of his was the Apprentices School at Halton, and those who passed out from there were quickly dubbed 'Trenchard brats'! He encouraged the formation of the Auxiliary Air Force, which provided a fine reservoir of trained pilots to call upon. It was the officers and men who had passed through such institutions, and later served with the Volunteer Reserve, that formed the backbone of the RAF for most of the critical early war years.

The story of the RAF during the early 1930s is a rather sorry tale of a variety of expansion schemes being approved only to be set aside and then abandoned by the politicians. Nevertheless, the redeeming features of the many schemes were that they brought forward specifications for various new aircraft that ultimately saw

Balloon barrage over London.

War is declared! (Daily Telegraph)

war service – the Wellington, Hampden, Stirling, Defiant, Hurricane and Spitfire. It was during this period that flying had so captured the public's imagination, largely through the Hendon Air Displays, Empire Air Days, the long distance record flights and the Schneider Trophy successes. Due to this great interest in aviation the RAF managed to attract many young men into the Service through their short service commission scheme and the Volunteer Reserve (formed in 1937).

The increasing belligerency of Nazi Germany and the rapid and frightening growth of the German Air Force greatly concentrated the minds of the politicians. Already, in June 1936, the Service had been divided into four separate and distinctly functional Commands – Bomber, Fighter, Coastal and Training – with the respective strengths of six, three, three and four Groups. The provision of new airfields, mainly in the east of the country, was accelerated and at long last resources were made available for a rapid expansion of aircraft production in a rather desperate attempt to make up the leeway that had been lost in 'The Days of the Locust', as the period was called when the RAF had suffered from a sad lack of interest.

In September 1939 the RAF numbered some 18,000 officers and men – about 15% of its total in the last year of the war. However ill-equipped and outnumbered the Service found itself in the early war years, all its members – be they regulars, reservists or volunteers – were utterly dedicated to their Service; this spirit and enthusiasm remained stern and steadfast throughout the darkest days of the war despite the intolerable demands that were placed upon them and the enormous sacrifices made by the aircrews. When faced by quite crippling losses of aircrews in the early years, the RAF never had to resort to conscription to replace their pilots and crews. Throughout the war all were volunteers, such was their devotion and dedication to the junior Service.

Although the RAF maintained a strong presence in Suffolk throughout the Second World War, it was mainly in the shape of Bomber Command rather than the other two operational Commands. However, for the last two years of the war the RAF was greatly outnumbered by the many Groups – both Bomber and Fighter – of the Eighth Air Force of the USAAF, who found welcoming homes in the Suffolk countryside. In order to understand the vital contribution made by Suffolk airfields during the war, it is necessary to examine these two mighty Air Forces in some detail and their aims and objectives during the air war over Europe.

Bomber Command

Although during the inter-war years there may have been many times when the very existence of the RAF as a separate and independent Service was called into doubt, there was never uncertainty as to its role in any future war. The overriding concept was that of a heavy and powerful bomber force striking into the heart of the enemy's territory, to destroy the enemy's means and will to wage war and thus obviate the need for crippling land battles as experienced in the First World War. The leading proponent of this doctrine was Sir Hugh Trenchard, who was utterly convinced that the main, if not the sole, reason for the RAF lay in the use of heavy bombers as a strategic strike force, with fighters playing a very minor role. Not for nothing was Trenchard called 'the patron saint of air power' by certain American Army Air officers.

Although Trenchard retired in 1929, his theories remained deeply ingrained in the Service and two of his most dedicated disciples – Sir Charles Portal and Sir Arthur Harris – were in positions of such power during the war that this concept of the all-powerful bomber force prevailed. Indeed, it would be argued that Bomber Command's tardy appreciation of the admirable Mosquito as a strike aircraft can be attributed to Trenchard's legacy.

The importance of the bomber force in the pre-war Service resulted in the bomber pilots becoming the elite of the RAF, almost a privileged class, and its most prestigious trophies – the Laurence Minot and Sasoon – were competed for by squadrons on the accuracy of their bombing. It was not until the Battle of Britain that the daring and valiant exploits of 'The Few' stole the thunder from their colleagues in Bomber Command.

In September 1939 Bomber Command had at its disposal 850 aircraft in 53 squadrons. However, within days ten squadrons of Fairey Battles were despatched to France to form the Advanced Air Striking Force (AASF), later to be followed by two squadrons of Bristol Blenheims. Furthermore 17 squadrons were immediately withdrawn from the front line to form Operational Training Units and another three were non-operational. So effectively the Command's strength was 23 squadrons or about 350 aircraft.

Nos 2 and 3 Groups were mainly based in East Anglia and equipped with Bristol Blenheims and Vickers Wellingtons

Air Chief Marshal Sir Arthur Harris with his deputy, Air Marshal Sir Robert Saundby. (RAF Museum)

respectively. The much loved Wellingtons were the Command's newest heavy twin-engined bombers, having come into service in the early months of 1939. In Suffolk there were two squadrons of Bristol

13

*The badges of two famous bomber squadrons: No
9 served at Honington, No 15 at Mildenhall.*

Blenheims at Wattisham. At Mildenhall and Honington there were a
total of three squadrons of Wellingtons, but Stradishall, despite being
a permanent airfield, was then under 'care and maintenance'. No 4
Group with airfields in Yorkshire had five squadrons of Armstrong
Whitworth Whitleys and further south in Lincolnshire were based six
squadrons of Handley Page Hampdens of No 5 Group. This Group
would, within weeks, be commanded by Air Vice-Marshal Arthur
Harris – who would ultimately become *the* most redoubtable Chief
of Bomber Command. These Whitleys and Hampdens, the first of the
new generation of heavy bombers to see service in 1938, along with
the Wellingtons and Blenheims would form the Command's strike
force for the early years of the war. In France the single-engined
Battles, along with the Blenheims from No 2 Group, would fight a
short but valiant battle against overwhelming odds and superior
opposition.

In the early months of the war the main objective of Bomber
Command was to aid the Royal Navy in imposing and maintaining
a strict blockade of German ports as well as to seek out the German
fleet and attack it, providing, of course, that it was at sea at the time!
In France the Battle squadrons, aided by Blenheims, were to give
tactical support to the British and French armies. Allied to these tasks
the Command was involved in dropping propaganda leaflets over
Germany by night. The official code-name for these operations was
'Nickel', but the aircrews referred to them as 'confetti throwing' and
Air Vice-Marshal Harris was more trenchant in his comments,
likening the whole operation to 'supplying the Continent's
requirements for toilet paper for the next five years'! Nevertheless,
these operations did provide valuable long-distance night flying
experience, especially in the early months of 1940 when the targets
were extended as far afield as Austria, Poland and Czechoslovakia.

Many of the early anti-shipping missions, mostly photo-reconnaissance flights, were made by the Blenheim squadrons. They turned out to be rather costly (about a loss rate of 19.5% of the sorties flown). But it was not until December 1939 that the Chiefs at Bomber Command were abruptly forced to recognise that the hallowed ethos of strategic daylight bombing was likely to prove very costly in men and machines. In two utterly disastrous operations on 14th and 18th December no less than 17 Wellingtons out of a total bombing force of 34 failed to return from shipping strikes near Wilhelmshaven. These two ill-fated missions made nonsense of the theory that a close formation of heavy bombers flying in daylight would defend themselves against enemy fighters.

There was no dramatic announcement of Bomber Command's volte-face, it was more a matter of reluctantly accepting the reality that if the German industries were to be attacked by day then the heavy bombers would require fighter escorts – Spitfires. However, the Spitfire, then, lacked the range and in any case the precious few squadrons were needed for the air defence of Great Britain. Therefore the only other alternative available to Bomber Command was to use its heavy bombers unescorted and by night. It was a policy that would be pursued whole-heartedly by Bomber Command and with great courage and determination by its heavy bomber crews for most of the war. Daylight operations were largely left to the Blenheims and their successors – Bostons, Venturas, Mitchells and, of course, Mosquitos.

If there were any residual doubts about the wisdom of the change of strategy, these were rapidly dissipated after 12th April 1940, when the largest bombing operation of the war was mounted against shipping at Stavanger in daylight. Of the 60 Wellingtons and Hampdens engaged in the mission nine were lost to heavy flak and fighters – a loss rate of 15%. This operation proved to be decisive for Air Chief Marshal Charles Portal, who had taken over Bomber Command at the end of March, and in future he used his heavy bombers solely at night.

The so-called Phoney War – a term conjured up by an American politician to describe the apparent lack of action up to the end of March 1940 – came to an abrupt end with the German invasion of Denmark and Norway on 9th April followed one month later (10th May) by their offensive against the Low Countries and France. The war in the air took a most dramatic turn and on the night of 11/12th May 37 aircraft – Hampdens and Whitleys – bombed München

Gladbach, the first raid of the war on a German town. Four nights later over 100 bombers attacked 16 different targets in the Ruhr. These raids signalled the start of Bomber Command's strategic offensive against Germany, which would continue almost unabated for the next five years.

By the end of May the Air Ministry had issued certain bombing directives. There were to be four specific 'priority' targets – aircraft factories, ammunition factories, oil-producing plants and road and rail communications. It was then thought that 75% of Germany's industrial production was centred in the Ruhr and names such as Dortmund, Duisburg, Düsseldorf, Cologne, Essen, Münster, Hamm and Krefeld were regularly heard on BBC news broadcasts as heavy targets for 'strong forces of Bomber Command', followed later in the year by Kiel, Bremen, Hamburg, Mannheim, Osnabrück and Hanover as the Command's operations became more ambitious.

With the entry, in June, of Italy into the war, Italian targets were bombed, which resulted in a round trip of 1,350 miles and even though the bombing results were not that successful, it was a striking demonstration of the growing confidence of Bomber Command. However, the next priority for Bomber Command was to attack the so-called 'invasion ports' along the Dutch and French coasts, as well as the airfields in occupied countries ranging from Southern Norway to Northern France in an attempt to hinder the mass attacks being launched against the country. These latter attacks were undertaken with great bravery by Blenheim crews and they proved to be very costly.

Avro Lancaster II: the most outstanding heavy bomber of the war.

On the night of 24/25th August 1940 the first German bombs fell, in error, on central London and on the following night about 50 Hampdens and Wellingtons attempted to bomb specific targets in Berlin, but because of heavy cloud they were frustrated. A couple more missions were mounted in the next few weeks and were equally unsuccessful. However, they did strike a blow at the morale of Berliners, who were reported to be 'stunned' as they were firmly convinced that such raids would never happen. These raids were purely and simply reprisal or morale-boosting operations that had been demanded by Winston Churchill. Bomber Command was not in a position to launch a major offensive on the German capital until March 1943. These early operations did, however, result in the Luftwaffe unleashing its all-out bomber offensive on London and other cities and towns.

Largely as a result of Coventry and Southampton being heavily bombed in November 1940, the War Cabinet authorised Bomber Command to mount its first major 'area' operation – a general attack on a German city centre. The operation was code-named Abigail Rachel and Mannheim was chosen as the target. On the night of 16/17th December 134 aircraft, the largest force launched so far, bombed but not too successfully. In the next three months Düsseldorf, Bremen, Wilhelmshaven, Kiel, Cologne and Hamburg were targeted for 'area' bombing, although the Germans called them 'terror raids'.

In February 1941 the first of the new four-engined bombers came into service. The Short Stirling arrived at squadrons, to be followed two weeks later by a small number of Avro Manchesters; the latter turned out to be not a particularly successful aircraft and its chief claim to fame was as the forerunner of the mighty Lancaster. The following month saw yet another new heavy bomber make its appearance – the Handley Page Halifax. This proved to be a most popular and very successful aircraft and it spearheaded Bomber Command's raids to Germany until the appearance of the Lancaster in March 1942.

March saw a change of operations with a directive to attack the French Atlantic ports, which not only harboured the U-boats but also some of the German Navy's major vessels – the *Scharnhorst* and *Gneisenau* (nicknamed Salmon and Gluckstein by the RAF crews after a well-known group of tobacconists). These operations proved to be most costly – the ports were heavily protected by flak batteries – without producing many positive results, as the bombs used were quite inadequate to cause other than superficial damage to the deep

Handley Page Halifax: a most successful and popular bomber.

defences of the U-boat shelters. It was soon recognised that the Command's resources would best be employed against German industries, so it was back to the 'Happy Valley' as the Ruhr was called by the airmen.

From July to mid-November 1941 the Command's aircraft were active almost every day and every night. Many of the night operations exceeded the critical 5% loss rate – the maximum acceptable operational limit; indeed several missions to Berlin exceeded 10%. The daylight operations were also proving very costly – the famous Blenheim raid on the Cologne power stations resulted in over 15% losses and they were also suffering heavily for their part in the anti-shipping offensive in the English Channel. Clearly no Command could sustain such heavy losses for very long and still remain operational. During this period the Command lost no less than 526 aircraft, which was effectively their total front line strength.

However, what was even more damaging was the report requested by the Air Ministry and which was based on two months' (June and July) photographic evidence of bombed targets. This report, compiled by R.M. Butt, a senior civil servant, revealed that only one quarter of aircraft came within five miles of the aiming point and in the raids over the Ruhr, where the intense flak and industrial haze greatly affected the bombing, this figure dropped alarmingly to barely one-tenth. Furthermore it was already known from de-briefings that almost one-third of returning crews freely admitted that they had not managed to bomb the primary targets. Faced with such a damning indictment, serious questions were raised about the whole of the Command's strategic bombing policy, which was proving so very costly in men and machines. The crisis came to a head on the night of 7/8th November when Sir Richard Peirse, the Chief of Bomber Command, mounted a major operation on Berlin. No less than 21 aircraft were lost (12.4%), and on the night's operations – Mannheim and Cologne were also bombed – the Command lost a total of 37 aircraft.

This very serious crisis of confidence obviously did not filter down to the aircrews, or indeed to the British public; both firmly believed the Air Ministry's confident and brash propaganda that heavy damage was being inflicted nightly on Germany, which was materially affecting its war efforts. Somewhat strangely when Bomber Command was at such a low ebb, a documentary film about its operations *Target for Tonight* was released and quickly proved a resounding success. This film along with the publication *Bomber Command* graphically portrayed the bravery and dedication of the bomber crews, or 'the gentlemen of the shade, minions of the moon' as they were described by the Air Ministry.

Sir Richard Peirse was made somewhat of a scapegoat for the ills of his Command although they were not of his making. Perhaps in recognition of this, he was given command of the Allied Air Forces in south-east Asia, which enabled Sir Charles Portal to appoint the one officer he wanted to lead Bomber Command and furthermore to carry out an offensive 'focused on the morale of the enemy civil population and in particular that of the industrial workers'. This latest bombing directive was issued on 14th February 1942, with the added caveat 'to use the utmost resources at all times'. Not only had Bomber Command survived but it had been given the green light to expand.

Just eight days later the new Commander-in-Chief arrived – Air Chief Marshal Arthur Harris – who was destined to direct operations for the duration of the war. It is reputed that Winston Churchill coined the sobriquet 'Bomber', although to his crews he was known as 'Butch'. Harris prosecuted the bombing offensive with a grim determination and, at times, an unbridled ruthlessness. A born leader, he quickly gained a fierce and undying loyalty from all the men under his command.

Very swiftly, Harris showed his mettle as a commander with the famous raid on the old town of Lübeck on 28/29th March. Four similar raids were made on Rostock towards the end of April, when

Goebbels called them 'terrorangriff' or 'horror raids' and was forced to admit that 'community life in Rostock is practically at an end'. They did, of course, bring forth the retaliatory 'Baedeker' attacks on Bath, Canterbury, Exeter, York and Norwich.

The following two months saw the three famous 1,000 bomber raids on Cologne, Essen and Bremen. Every possible aircraft was brought into action, including training flights and some aircraft 'borrowed' from Coastal Command. These 'Greatest Air Raids in History', as the newspapers proclaimed them, did much to lift the morale of the British public. Bomber Command seemed to be the only force taking the offensive to the enemy. Harris put it very succinctly: 'They have sowed the wind, now they will reap the whirlwind.'

A most important step was taken in August when the first Pathfinder squadron was formed. This was in spite of Harris's scepticism as to its need or indeed worth, in fact he was against any move that smacked of elitism in the Service. The task of the Pathfinders was to mark the target areas in front of the main bomber force. This squadron was not overly successful in its early operations but it quickly developed into a potent and influential force, which in January 1943 would become a new Group of Bomber Command – No 8.

At the beginning of 1943 the major Allied conference at Casablanca came to an agreement on the Allied bombing strategy for the remainder of the war – at least except for certain minor changes in the priorities. The directive known as 'Pointblank' stated that 'the primary aim will be the progressive destruction and dislocation of the German military, industrial and economic system and the undermining of the morale of the German people to a point where their capacity for armed resistance is fatally weakened'. It listed the essential targets in order of priority – U-boat yards and bases, the German air force and its factories, ball-bearing plants, the oil industry and rail and road transportation. Air Marshal Harris was utterly confident that his Command was ready, willing and equipped for this next phase of the air offensive.

Certainly this confidence was not misplaced. The Lancasters and Halifaxes were now fully established as the main heavy strike force, with new light or medium bombers such as the Venturas and Mitchells coming into operational use. The 'wonder' aircraft – the de Havilland Mosquito – made its first famous raid on Berlin on 30th January and would play an increasing part in the Command's operations. Technical improvements were on the up and up with the blind-bombing device, Oboe already proving highly successful. At

Runnymede Memorial commemorating 20,455 members of the British and Commonwealth air forces who lost their lives operating from Great Britain and Europe, and have no known graves.

the end of January the airborne ground-scanning radar set – H2S – was first used by Pathfinder aircraft. Later in the year an increasing number of technical aids, radar jamming equipment and other devices would be brought into operational use.

Much of February 1943 was taken up with operations against the U-boat bases on the French Atlantic coast but in the first week of March Bomber Command was back to German targets with a vengeance. What is now known as the Battle of the Ruhr started on 5/6th March with an attack on the Krupps works at Essen, and the raids continued until July. This was shortly followed by Operation Gomorrah – the devastating fire-raids on Hamburg. In May and August there were the highly publicised individual operations against the three dams and the rocket research centre at Peenemunde. The 23/24th August saw the opening of the Battle of Berlin, which continued until March 1944, by which time over 30,000 tons of bombs had been dropped on the German capital. The 19 major raids which formed this bitter battle resulted in the loss of over 600 aircraft and their crews.

The threat of the V1 rockets at the end of 1943 resulted in a large amount of the resources of Bomber Command being diverted to their sites in northern France. However, when they returned to German targets in early 1944 the Command suffered some heavy losses, which could only be sustained because of the numbers of aircraft and trained crews that now were coming forward. Magdeburg in January and Leipzig in February were particularly costly operations but both paled into insignificance with the Nuremberg raid of 30/31st March, when 795 aircraft set out for this vital industrial centre and railway junction in southern Germany and 95 aircraft failed to return; another twelve crashed on reaching the English coast. It was the heaviest loss sustained by Bomber Command throughout the war. Just two weeks later the overall control of Bomber Command (and the USAAF) was passed to General Eisenhower, the Supreme Allied Commander in Europe, and much of the Command's forces were diverted to the preparations and support of Operation Overlord – the invasion of mainland Europe.

The targets now were the coastal batteries along the French coast, German airfields in France and road and rail communications in France and Belgium, particularly those within a 150 mile radius of Caen. These latter targets were all part of the Transportation Plans, which had been closely debated because of the high risk of heavy civilian casualties. Both Harris and General Spaatz, the Commander of the US Strategic Air Force were opposed to the operations mainly on the grounds that their combined air forces would be better deployed in continuing their offensive on Germany's oil industries and its airfields. Nevertheless the plans were approved and Bomber Command was allocated 37 rail targets in northern France and Belgium and by D-Day well over half of these targets were utterly destroyed. After the Normandy landings the Command was involved in giving support to the Allied armies, notably at Caen and the Falaise Gap.

The first V1 rocket fell on Britain on 13/14th June 1944 and from then until the middle of September the Command was heavily engaged on attacking the rocket sites. But by mid-August the Lancasters and Halifaxes were back over Germany and on 27th August it launched its first major daylight operation for over three years. The target was an oil refinery at Homberg and the bomber force was escorted by Spitfires there and back and not a single aircraft was lost. In mid-September the battleship *Tirpitz* was attacked in a fjord in northern Norway – the Lancasters used the 12,000lb Tallboy bombs with great success as they did ten days later to breach the Dortmund-Ems Canal.

On 13th October a directive for Operation Hurricane was issued 'to apply within the shortest practical period the maximum effort against objectives in the densely populated Ruhr'. The following day Duisburg was attacked by over 1,200 bombers and on the following night by another 1,000 bombers. In just 24 hours the Command made 2,589 sorties for the loss of 24 aircraft, a record not to be exceeded. Then, to close a most successful year of bombing, there was the famous and dramatic low-level attack by Mosquitos on the Gestapo headquarters in Oslo.

By January 1945 Bomber Command was at the zenith of its power. With over 1,600 aircraft at its disposal it was a highly technical and superbly professional force that could attack with terrifying and awesome power. In the first four months of the year it conducted 36 major operations over Germany dropping 180,000 tons of bombs, which was one-fifth of the total tonnage used throughout the war. On the 16th April it was announced that all the objectives of 'Pointblank' had been achieved and that only necessary operations should be mounted over Germany. The night of 20/21st saw the last Mosquito raid on Berlin, the end of the so-called 'Berlin shuttle'. Then on 25th April Air Marshal Harris rather indulged himself with two separate operations; one against the island of Wangerooge, where over five years earlier Bomber Command had suffered its first defeat, and the other against Hitler's mountain retreat, the Eagle's Nest at Berchtesgaden. The following night 107 Lancasters with 12 Mosquitos attacked an oil refinery at Tonsberg in southern Norway. One of the Lancasters came down in Sweden, the last of more than 3,300 Lancasters lost during the war. But by now victory in Europe was assured and so close at hand. The last offensive action by Bomber Command took place on 2/3rd May against Kiel and was undertaken rather appropriately by Mosquitos. The final operations were Exodus and Manna. The first brought home prisoners of war and the second, as its name suggests, involved flying food missions to the starving Dutch people.

In the last 20 years or so much heated debate has centred on Bomber Command's contribution to the defeat of Germany, and perhaps even more has been written on Air Chief Marshal Harris's methods and the use of the forces under his command, especially during the last six months of the war – the destruction of Darmstadt and Dresden have both been strongly condemned.

Without doubt the strategic bombing policy was very costly in human terms – 55,500 airmen killed, 8,403 wounded and 9,838 made prisoner of war with the loss of 10,724 aircraft. It is most sobering to reflect that Bomber Command's casualties amounted to one-seventh of *all* British deaths by land, sea and air for the whole of the war. Of the 32 Victoria Crosses awarded during the war, 19 went to members of Bomber Command. The contribution made by the crews of Bomber Command to the ultimate victory was massive.

Air Chief Marshal Harris stoutly maintained that insufficient official recognition was made to his men of Bomber Command. Indeed more honour has been given to the airmen of the Battle of Britain, although fewer airmen died in that battle than were lost in just *one* Bomber Command operation to Nuremberg in March 1944! The enormous sacrifice made by the young men of Bomber Command has probably been best remembered by their own Commander, 'Bomber' Harris, who wrote in 1947: 'There are no words with which I can do justice to the aircrew who fought under my command. There is no parallel in warfare to such courage and determination in the face of danger over so prolonged a period...It was the courage of men with long drawn apprehensions of daily "going over the top". Such devotion must never be forgotten.'

The United States Army Air Force

In retrospect 20th February 1942 may be seen as a major turning point in the strategic air offensive against Germany. It was on that day that a Douglas DC-3 of the USAAF landed at RAF Hendon bringing Brigadier General Ira Eaker and six of his fellow Air Force officers; their orders were to prepare the way for the entry of the American Army Air Force into the 'European Theater of Operations' (ETO).

The timing of the American airmen's appearance could really not have been more propitious. It almost coincided with the appointment of Arthur Harris as the new Commander-in-Chief of Bomber Command. Harris had only just returned from America where for much of the previous year he had been based in Washington. He was therefore well acquainted with many senior American Air Force officers, understood and appreciated their different methods of operations and furthermore was well aware of their needs. It was

Lieutenant General Ira A. Eaker, C.O. of the Eighth Air Force from 1942 to 1944.
(Smithsonian)

vitally important for the future conduct of the European air war that the two Commanders should work well together, and indeed Eaker and Harris became personal friends.

There was, of course, a very sharp dichotomy over the methods of bombing. The Americans were completely dedicated to high-altitude precision bombing with large formations of self-defending bombers operating in daylight. For this kind of aerial warfare they considered that they had the best weapons – the Boeing B-17 and the Consolidated B-24 – better known to the British as the Flying Fortress

25

and the Liberator respectively. Each was equipped with an excellent oxygen system and the 'wonder' Norden bomb-sight, which had been developed in 1933, and was believed to be deadly accurate. Eaker was well aware of Bomber Command's rather unsuccessful operations with a small number of Flying Fortresses in the previous summer but was undeterred by those experiences, as he and other American officers were firmly convinced that the aircraft had not been used to their best advantage. All the faults that had been found by the RAF operations were being rectified by the Boeing company back in Seattle, so it would be vastly improved aircraft that would arrive to serve with the Eighth Air Force. The B-24 or Liberator, because of its long range was used by the RAF mainly in an anti-shipping role with Coastal Command.

Eaker represented a fledgling organisation. The American Army Air Force, as such, had only been redesignated on 20th June 1941 with Major General H.H. 'Hap' Arnold as its Commander, and the Eighth Air Force had been formed on 2nd January 1942 , though it was first known as the 'Fifth' only to be renumbered just four days later. This Air Force was originally planned to provide the air support for an invasion of North Africa but when that operation was postponed, Major General Carl Spaatz, the designated Commander in Europe, persuaded the Army chiefs in Washington that the Eighth should move to England to form the nucleus of the USAAF in Europe.

The original planned build-up of the Eighth Air Force was not only most ambitious but quite staggering in its immensity – no less than 60 combat groups comprising 17 Heavy, 10 Medium and 6 Light Bombardment (Bomb) Groups, 12 Fighter, 8 Transport and 7 Observation Groups, making in all a total of 3,500 aircraft by April 1943 with all the other backroom units to support this massive force. If this figure was realised then the Eighth Air Force would be larger than the whole of the RAF's three operational Commands then serving in Great Britain. That this original plan was modified and changed by the dictates of the supply of aircraft, operational needs and the demands of other theatres of war, did not alter the fact that the Eighth became an enormously powerful Air Force. Its famed sobriquet, the 'Mighty', was not solely related to its sheer size, but also for the brave and valiant operations that it mounted, sometimes at a very heavy cost.

Obviously the first demand of such a force was airfields and it was estimated that no less than 75 would be required, virtually all in the east of England. Bomber Command airfields normally housed two squadrons and since the American Bomb Groups comprised four squadrons, it was anticipated that each Group would need to occupy two airfields, although this policy was changed quite early on, with the result that each Group – Bomb or Fighter – ultimately had its own airfield. The sheer amount of planning and all the logistics involved in accommodating such a vast Air Force was a massive undertaking and the debt the Eighth Air Force owed to Eaker and his small band of dedicated and hard-working officers was immense.

The Eighth comprised a separate Bomber and Fighter Command. Eaker was the Bomber Commander-in-Chief until the end of 1943 and he took it through its growing pains and its most critical period. The Bomber Command would ultimately be composed of three Bomb Divisions (later redesignated 'Air'). The Fighter Command, under Brigadier General Frank Hunter, was planned to have three Wings. However, the nature of the bombing offensive, a serious shortage of suitable fighters and the pressure of the North African campaign resulted in its build-up becoming that much slower.

The first units began to arrive in May 1942 with the first B-17s

'Big Picture' completed by S/Sgt Waldschmidt of 92nd Bomb Group – now on display at IWM, Duxford.

appearing in July along with the Lockheed P-38s (Lightnings), then without doubt the best long-range fighter in operation. The B-17s moved into Polebrook and Grafton Underwood in the East Midlands and the other Groups of the First Bomb Wing (later First Division) would mainly find homes in the same area, whilst subsequently the Bomb Groups of the Second and Third Divisions would be based in Norfolk and Suffolk.

The first USAAF involvement in the European air war came on 29th June 1942 when just one American crew joined No 226 squadron at RAF Swanton Morley in Norfolk for a raid on northern France. Then on 4th July (Independence Day) six crews from the 15th Bomb Squadron (Light) 'borrowed' six RAF Douglas Bostons to accompany six RAF aircraft on a bombing mission of enemy airfields. This was the first Eighth Air Force operation of the war and resulted in its first casualties and first medal awards. However, two aircraft failed to return, which made it a not too auspicious start.

It was not until 17th August that the first heavies were ready to try their luck over enemy territory. On this historic mission twelve B-17s of 97th Bomb Group took off from Grafton Underwood. The formation was led by Colonel Frank Armstrong, the Group's Commanding Officer and one of the original six officers that arrived with Eaker. On this first mission Eaker sneaked a ride in the rather appropriately named *Yankee Doodle*. The target was Rouen and the bombers were escorted by RAF Spitfires. All the aircraft arrived back safely though two were superficially damaged by enemy flak. Air Marshal Harris sent a congratulatory message to Eaker: 'Yankee Doodle certainly went to town and you can stick another well-earned feather in his cap'! However, it would be another six months before the Eighth would make a significant contribution to the air offensive over Germany.

The two Fighter Groups – No 31 equipped with Spitfires, and No 1 with the very scarce and valuable P-38s – saw some action towards the end of the month. Then on 29th September the three 'Eagle' squadrons of RAF Fighter Command were formally handed over to the Eighth Air Force to become the 4th Fighter Group. Ten days later the first B-24s entered the action over Lille and of the 24 aircraft sent on the mission, one was lost to enemy flak. Indeed, on the operation (9th October) the Eighth managed to despatch no less than 108 heavy bombers, which was quite an achievement in such a short space of time, and this figure would not be bettered until April 1943.

The build-up of the Eighth was slow and painful and it was not until 27th January 1943 that it was able to launch its first operation over a German target – Wilhelmshaven naval base – and on this occasion three aircraft were lost. In the first six months of its operations the Eighth had lost over 70 heavy bombers missing in action or damaged beyond repair as well as many destroyed in accidents. This was a large proportion of what Eaker once described as 'my piddling little force'. It had become patently obvious that the theory of the self-defensive bomber formation was not really working in practice and that such crippling losses would still continue, or even increase, until a strong fighter escort force became available. However, the P-38s had been diverted to the Twelfth Air Force, which was involved in Operation Torch – the North African campaign – and they would not reappear in England for another year. In their place came the Republic P-47s (Thunderbolts), which although proving themselves to be very strong and effective fighters, were rather limited in their operational range even when supplied with special drop fuel tanks.

Throughout the spring and early summer of 1943, the Eighth, despite heavy losses, continued to wage a most courageous and valiant offensive against the targets laid down in the 'Pointblank' directive. Some of the missions proved to be very costly – Bremen in April a 14% loss – but nevertheless the Eighth's chiefs held their nerve and doggedly persevered with the daylight operations, convinced in their own minds that ultimately such bombing would prove decisive. Little did they know that losses sustained in some major operations later in the year would put even greater strain on their faith in daylight formation bombing.

However, there was one major change to the original operational plans of the Eighth. The early missions with the medium bombers – B-26 Marauders – had proved anything but successful and some were very costly affairs. Eaker did not consider that these squadrons sat easily in a Command which was dedicated to a heavy bomber offensive and therefore he 'retired' them to purely support duties, at least until they could be transferred to the Ninth Air Force later in the year.

The high losses sustained by the Eighth in the second half of 1943 can be largely attributed to the lack of long-range fighters but were also brought about by the massive increase in the Luftwaffe's day-fighter force. In the early months of 1943 the German High Command had not taken the American daylight offensive too seriously, but as the numbers of heavy bombers slowly increased over German

A B-17 being bombed up with a suitable message! (Daily Telegraph)

targets, it was decided to vastly increase the Luftwaffe forces based in Germany and fighters were pulled back from other war fronts, especially in the east. In a few short months the Luftwaffe day-fighters had almost doubled to 800, mainly Me109s and Fw190s. This proved to be a most critical air battle, which continued until the last months of the war.

The first major contest came in August 1943 on the anniversary of the Eighth's first full operation in Europe. The names of Schweinfurt and Regensburg have now passed into the annals of American Air Force history, so brutal and bloody was the mission – 60 aircraft out of a total force of 376 were lost! Far worse was to follow. On 6th September came the most costly mission to Stuttgart, now considered the Eighth's most disastrous operation of the war. Before the end of the month (27th) the Eighth had launched its first Pathfinder (PFF) mission with some of their B-17s using the RAF's H2S device. Then in October, in just seven days, the Eighth mounted major raids to Bremen, Anklam, Marienburg, Gdynia and Münster before finally returning to Schweinfurt again. Over 1,400 sorties were flown and

173 aircraft were lost along with 1,500 airmen; another 60 aircraft and 600 men failed to return from the second Schweinfurt raid and this day became known as 'Black Thursday'.

In October the USAAF in England suddenly increased in size when the Ninth Air Force was reformed after service in the Middle East. It was intended to operate alongside the RAF's 2nd Tactical Air Force in preparation for the ultimate invasion of Europe and subsequently to give air support to the Allied armies. It operated with medium bombers – A-20s and B-26s – from airfields mainly in Essex, with most of the Fighter Groups installed in advanced landing grounds in Kent. Although it became a large Air Force in its own right, with over 20,000 personnel, because it did not occupy any Suffolk airfields (except for Raydon for a short period) its operations have not been detailed.

On 1st December the first North American P-51s (Mustangs) began to appear in the USAAF. This legendary long-range fighter, which was destined to make such an impact on the air war, was first placed with the Ninth Air Force in a ground attack role, and it was almost three months before its true metier was recognised – as a superb long-range pursuit fighter.

January 1944 ushered in several changes. It saw the formation of the United States Strategic Air Force in Europe (USSTAF) with General Spaatz returning from North Africa to take over the new organisation. He brought with him Lt General James H. Doolittle, who was given command of the Eighth Air Force, whilst Eaker was sent to oversee air affairs in the Mediterranean. Doolittle was destined to command the Eighth Air Force for the rest of the war, even after it had moved from Europe to the Pacific.

On 11th January, only five days after his arrival, the Eighth's B-17s encountered very heavy fighter opposition over Oschersleben and Halberstadt – both having important aircraft factories, when 42 were lost out of a total of 291 aircraft. It did not augur well for Doolittle's planned major offensive against the German aircraft industry, which was code-named Operation Argument. In just five days of concentrated action, from 20th February, over 3,000 aircraft were involved in bombing targets throughout Germany for the loss of 177 aircraft with nearly 500 enemy fighters claimed to have been destroyed. These operations became known as 'The Big Week' and although expensive in terms of men and aircraft, such losses could now be contained because of the avalanche of new crews and replacement aircraft arriving almost daily from the States.

As the RAF's long and bitter Battle of Berlin was reaching a conclusion in the early spring, the Eighth Air Force's chiefs knew that it was time for their Force to attack the same ultimate target in Germany. Five operations were mounted in March. The first resulted in just a handful of aircraft making their way and bombing the target and the first full raid, on the 6th, proved to be a rather costly affair. The American aircrews, like their counterparts in RAF Bomber Command, felt some dread and apprehension when the red ribbon on the briefing map disclosed the long haul to Berlin and they knew they would have to face its intense and fearsome flak defences.

On 12th May, the Eighth commenced their assault on the German oil industry; the targets that day included Merseburg, Lutzendorf, Zwickau, Brux, Bohlen and Zeitz. These places, along with many others, would figure large in the minds of American crews over the next six months or so. Indeed the Eighth's concentrated offensive against the oil industry was a major contribution to the demise of the Luftwaffe as a fighting force, their aircraft, as well as the Wehrmacht's armoured divisions, slowly being starved of fuel. But it was a victory that exacted a very high cost; no other single priority target caused the loss of so many American airmen and aircraft.

By June 1944 the Eighth Air Force was at the height of its strength and power – a massive force of heavy bombers with B-17s in the preponderance and backed by a huge number of fighters, still mainly P-47s. On D-Day over 2,500 bomber sorties were made with the fighters flying almost continuous escorts and patrols. During the day Lt General Doolittle and his deputy Major General Earle Partridge each flew a P-38 to view their Force's performance over the beachhead and behind the enemy's front lines.

However, before the month was out the Eighth was back to German targets and more specifically oil. From now on until the end of the war their operations would be mounted at a rapid rate, in great numbers and on a grand scale. On many operations the Eighth worked much closer with RAF Bomber Command and several targets were being bombed both day and night – a notable example was Dresden in February 1945. Certainly 'round the clock' bombing had become a grim and dread reality for many German cities. This was a bombing philosophy that both Eaker and Harris had envisaged in 1942, but which had all too infrequently been achieved.

During September B-24s were dropping supplies to the US airborne forces at Nijmegen and Eindhoven and then two months later the

'Wall of the Missing' in the American War Cemetery and Memorial at Madingley, near Cambridge.

heavies were bombing German positions around Aachen prior to a ground offensive. However, their biggest role as a tactical strike force came in December in support of the Ardennes campaign. On Christmas Eve a maximum effort was called for and over 2,000 heavy bombers attacked targets in western Germany. This proved to be the largest air strike ever mounted by the Eighth Air Force, although it was almost equalled on 24th March 1945 in support of Operation Varsity – the Allied armies' crossing of the Rhine.

As an increasing number of P-51 fighters came into operation so they made their presence felt on mission after mission. However, the appearance of both the rocket propelled Me163 and the Me262 jet fighter did cause deep concern. It was readily acknowledged that should they arrive in sufficient numbers then they would pose a great threat to the Eighth Air Force. This dangerous menace resulted in a more intense bombardment of aircraft factories and the airfields known to be their bases. One of the last major operations of the war, on 10th April, was directed at such airfields, although the final battle with the Luftwaffe day-fighters took place nine days later.

With all the objectives of 'Pointblank' being achieved, the final bombing mission (No 968) took place on 25th April. For almost three years the Eighth Air Force had fought a most harsh, harrowing and costly battle, and in the process it lost well over 40,000 airmen. The ultimate sacrifice made by these brave young Americans has not been forgotten. Countless poignant and dignified memorials abound in the eastern counties, most of them discreetly placed close to the sites of the old airfields which were the airmen's homes during those grim wartime days. Many of the young men who failed to return to these airfields are commemorated on the Wall of the Missing at the fine American Military Cemetery and Memorial at Madingley near Cambridge. Perhaps the most sincere testimonial to them was made by Air Chief Marshal Harris: '. . . As far as the American bomber crews, they were the bravest of the brave, and I know that I am speaking for my own bomber crews when I pay this tribute.'

The Airfields

It has often been said that during the Second World War Britain tended to resemble a gigantic aircraft carrier moored just off the north-west coast of Europe. This impression would seem particularly appropriate as far as Suffolk was concerned. It is about 30% smaller in area than Norfolk and yet it contained almost the same number of airfields – 32 compared with 37 – and indeed was planned to have more, but three sites (Assington, Crowfield and Fressingfield) were finally dropped. There was a greater preponderance of heavy bomber stations in Suffolk and the B-17s, B-24s, Wellingtons, Stirlings and Lancasters, all tended to make their presence felt in more ways than their sheer bulk and noise dictated. The very aptly named 'Friendly Invasion' of the USAAF during 1942-44 impinged greatly on the life of the county with no less than 19 combat groups operating from its airfields.

Well before 1939 Suffolk residents were accustomed to aircraft of all shapes and sizes flying in their skies. Since the First World War Martlesham Heath had been an experimental station where the Service's latest aircraft were tested and trialled, and the important sea-plane base at Felixstowe was also engaged in experimental work. The expansion of the RAF during the 1930s saw four new stations being built in Suffolk – Mildenhall, Honington, Stradishall and Wattisham. The first to open was Mildenhall and it quickly became one of the most famous in the land, largely as a result of the much-publicised international race to Melbourne held in October 1934 which so captured the public's imagination. In addition to these Service airfields, there were three private aerodromes in the county – Westley (near Bury St Edmunds), Ipswich and Newmarket Heath.

Thus at the outbreak of the war there were five permanent RAF airfields plus Felixstowe, with Ipswich and Newmarket Heath being quickly commandeered under the Emergency Powers (Defence) Act of 1939, and Westley was closed. The pre-war RAF airfields had been built to a very high standard, certainly compared with those constructed in great haste during the war. All the buildings were of brick construction and normally supplied with central heating, with the officers and men being provided with a fair degree of comfort and good sporting amenities. The headquarters and some of the other

Wartime control tower, which were all built to a standard design. (USAF)

blocks were designed in an almost neo-Georgian style, which was aesthetically pleasing to the eye, and many have survived to this day. These permanent stations seemed outwardly to confirm the ascription that the RAF 'was the best flying club in the world'.

Almost without exception these pre-war airfields were grass surfaced, as indeed were those completed in 1940, despite the fact that it had been recognised in 1937 that the new generation of aircraft about to enter the Service would require concrete runways. The main objection was based on grounds of cost but also the problem of camouflage was cited as a disadvantage, as was the lack of natural braking power of concrete! Stradishall was almost unique in being built with concrete runways in 1938. It was essential with grass airfields that the site be chosen with the utmost care. They required well-drained land, hence Mildenhall and Honington were selected as they were on the edge of the Breckland where the light loamy soils with underlying chalk afforded good drainage. Martlesham Heath, as its name implies, was built on open heathland well suited for its ultimate use.

The desperate need for new airfields during the early years of the war meant that there was little time for such fine deliberations. The main requirements were relatively flat land between 50 and 600 feet above sea level, with as few natural and other obstructions as

36

possible. The provision of concrete runways was thought to have resolved any problems of flooding, though many wartime airfields suffered from severe drainage problems especially during the winter months when they became reminiscent of the Flanders landscape of the First World War. There was enough urgency to find sites for the RAF's needs but when the United States entered the war in late 1941 and the planned massive development of USAAF in Europe became apparent, the demand for new airfields rose quite dramatically.

However, by now most new airfields were being built to a standard design – the 'Class A Bomber'. This plan provided for three intersecting concrete runways, the main one normally about 2,000 yards long with a standard width of 50 yards, with the other two runways each about 1,400 yards long. The main runway was normally aligned to the prevailing wind providing the area around the airfield was suitable. The runways were joined by a 50 foot wide perimeter road; which could stretch for up to three miles. Concrete hardstandings and dispersal points were provided off the perimeter road; these could number up to 36 on an RAF airfield and more likely up to 50 or more at USAAF airfields.

The watch-house (although the Americans called them 'control towers') had by now become a most functional design – a plain, two-storied brick building provided with a railed balcony around it. Perhaps the most lasting and evocative image of all these wartime airfields is that of the balcony crowded with anxious officers scanning the skies overhead and straining to hear the first sounds of the returning aircraft. Some of these towers have survived and look empty and forlorn alongside the ploughed fields. A precious few have been lovingly restored to provide fitting memorial musems to American combat groups, and some of the others have been put to more mundane uses.

Another permanent feature of these wartime airfields was the gaunt and rather ugly water tower, essential in such a flat region. All the wartime airfields were provided with two T2 type hangars with a span of 120 feet and a height of 39 feet. They became the unmistakeable trademark of an airfield; some survive today as grain stores. The multiplicity of buildings – headquarters, technical workshops, stores, briefing rooms, messes and sick-quarters – were all pre-fabricated huts, some of timber and plasterboard, others of pre-cast concrete slabs – 'Orlit' and 'Maycrete' huts seemed to be the most prevalent. The living quarters were normally provided by the curved Nissen huts, which owe their origin to the First World War and a Colonel P. Nissen, although the Americans normally referred to them as 'Quonsets'.

Other than the headquarters and technical sites, the domestic buildings were usually well spread out in the surrounding countryside and neighbouring villages in separate units of up to ten or a dozen, to lessen the impact of any enemy air attack. Some were a sufficient distance from the main site to make the possession of a bicycle almost an essential part of life. Normally the living quarters were the last buildings to be erected and often the first occupants arrived to find very basic living conditions which prevailed until the huts and all the necessary services were finally completed.

For obvious safety reasons the bomb and ammunition stores were also sited well away from the airfield – usually on the opposite side to the working and living quarters. Two underground fuel tanks were normally built, each containing 100,000 gallons of aviation fuel, and the firing butts were mostly positioned at the furthest point of the airfield and quite near the end of the main runway.

Most of these wartime airfields were tucked well away in the countryside and with close on 3,000 officers, men and some women, they soon melded into close, tight-knit and largely self-sufficient communities in their own right, well outnumbering the local inhabitants. Certainly the USAAF airfields quickly became little enclaves of American life and customs.

The building of these airfields, which reached a peak during 1942/3, was a construction programme on a massive scale, involving a large workforce – over 60,000 men were said to be engaged on airfield construction. It was also a most costly business, each completed airfield representing an investment of about £900,000! Most of the

Laying concrete runways. (John Laing plc)

38

The old parachute store, which still stands at Bury St Edmunds.

large construction companies were engaged in the operation, household names such as John Laing, McAlpine, Wimpey, Taylor Woodrow, Richard Costain and Constable Hart, as well as hundreds of smaller sub-contractors – it was very big business indeed.

The amount of construction work in just one airfield was quite staggering – half a million cubic yards of concrete, 20 miles of drains, six miles for water, for for sewers and so on. It was said that six trains ran daily to East Anglia, each bringing 400 tons of hardcore; this was the rubble of bombed London and there is a bitter irony in the concept that the result of the Luftwaffe's raids was being used to build airfields from which Germany would be bombed! The runways could take up to six months to complete and then it would be another six to nine months before all the ancillary buildings and services were in place. In the middle of 1942 the first parties of the American Engineers (Aviation) arrived to help build some of the American airfields. In Suffolk Debach, Eye and Raydon were largely constructed by the American engineers. When the last Suffolk airfield – Bentwaters – came into service towards the end of 1944, it brought to a conclusion three long years of construction work in the county.

All the permanent RAF stations survived for a long time and some still do to this day. Others, such as Bentwaters, Lakenheath,

Shepherd's Grove and Woodbridge changed allegiance and became the homes for new generations of American airmen.

In the case of the wartime RAF stations, most served in No 3 Group of Bomber Command and as such were involved in similar operations, some of which have been highlighted under the individual airfields. Furthermore, it has not been the intention in this book to list all the squadrons that served at them or indeed all the missions mounted from these airfields. The majority of Bomb Groups in Suffolk served in the Third Air Division of the Eighth Air Force, along with just three Groups of the Second Air Division. Although Suffolk could be considered predominantly 'bomber country', the fighters of both the RAF and the Eighth did play an important role in the county's wartime history.

From 1939 to 1945 those Suffolk skies much beloved by John Constable saw thousands upon thousands of brave and valiant airmen leave on their missions of war and those who were not fortunate to return are remembered still by the many memorials that can be seen in the Suffolk towns, villages and countryside. It is to those young men that we all owe an immense debt of gratitude.

2
BECCLES

Beccles was not only the most easterly wartime airfield in England but it was also one of the last in Suffolk to be completed. Right from its inception, in August 1942, it had suffered a rather chequered career. It was planned and constructed for use by the USAAF as a heavy bomber station, and it was then generally known as Ellough – taking the name from the neighbouring village, although the locals persisted in using this name for the airfield throughout its existence.

During its construction it was used as an emergency landing strip by several badly damaged bombers returning to their airfields in East Anglia. These were mainly American aircraft and the first – a B-17 belonging to the 95th Bomb Group at Horham – used the partially completed runway on 10th October 1943. In March and April 1944 the airfield was used on several occasions by both B-17s and B-24s and later on in the year by the odd American fighter. This was despite the fact that by now Woodbridge, just down the coast, had opened as a specially designated Emergency Landing Ground.

When the Eighth Air Force found they did not really need the airfield as they had finally reached their planned complement of Groups, Beccles or Ellough was handed over to the RAF. Bomber Command was given the first option, but after some deliberation it was decided that they, too, did not require another airfield in the area. The Air Ministry offered the airfield to Coastal Command and they gladly accepted. Thus, on 14th August 1944, Beccles came under the control of No 16 Group, which already had several airfields in Norfolk – Bircham Newton, Docking and Langham. Quite evidently, because of its close proximity to the coast, the airfield would ultimately feature in one of the Command's important roles – Air Sea Rescue (ASR).

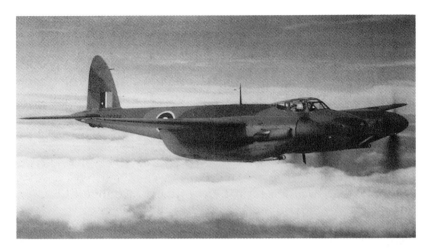

De Havilland Mosquito: No 618 Squadron brought its Mark IVs to Beccles in August 1944.

Despite having such a relatively short existence as a wartime airfield, Beccles nevertheless managed to play host to quite a variety of different aircraft – Swordfish, Albacores, Barracudas, Warwicks, Walruses, Sea Otters and Mosquitos as well as the odd heavy bomber dropping in unannounced! Indeed it was quite a selection in a matter of just nine months.

Of all these aircraft the most unlikely one to use a Coastal Command airfield was the 'wonder' aircraft of the Second World War – the de Havilland Mosquito. They arrived in August and belonged to No 618 squadron, which was a sister unit of the more famous No 617 squadron, better known as 'The Dambusters'. No 618 had been specially formed in April 1943 from the crews of two famous Mosquito squadrons – Nos 105 and 139 – to experiment with another type of bouncing bomb or spinning mine – the 'Highball'. This weapon had been specifically designed to be used against German battleships and the *Tirpitz* in particular. However, the squadron had also developed their Mosquito IVs and VIs as most effective anti-shipping and anti-U-boat strike aircraft. Indeed, in March 1944 the first Mosquito had been successfully landed on an aircraft carrier, so another new role had opened up for this most amazing and versatile aircraft. The squadron had gained a fine reputation whilst serving with Coastal Command. During their short stay at Beccles they were engaged in various bombing and target

42

practices but by the middle of October they had departed to Scotland. The 'Highball' was never used in action.

During September there appeared two types of aircraft that had both seen sterling service with Coastal Command and the Fleet Air Arm. Each had been designed and built by Fairey Aviation; they were the Swordfish and the Albacore. The Swordfish was really a quite remarkable little bi-plane, which had been in service since 1936 and had been nearing the end of its natural life at the outbreak of the war. However, because Coastal Command was so short of aircraft the Swordfish was retained and was used as a torpedo bomber, mine layer, rocket projectile carrier and trainer. Though it barely exceeded 140 mph, the Swordfish squadrons served with great distinction throughout the war. The Albacore, another bi-plane, had been designed as a torpedo bomber with the intention of replacing the Swordfish, but in fact the latter survived it, and in the early months of 1945 the Swordfish XIs were actually replacing Albacores in operational squadrons!

Yet another Fairey aircraft arrived at Beccles in October – the Barracuda. This had proved to be the Royal Navy's most versatile wartime aircraft, able to launch a torpedo and used as a dive bomber, mine layer, anti-U-boats and in a reconnaissance role. It had first entered the Fleet Air Arm in January 1943 and was developed into three marks, all of which saw wartime action. The later model was equipped with a radar scanner to aid in its anti-shipping role. The Barracudas of No 827 squadron of the Fleet Air Arm stayed at the airfield for about two weeks, just sufficient time to mount some east coast convoy patrols.

At the end of the month the airfield received its first permanent residents – a squadron of Vickers Warwicks. This squadron – No 280 – had been one of the first of Coastal Command's ASR units. It had been formed at Bircham Newton at the end of 1941 when the Command had been made responsible for all rescue work up to 40 miles from the coast. The squadron was first equipped with Avro Ansons but by October 1943 the 'Faithful Annies' were phased out and replaced by Warwicks.

The Warwick had originally been designed as a heavier contemporary bomber to the very successful Wellington, and was built on similar lines. However, it proved to have a quite disappointing performance and the Warwicks were quickly passed over to Coastal Command and it was left to them to find a useful role for these aircraft. Their ultimate salvation was found in ASR work.

Vickers Warwick V: The Warwick found its metier in Air Sea Rescue work. (Via J. Adams)

Provided with ASV (Air Surface Vessel) radar, an increased fuel capacity and also adapted to take the two models of airborne lifeboats, the Warwick ASR MkIs – as they were designated – ultimately formed four ASR squadrons within Coastal Command, each 20 aircraft strong. The early success of these ASR squadrons in the last months of 1943 was fully acknowledged by Lieutenant General Eaker, Commander of the Eighth Air Force, in December of that year. 'Your superlative ASR Service has been one of the prime factors in the high morale of our own combat crews. This organisation of yours has picked up from the sea nearly 600 of our combat crew men since we began operations in this theater. This is a remarkable achievement, made possible by only the highest efficiency and the greatest courage and fortitude.'

By the time No 280 started operations from Beccles in November, there had been a major reorganisation of ASR operations. The Air Defence of Great Britain (previously Fighter Command) were now responsible for rescue services in the English Channel and the southern North Sea, and also the USAAF had established their own very effective rescue service, first from Boxted in Essex and later from Halesworth. Therefore the Warwicks of No 280 squadron were engaged in 'deep search' missions across the North Sea and in co-operating with units of the Eighth Air Force to ensure that distress signals were quickly answered. In late February 1945 a detachment of Supermarine Walruses of No 278 squadron arrived to help the Warwicks, the rest of the squadron remaining at Thorney Island in Hampshire. The airfield was now virtually dedicated to Air Sea Rescue.

The Walrus was a rather strange looking aircraft almost antediluvian in appearance. It was an amphibious bi-plane distinctive for the single engine mounted above and behind the crew's quarters. It had entered service with the Royal Navy in 1936 as an amphibian reconnaissance and spotter aircraft capable of being catapulted from Naval vessels. Perhaps, like the Warwick, it found its true metier in ASR work. The original aircraft had a metal hull but the later and more numerous Mark IIs, built by Saunders Roe, were constructed of wood. Despite its looks and limitations – not least of these was its top speed of 135 mph – it served in all areas, from Iceland to the Pacific, and many a ditched airman owed his life to these doughty aircraft. In May 1945 the Walruses were finally replaced by another Supermarine sea-plane or flying boat – the Sea Otter. It was also a bi-plane and did not enter the service until late 1943, in fact the Sea Otter IIs were the last bi-planes to be operated by the RAF. It is worth noting in passing that during the war the various ASR services were responsible for saving the lives of no less than 13,269 persons and 8,604 were Allied aircrews.

Briefly during April 1945 the airfield became more offensive when Barracuda IIIs of No 810 squadron of the Fleet Air Arm arrived from Thorney Island. Their specific task was to seek out the German midget submarines. These craft, crewed either by one or two men, had caused deep concern in the Admiralty. They had been produced in great numbers and were capable of carrying either torpedoes or mines. No 16 Group of Coastal Command devoted considerable resources to this campaign. From December 1944 to the end of the war over 1,100 sorties were mounted involving some 3,000 flying hours, with 16 definite 'kills' and another ten possibles. The squadron left Beccles in June for Scotland for service on HMS *Queen* in the Far East.

When No 280 squadron left Beccles during October 1945 after a tenure of twelve months, the days of the airfield were numbered. By the end of November it was non-operational and was closed for flying. Nowadays much of the site is given over to an industrial estate, although there is still some flying activity with helicopters operating to the various oil and gas rigs in the North Sea. The airfield is about two miles south-east of Beccles along the B1127 road, which in fact crosses the site.

3

BENTWATERS

Perhaps there was an inevitability about the fact that Bentwaters would one day become a major USAF base and the American presence would last for over 40 years. It was in August 1942 that the site was first identified for airfield development, at a time when there was a desperate and hectic search to meet the requirements of the planned massive build-up of the Eighth Air Force in England. Certainly it can be appreciated why the site was thought so favourable – flat terrain, few natural obstructions, well away from any large communities and moreover just five miles from the coast.

During its early development the airfield was known as 'Butley' from the small village a mile or so to the north-east. Construction work commenced towards the end of 1942 but by the following March building work had ceased with the labour force being moved elsewhere to hasten the completion of other airfields in East Anglia. When the contractors finally returned to the site in the winter of 1943 the embryo airfield had been renamed Bentwaters, said to have been chosen from the name of an old house which had stood on the site of the main runway. Work slowed down during the early summer of 1944, when its future use was in considerable doubt. In May the fortieth and last heavy Bomb Group had settled into Debach in Suffolk and there were no immediate plans for any further development of the Eighth Air Force. Thus Bentwaters or 'Station 151' – traditionally all USAAF bases were so numbered – seemed to be surplus to requirements. The airfield was duly completed and placed under 'Care and Maintenance', which included the provision of runway obstructions, whilst its ultimate operational use was considered.

As the airfield lay empty and inactive, it did, however, provide a blessed haven for several badly damaged aircraft returning from missions and unable to quite make it back to their home bases. The first to limp in, on 20th July, was a badly damaged B-17 of 96th Bomb Group at Snetterton Heath, followed in September by a B-24 from North Pickenham. Three weeks later another pilot of a B-17 found the 30 or so miles to home at Horham was just a little too much and he attempted a forced landing at Bentwaters; this incurred even more damage to his aircraft due to the runway obstructions. After this sad accident the obstructions were wisely removed just in time (24th October) for three P-51 fighters, belonging to 359th Group at East Wretham, to land there because they were running very low on fuel. They had returned from a fighter/bomber mission to Nienburg on the Weser which was not far from Hanover. These P-51s proved to be the harbingers of their British counterparts – the squadrons of RAF Mustangs that arrived at Bentwaters towards the end of the year.

The USAAF decided to relinquish their control of the airfield and as it was a Type A heavy bomber station the Air Ministry offered it to Bomber Command. However, as No 3 Group had only recently (in April) taken over another redundant American airfield – Shepherd's Grove – they had no pressing need for yet another heavy bomber station in East Anglia. It was decided that the airfield would be taken over by No 11 Group of Fighter Command.

During the latter months of 1944 Bomber Command had begun to mount more major daylight operations by heavy bombers, especially the Lancaster squadrons of No 3 Group. In November 14 out of 22 major raids were conducted by day with a heavy fighter escort – normally Mustangs. Therefore it was not really surprising that it was decided to form a Mustang Wing at Bentwaters, which was placed under the command of Wing Commander H.A.C. Bird-Wilson, who later became the Commanding Officer at Coltishall and ended his RAF career as a much decorated Air Commodore.

The North American P-51 or Mustang was, without doubt, the finest of all American wartime fighters. It surpassed the other two main American fighters – P-38 and P-47 – in speed, range, fire-power and manoeuvrability. However, the aircraft really owes its origin to the British Air Purchasing Commission, which had visited America to seek from its aviation industry a new fighter that would be capable of long-range escort duties. The North American Company responded to the challenge very swiftly and completed a prototype in no less than 117 days, which, after certain modifications,

Mustang IV of No 234 Squadron at Bentwaters. (RAF Museum)

first flew in September 1940. The RAF were quite impressed with the design and specifications of the aircraft and immediately placed an order for the fighter. The first Mustang Mark Is (as they were known by the RAF) arrived in Britain during October 1941. At this stage the USAAF showed little interest in the aircraft as they were quite satisfied with the performances of their existing fighters in service.

In this respect the American apparent disinterest seemed fully justified when the RAF quickly discovered that although the aircraft's performance at low altitude was quite impressive, it appeared to be greatly handicapped at high altitudes by lack of power and therefore was not really suitable for escort duties. Fighter Command relegated their Mustangs mainly to reconnaisance and army support duties, and they first entered the Service with No 2 squadron at Sawbridgeworth, which was operating in the Army Co-operation Command. Nevertheless, in October 1942, it still became the first single-engined RAF fighter to penetrate the German skies. In the autumn of 1942 the RAF suggested that the original low-powered Allison engine be replaced by a Rolls Royce Merlin power unit, which had proved so successful in the Spitfire. This was agreed and Packard built the new engines in America. It was almost a miraculous recovery and from this time the Mustang or P-51 never looked back.

The new Mustang IIIs were capable of a top speed of 425 mph at 24,500 feet – an improvement on the latter marks of Spitfires. With a service ceiling in excess of 42,000 feet and strongly armed with four .50 cannons, it had developed into a most redoubtable escort fighter considering that it also had a normal range of 1,000 miles. The Mustang was also able to take two drop tanks which further increased

48

its range and endurance or to carry two 500 pound bombs, which added to its strike capabilities. Suddenly the USAAF became decidedly interested in this now very impressive fighter, especially for long range escort duties but it would not be until December 1943 that the first Mark IIIs or P-51Cs entered service with the USAAF in Europe.

It was not until the spring of 1944 that some 300 Mark IVs were delivered to the RAF and most of them served with the 2nd Tactical Air Force. This fighter was now in great demand and the majority of the production went to the USAAF; ultimately 14 out of 15 Fighter Groups serving with the Eighth Air Force were equipped with P-51Ds, such was their reputation. These later marks were supplied with a more powerful engine giving a maximum speed of 440 mph with a range of over 2,000 miles and an endurance of some eight hours. Their appearance in great numbers in the German skies virtually brought the Luftwaffe to its knees.

The first squadron of Mustang IIIs arrived at Bentwaters on 1st December 1944; it was No 129, whose pilots already had considerable experience with these fighters, having used them operationally since the previous April. Because of their great speed the Mustangs proved very effective against the V1 rockets and by September 1944 had claimed no less than 232 destroyed. No 129 squadron was quickly followed into Bentwaters by what could be considered a 'local' squadron – No 64. This famous squadron, which dated from First World War days, had been reformed at nearby Martlesham Heath in 1936 and stayed there for almost two years. After sterling service in the Battle of Britain from RAF Kenley, the squadron had spent several periods of service at RAF Coltishall. The third squadron, No 234, arrived from North Weald where it had been re-equipped with Mustang IIIs. This squadron received half a dozen of the more powerful Mark IVs in March 1945. Three other squadrons, Nos 118, 126 and 165, arrived at Bentwaters during the month and all were converting from Spitfire IXs to Mustangs and would not see any action until the New Year.

The first time that Bentwaters became operational was on 23rd December when three squadrons escorted 153 Lancasters from No 3 Group to the railway yards at Trier, which was situated on the German/Luxembourg border. This daylight mission was just a small part of the huge Allied Air Forces' offensive to support the beleaguered American land forces engaged in the Ardennes offensive; on this day only one Lancaster failed to return so the

Mustangs had completed their task successfully. On 3rd January 126 squadron entered the fray escorting 99 Lancasters on another daylight raid to the Hansa oil plant at Dortmund, and again only one Lancaster was lost. By the 29th of the month yet another squadron became available for operations – No 165. Their first mission was to escort No 3 Group Lancasters to the railway yards at Krefeld in the Rhine valley. Finally on 14th February the whole Wing was fully operational for the first time when No 118 went out on their first escort duty.

The Wing was mainly engaged on daylight escort missions mounted by the Lancaster squadrons of No 3 Group from its various airfields in East Anglia. However, on 20th March, No 64 squadron acted as escort for 18 Mosquitos which set out from Fersfield in Norfolk to undertake the last of those many daring daylight precision raids for which they were justifiably famed. This time the target was the Gestapo buildings in Copenhagen and although the raid was successful, one Mosquito and two Mustangs were lost.

The Mustang squadrons were engaged in the last of Bomber Command's major operations of the war – to Hitler's Eagle's Nest chalet and the local SS headquarters at Berchtesgaden. This rather spectacular raid, which achieved very little, resulted in two Lancasters being lost to enemy flak. No Luftwaffe fighters were evident despite the long haul across Germany. On 9th May, the day after VE Day, the Bentwaters' Mustangs were active providing escorts for the force that was sent to liberate Guernsey. This last mission brought to a close the very short operational life of Bentwaters as a Second World War airfield.

By September the Mustangs had left and Bentwaters remained active for another four years when it was put into 'moth balls'. In March 1951 the airfield was transferred to the USAF, the first of many American jet fighters appeared in September and the rest can be considered as recent history. The airfield, after a long American occupation, closed in 1993.

4

BUNGAY

In a rather delightful and unspoilt corner of north-east Suffolk, known locally as 'Saints Country', was sited a wartime airfield which became the home of one of the most renowned Groups of the Second Bomb Division – the 446th. They were more familiarly known as 'The Bungay Buckeroos', a name which was taken from the old market town some two miles to the north-east.

Bungay, or Flixton as it was first called, was one of the earliest sites to be allocated to the USAAF – it was included on a list dated 4th June 1942. The first intention was that the airfield would become a satellite for the main station of Hardwick, just across the boundary in Norfolk. However, when plans changed and it was decided that each Bomb Group would occupy just a single airfield, in the fullness of time a heavy Bomb Group would arrive at Bungay. During the summer of 1942, long before the airfield was completed, the first American aircraft arrived to use its very basic facilities. They were North American B-25Cs of No 428 squadron of the 310th Bomb Group.

These twin-engined light/medium bombers had first flown in late 1940 and saw service with the USAAF just six months later. They were better known as Mitchells, named after the famous General 'Billy' Mitchell, one of the pioneers of American Service aviation. These B-25s at Bungay proved to be nothing more than birds of passage en route to warmer climes to join the Twelfth Air Force in North Africa in November 1942.

They were, however, followed into Bungay by a squadron of Consolidated B-24s. These four-engined heavy bombers would grace the airfield for the duration of the war; although 'grace' is hardly the most appropriate word, because even to its most devoted admirers, of which there were many, the B-24 (Liberator) did not look a particularly elegant aircraft with its twin tails and rather heavy and slab-like appearance. The B-17 crews used to contemptuously refer to it as 'the crate that ours came over in'! Nevertheless the B-24 proved to be the most versatile of all American Second World War bombers, serving as a most effective heavy bomber, a transport carrier and also an anti-submarine aircraft. In its many and various models it served with 15 Allied Air Forces and in every theatre of war. Throughout the duration of the war the Second Division operated only B-24s and mainly from airfields in Norfolk.

Compared with its close rival, the B-24 was a new aircraft; the first prototype had only flown in 1939 and the 'D' version was the first to be mass-produced for the USAAF. Its four Pratt & Whitney engines gave it an operating speed of about 216 mph at an altitude of 23,000 feet and it had an average bomb load of 5,000 pounds. The name 'Liberator' came as a result of a competition held in the manufacturer's works in San Diego, California, although originally the name 'Eagle' was thought to be more fitting.

For about three months 329 squadron of 93rd Bomb Group (the other squadrons had been detached for operations with the Twelfth in North Africa) operated from the rather basic airfield at Bungay.

Typical layout of a wartime airfield. (Crown copyright)

They were engaged in conducting experiments with the RAF's GEE equipment. This was a radio-pulse navigational aid, which enabled a navigator to fix the position of his aircraft by reference to pulses transmitted from three stations in England. The RAF had introduced the system into operations in March 1942. Ultimately the Eighth Air Force brought it into service, first providing GEE sets for twelve aircraft in each Bomb Group and then by the beginning of 1944 in every bomber. Early in March 1943 this squadron had left Bungay to rejoin the rest of the Group, which had now returned to its new home at Hardwick. It would be another eight months before the airfield became active again.

The 446th had been first activated or formed at the beginning of April 1943 and throughout that summer the crews were busy training in New Mexico and Colorado. They finished their final training in Nebraska towards the end of October but the crews still did not know to which theatre of war they would be posted. It was not until they had been airborne from the United States for one hour that they were allowed to open their sealed orders and so discovered they were bound for the Eighth Air Force in England.

Two different ferry routes to Great Britain were used – the northern and the southern. The former took the crews up to Gander in Newfoundland and from thence across to Prestwick in Scotland, often via Iceland. The other route was much longer and far more time consuming, following a route from Florida to Puerto Rico or Trinidad, Brazil then across the Atlantic to Dakar and Marrakesh in North Africa. The final leg was flown due north to Cornwall carefully avoiding the Spanish and French air-spaces for obvious reasons. The northern route was only used in the summer months so the 446th crews came over by the southern route.

By the last week of November the airfield was coming to life with the ground crews settling into their accommodation and awaiting the arrival of the first aircraft. Unfortunately two of the original aircraft were missing, one had crashed on the Puerto Rico leg and a second had been shot down over France when it had wandered off course. All the personnel were subjected to mandatory lectures on the social niceties of serving in England and were generally confined to camp in the early weeks. The aircrews were busy in obtaining assembly skills, practising tight formation flying and becoming conversant with all the RAF's flying control and radio procedures. They also had to acclimatise themselves to their new homes – the Nissen or 'Quonset' huts (as they called them). As one of the airmen commented, 'The

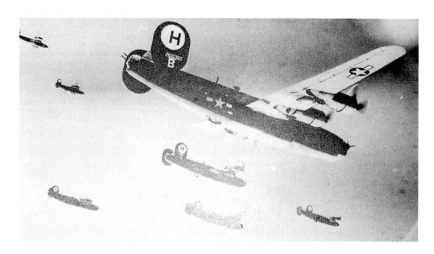

Formation of B-24Js of 446th Bomb Group. (USAF)

raw and damp North Sea cold . . . was as nothing we had experienced before. It cut through six blankets at night and we lay around the small coke stoves like wolves about a dying doe . . .'

The Group formed part of the 20th Combat Bomb Wing along with the experienced 93rd Group at Hardwick and another novice unit – the 448th based at Seething near Norwich. Most missions would be flown with these Groups. It was not until 16th December that the Group's Commanding Officer – Colonel Jacob Brogger – felt sufficiently confident of his crews to let them out on their first mission. Along with the rest of the Eighth, now numbering 24 Bomb Groups, 24 of their aircraft attacked the port area of Bremen. On return to Bungay two aircraft unfortunately crash-landed on and near the airfield but with no loss of life. On the 20th the target was again Bremen, indeed Lt General Eaker had made it clear to the Eighth's crews, 'if you don't do the job properly the first time, you will be sent back and back again.' On this second mission the Group sent just a single aircraft and that failed to return. However, two days later 25 aircraft were in action over Osnabrück, with two B-24s lost on this mission. The Group's first week of operations had not been particularly successful but this could be put down largely to inexperience, as it ultimately achieved a very high safety record.

On Christmas Eve the Group went out on its first No Ball mission – the code-name given to the operations against V1 rocket sites in northern France and particularly the Pas de Calais. At the briefing it was made very clear that these operations were of the utmost importance, London and south-east England were at grave risk and there was a possibility that the planned invasion of Europe might even have to be delayed. The crews responded well, they felt that this was different to their normal missions, as at long last they were going to do something positive for the war effort. In the first three months of the New Year the 446th were engaged in half a dozen No Ball targets for the loss of just one aircraft, which was so badly damaged on 21st January's mission that it crash-landed near Dover.

The year came to a close with a long and exhausting flight with the crews being airborne for over eleven hours. The target had been the docks at Bordeaux but because of heavy cloud over the area, they turned to the secondary target, the airfield at Cognac. The Group lost two aircraft and a third was so badly damaged that it was considered a write off. In their short time at Bungay the young crews were only too aware that they were engaged in a most bitter war.

On 24th February as part of Operation Argument or 'The Big Week' – the Eighth's major offensive against aircraft factories – the Second Division was allocated a target deep in central Germany. It was Gotha and its complex of Me110 factories. This proved to be one of the hardest and most costly missions of the war as far as the B-24 Groups were concerned. Of the 239 aircraft despatched, 33 failed to return – a 14% loss – with 327 airmen killed, a very harsh day, especially for the Group at Tibenham, which lost 13 crews. The 446th escaped relatively lightly losing two aircraft over the target area and a third which crashed near Sternfield killing the pilot. The whole operation had lasted seven hours – as one crewman commented, 'it was the longest seven hours in my short life'!

The months leading up to D-Day proved to be a long and grinding stretch of quite harrowing missions – Fürth, Pforzheim, Berlin, Wilhelmshaven and Friedrichshafen. On the 8th April Brunswick was the target and the crews had good cause to fear the renowned Luftwaffe fighter gruppes in the area, indeed they had been nicknamed 'The Battling Bastards of Brunswick'. And on this day the Luftwaffe were out in force with the result that 30 B-24s failed to return and the 446th were fortunate to lose only two aircraft – some of the other Groups in the Division suffered quite severe losses. This became a feature of the Group's operations and it must speak volumes for the leadership of the 446th and the disciplined formation flying of its crews.

Most personnel on the station felt that something big was brewing in the first few days of June but it was still with some surprise that the crews were called for briefing at 11.30 on the night of the 5th, although they were aware that their aircraft had already been fuelled and bombed up. When they were informed of the operations taking place on the following morning there was a great feeling of relief and they were delighted to be told that the Group would be leading the Eighth Air Force over the Normandy beaches on D-Day.

Considering the number of aircraft that would be airborne over southern England during the day, the operating orders were lengthy and very precise. It was stressed that the operating altitudes and flying corridors had to be strictly observed. The sheer logistics in mounting such an operation were staggering as waves of heavy bombers (nearly 2,400) left their bases at various times during the night and early morning.

With Colonel Brogger leading the Group in *Red Ass*, the aircraft left Bungay shortly before 2 am and flew directly north-west to the 20th Wing's assembly area over the Manchester area before proceeding across central England to cross the English coast near Selsey Bill in Sussex. At precisely five minutes to six they arrived over the Normandy beaches and 20 minutes later the first formation had bombed and were returning to their airfields. The 446th arrived back safely, in fact only one aircraft was lost to enemy action on the day. The Luftwaffe did not show until two days later when the Group were suddenly attacked by Me109s near Jersey; one B-24 was shot down but the gunners claimed two fighters destroyed.

Soon, however, the Group were back over Germany and on 20th June 1944 they were part of a massive assault by the Eighth Air Force on oil targets in Germany. The Second Division were allocated targets in central Germany – Pölitz and Ostermoor. Two of the fighter groups were delayed, leaving just one Group of P-51s to cover the whole formation, a quite impossible task. With virtually no fighter protection the Luftwaffe attacked in strength and with great tenacity and at the end of this mission 34 B-24s failed to return, although 20 of these landed or crashed in Sweden, including three from the 446th. As will be noted later quite an American community was built up in Sweden from all the interned crews.

Colonel Brogger was certainly no mere 'paddlefoot' – as the aircrews called their non-flying officers – and, on 18th September, he decided to lead the Group on a rather special mission. They were called upon to supply stores and ammunition to the US airborne forces that had landed in the Nijmegen and Eindhoven areas. It

B-24 'Shady Sadie' lands at Bungay – March 1945. (USAF)

would mean that the B-24s would have to fly at a very low altitude and a relatively slow speed over the dropping area to ensure the accuracy of the supply drop. This made them virtually sitting targets for enemy flak batteries. As had been expected the B-24s faced quite murderous ground fire and although the 446th survived the mission without loss, which was no mean achievement, most of their aircraft were damaged and unfortunately Brogger was badly wounded, which resulted in a change of command.

Colonel Tony Crawford, who took over the Group on 23rd September, was another officer who firmly believed in leading from the front, indeed his deputy Lieutenant Colonel William Schmidt was of the same persuasion. It was Schmidt who led the Group on a very similar low flying mission on 24th March 1945; this was just a part of Operation Varsity – the Allied Air Forces' tactical support of the crossing of the Rhine. On this mission a force of 240 B-24s was despatched to drop supplies to the Allied armies. This required flying into the dropping zones at 330-400 feet – in fact the lower the better – and Schmidt brought the Group in over their dropping area at Wesel as low as 50 feet and at a speed of 145 mph to ensure an accurate drop. Needless to say the aircraft faced stiff ground fire and a total of 14 aircraft was shot down, another four written off, and well over 100 damaged by enemy fire. The Group lost two aircraft on this very dangerous mission.

Eleven days later (4th April) the Group had the misfortune to lose its Commanding Officer in a rather bizarre fashion. Crawford was aboard a Mosquito from 25th Bomb Group at Watton and was supervising his Group's assembly before the formation departed to

Wesendorf airfield near Dortmund. On some of these occasions, if the mission was a relatively short haul, the monitoring aircraft would also accompany the formation. Crawford decided in this instance to follow the bombers and when the Luftwaffe fighters were sighted, he decided to close up to the formation for added protection. Unfortunately the Mosquito was wrongly identified as a Me262 and was shot down by friendly fire from one of his own B-24s! Crawford managed to bale out but was captured. However, he and another 40 Americans escaped from a local prison and he finally arrived back at Bungay on 25th April to a hero's welcome.

Lt Colonel Schmidt took over the Group for what proved to be the last three weeks of operations. Their last mission was flown on 25th April when the Second Division made a long penetration flight into southern Germany to attack the railway yards at Salzburg, just across the border in Austria – all of the Group's aircraft arrived back safely. Indeed, April had proved to be a trouble-free month, save for a rather unfortunate accident on 11th April, when two aircraft returning from the infamous Regensburg collided over East Anglia killing 22 crewmen.

In almost one and a half years they had completed no less than 273 missions for the loss of 'only' 58 aircraft in action and another 28 due to other causes. This proved to be one of the safest records in the whole of the Eighth Air Force.

By the middle of June the Americans were beginning to leave 'Saints Country' but before they finally departed the Group presented new wooden gates for St Mary's church at Flixton, although the present ones are replacements provided by the veterans of the 446th. The return to the USA was not without mishap as unfortunately one of the B-24s was lost over the Azores with 15 passengers on board. The airfield was handed back to the RAF and a Maintenance Unit moved in. Some of the old airfield buildings still remain and are now part of a chicken factory. However, besides the various memorials to the Group in the village there is a display of aircraft and memorabilia at Flixton – the Norfolk and Suffolk Aviation Museum – which is open on Sundays and Bank Holidays and well worth a visit. It can be best reached by taking the B1062 road off the main A143 and following the signs to Flixton.

5
BURY
ST EDMUNDS

There is no doubt that the aircrews of the various Bomb Groups that arrived in England during late 1942 and the first half of 1943 would face the sternest of tests, and it was probably better that they were not aware of what was in store for them. These crews were the precursors of the many thousands of airmen that would, by 1944, make the Eighth Air Force truly 'Mighty'. One such Group was the 94th which was stationed at Bury St Edmunds from June 1943, and during their stay in England completed no less than 324 missions – a record for the Third Bomb Division.

However, almost nine months before the 94th arrived at the airfield, which had been completed by Richard Costain towards the end of 1942, other American units had occupied the base. In September some A-20s (Havocs) of the 47th Bomb Group arrived but just as quickly left for Horham, which was then almost completed. December saw the first personnel of 322nd Bomb Group arrive and settle into the accommodation sites that were placed to the east of the airfield towards the village of Rougham, from which the airfield had been originally named. Nevertheless it would be another four months before this Group's aircraft made their appearance – B-26s, perhaps better known as Marauders.

This aircraft was built on really classic lines – clean and very streamlined. It had been produced by the Glenn L. Martin Company as a response to a specification that called for a fast and heavily armed medium bomber. The USAAF were so impressed with the original design that they ordered no less than 1,100 aircraft straight off the drawing board, something that was quite unheard of in those days. The B-26s had first come into service in late 1941 and it was from this time that the aircraft began to gain its rather unfortunate and ill-deserved early reputation. Its high landing speed certainly presented problems for inexperienced pilots and as the accident rate with these aircraft soared, so the crews began to call it the 'widow maker' or the 'Baltimore whore'! Nevertheless, with a top speed of 315 mph, a range in excess of 1,000 miles and a maximum bomb load of 4,000 pounds, it was an impressive and formidable aircraft. Actually the B-26s proved to be one of the most successful medium bombers, with an amazingly low loss rate when operating with the Ninth Air Force; one aircraft, *Flak Bait* of 322nd Bomb Group, completed 202 missions and the nose section is now preserved in the Smithsonian in Washington DC.

During March and April 1943 two squadrons – Nos 450 and 452 – arrived with their B-26B-4s and were quickly engaged in low-level flying practice over East Anglia, losing one aircraft which crashed near Cambridge killing its five man crew. By the middle of May the Group's Commanding Officer, Colonel Stillman, was reasonably happy that his crews should test their mettle in battle. On 14th May twelve B-26s took off to bomb the power station at Ijmuiden on the Dutch coast. They flew very low over the North Sea in an attempt to negate the enemy's radar. Unfortunately one aircraft was damaged and had to return to base. The remaining eleven aircraft attacked the target but encountered quite severe and accurate flak and nine of them were badly damaged. On its return to Bury St Edmunds one aircraft crashed over the airfield; five of the crew managed to bale out but the pilot was killed. This was not a particularly auspicious entry of the B-26 into the European air war. Two days later the Group were informed that as most of the bombs had missed the target so they would have to return and try again!

On 17th May, because of the number of damaged aircraft and with just two squadrons operational, the Group could only muster eleven aircraft. The return mission to Ijmuiden was led by Colonel Stillman, with half the force led by Lt Colonel Purinton attacking another generating station at Haarlem. One aircraft aborted within 30 miles of the Dutch coast and the remaining B-26s took a wrong heading and entered a heavily defended area. Colonel Stillman's aircraft was shot down, another two collided and crashed and the resultant fierce explosion brought down another aircraft. One aircraft did manage to bomb a gas holder in Amsterdam but eventually that also crashed.

B-26 'Flak Bait' of 322nd Bomb Group. (Smithsonian)

Another aircraft was brought down by some Me109s over the North Sea and four that were badly damaged crashed into the sea. A total loss of ten aircraft – a disaster of some magnitude, one could say. Colonel Stillman, though badly injured, was taken prisoner of war, and Lt Colonel Purinton was later rescued from the sea by a German vessel. The only survivors – two gunners – were picked up from a dinghy off the east coast, five days after the mission.

This tragic operation really highlighted the inherent dangers of medium bombers making low-level attacks in daylight. The Group's new Commanding Officer, Lt Colonel Glenn Nye, ordered an intensive programme of low-level flying training, which unfortunately resulted in a crash almost on the airfield, adding fresh fuel to the aircraft's unfortunate reputation. However, by the middle of June the Group moved to Andrew's Field in Essex in a general reshuffle of airfields. Ultimately the Eighth's B-26 Groups would be transferred to the Ninth Air Force and were mainly based in Essex, which was thought to be more suitable and convenient for their operations over northern France.

As a result of the change the 94th Bomb Group moved from Earls Colne in Essex, from whence they had mounted their first operations, to Bury St Edmunds. Just 26 B-17s took off from Earls Colne for the last time on 13th June and it was planned that they would return to their new airfield. This was their ninth mission and the target was the U-boat yards at Kiel. On this day a 76 strong force of the 4th Bomb Wing faced severe flak from this strongly defended port. However, the 94th managed to survive intact and were within 30 miles of the Norfolk coast when they were suddenly attacked by twelve Junkers 88 night fighters. At the time some of the gunners had stripped their guns and were cleaning them – a chore that should have been undertaken after they had landed. In a matter of minutes nine of the Group's aircraft were shot down. What did their Commanding Officer, Colonel John Moore, have to say about this very costly lapse of discipline?

The 94th, like all Bomb Groups then in the 4th Wing (which later became the Third Bomb Division) were equipped with Boeing B-17s, the famed Flying Fortresses. These aircraft will forever epitomise the Eighth Air Force during their time in England, due in no small measure to William Wyler's famous wartime documentary film *Memphis Belle* and its fairly recent and successful remake of the same name.

The first B-17 had flown in July 1935 and as the first all-metal four-engined monoplane it was a most revolutionary aircraft for its time. The slender design made it visually a most attractive and almost elegant aircraft, which certainly was the exception to the general rule as far as military aircraft were concerned. Its several prominent gun turrets caught the interest and imagination of the American press, who described it as being 'like a flying fortress' and the famous name stuck. In 1939 the Army Air Force had a mere 39 in service and yet by September 1943 the Eighth Air Force alone had no less than 800 B-17s in England. These were B-17Fs, a model that was more modified and improved than any other. The aircraft had an operating speed of around 215 mph at an altitude of 27,000 feet, with a range of 1,300 miles when carrying a normal bomb load of 4,000 pounds. The Fortresses well merited their name, as they were strongly armed with twelve .50 guns. The aircraft in its various models formed the backbone of the Eighth Air Force, leading the American assault on Germany. It was fondly admired by all its pilots and crews, who had a terrific faith in the aircraft getting them safely home despite heavy damage.

The Group had lost no less than 17 aircraft and their crews in its first month of operations, the debacle over the North Sea had not

Some of the 'Top Brass' visit Bury St Edmunds. From left to right: Lt. Gen. Eaker, Gen. Arnold, Colonels Le May and Castle. (IWM)

helped matters and morale was quite low, especially as it had been made clear to the crews that their bombing was less than satisfactory. General Eaker and the 4th Wing chiefs felt a change of Commanding Officer was needed and Eaker turned to one of his original officers, and a personal friend, Colonel Fred Castle. The change of command was not well received by the Group's personnel but nevertheless Castle arrived at Bury St Edmunds on 22nd June 1943 and remained in charge of the Group until the following April.

Perhaps the best testimony to Castle's fine qualities of leadership came on 28th July when the 4th Bomb Wing, now doubled in strength to six Groups, was directed to attack an aircraft assembly plant at Oschersleben in central Germany. This would be the Eighth's deepest penetration raid so far and Castle acknowledged to his crews that it would be 'a hot mission'. Bad weather over Germany caused the formation to disperse, which resulted in several aircraft falling foul of Fw190s. Castle, who was leading the Group, managed to find a break in the clouds with the result that the primary target was bombed very effectively. It was later estimated that production had been halted for at least one month, which meant 50 or so less enemy fighters to face. Although the Wing lost 15 B-17s (12.5%), the 94th's crews arrived back intact but with twelve badly damaged aircraft – things were looking up!

On the first anniversary of the Eighth's entry into the European war – 17th August – a major operation was planned to suitably mark the occasion. The 1st Bomb Wing were to go to Schweinfurt and its important ball-bearings works, whilst the 4th Wing's target was the large complex of Messerschmitt assembly factories located at Regensburg. It was intended that the 4th Wing would then fly over the Alps and down Italy to land in bases in North Africa. The theory behind this tactic was that the Luftwaffe fighters had been attacking in strength as the bomber formations were on their return flight back to England. Regensburg was almost 750 miles from East Anglia, certainly the longest mission yet undertaken by the Eighth; it was estimated that the whole operation would involve about eleven hours flying time.

The take-off time was planned for dawn but misty conditions at the airfields delayed the start, but eventually by 9.30 am the 147-strong force was leaving the Suffolk coast behind. Castle was leading the 94th and it was placed in the middle formation, along with another Suffolk group, the 385th, which was probably the safest position, as the lead and trail formations were usually attacked first. It was planned that two Groups of P-47s would escort the bomber force as far as the German border, which was the limit of their range. However, one of the Groups failed to make the rendezvous on time with the result that the rear formation was left unprotected. Soon the force came under attack from Luftwaffe fighters, first Fw190s and

'The Flying Fortress' public house near Bury St Edmunds old airfield.

then later Me109s and 110s as well as Ju88s. These fighter attacks lasted for almost 90 minutes, which was 'sheer and unadulterated hell'. The bombing over the target area was said to be 'good and accurate', although some crews later confessed that they could see nothing because of the huge towering pall of black smoke covering the target area. The Force Commander, Major General Curtis Le May, later reported back to England: 'Objective believed totally destroyed.'

The battered and damaged remnants of the Groups finally landed at a variety of bases in Tunisia. Two B-17s had crash-landed in Switzerland, another eight had come down in the Mediterranean. The 94th had suffered the least harm with just one aircraft lost and another written off. As Lt Colonel Beirne Lay Jnr, a Headquarters observer flying with 100th Group, commented, ' . . We all felt the reaction of men who had not expected to see another sunset . . . One stint to Regensburg took more out of an airman than 20 normal missions . . .' An opinion that would be shared by all that took part in this famous mission. The two operations had cost the Eighth no less than 60 aircraft and over 600 men killed or missing in action. The 94th, along with the other Groups involved in the Regensburg shuttle, was awarded a Distinguished Unit Citation. The USAAF reserved this highly coveted award for a Group's meritorious achievement or performance either for a single mission or a succession of operations, and, of course, they were highly prized by the Group's personnel.

Almost two months later the Eighth, with that dogged perseverance that was a hallmark of their operational strategy, mounted a second mission to Schweinfurt. On 14th October 1943, 291 B-17s left in two waves but because of fierce fighter opposition only 229 were able to bomb the target. Once again the 94th did well on the outward leg and all of their 21 aircraft managed to reach the target. However, on the return leg they lost six aircraft, or just one tenth of the total losses. The two operations had been most costly – 120 aircraft lost – and they cast grave doubts on the whole policy of daylight bombing.

In between these two ghastly operations the 94th, along with other Groups in the 4th Bomb Wing, undertook a mission to the Focke Wulf plant at Marienburg on 9th October, which was hailed by the USAAF as 'the bombing event of the year'. Ninety six B-17s made the 1,500 mile round trip to this target in central Germany, and although the aircraft were airborne for over ten hours very little Luftwaffe opposition was met. The weather conditions over the target were clear and bright with the result that excellent bombing results were achieved. Only two aircraft were lost on this mission and the 94th returned home intact. However, it must be said that such successful missions were very rare during 1943.

Missions came and went, as did crews; some of the more fortunate ones completed their tours and 'went back stateside'. Replacement crews arrived weekly and to the veterans of the Group they seemed to be getting younger and younger – as indeed they were! The onset of the European winter brought even further strains on the crews. All had to get used to the cold and damp winter conditions of East Anglia. Ground crews found the routine servicing, bombing and arming the aircraft a thankless task and soon, at many airfields, small huts made out of surplus wood began to appear on the edges of the airfields; they at least afforded some warmth and protection from the bitingly cold winds that cut across the flat countryside. Flying at high altitudes even during the summer months created enough problems but northern European winters made operational life much more uncomfortable and placed quite intolerable physical strains on the aircrews. Sweat bands froze, icicles formed inside oygen masks, and frost-bite was quite common. Winter weather, such as ice, snow and freezing fog, only provided additional hazards to operating aircraft both on the ground and in the air, and the incidence of accidents greatly increased during the winter months.

In January 1944 the Group experienced yet another rugged mission, this time to Brunswick. It has already been noted that this target was not only heavily defended by flak batteries but was feared for its experienced and determined Luftwaffe fighter pilots stationed in the area. On the 11th of the month the mission was led by Lt Colonel Louis Thorup, the Air Executive Officer. After the bomber formations had assembled and departed for Germany the weather conditions seriously deteriorated, so much so that the operation was recalled when within 30 miles of the target – the Me110 assembly plant at Waggum. However, Lt Colonel Thorup considered that there was more than a good chance of visual bombing and he decided to continue the mission. The now rather small bomber formation came under almost continous fighter attacks but despite this onslaught and the barrage of heavy flak 47 aircraft managed to bomb the target. It was later disclosed that the bombing had been most accurate, all within 2,000 feet and many of the bombs falling even closer. As the aircraft headed for home their speed was reduced by a very strong head wind, and it was at this stage that most of the casualties

B-17s of 94th Bomb Group leave Marienburg. (IWM)

occurred. Unfortunately eight of the Group's aircraft were missing and all but one of the surviving aircraft suffered heavy damage. Lt Colonel Thorup was awarded the Silver Star for his brave leadership and the Group received their second Distinguished Unit Citation for their determination and their high standard of bombing.

April proved to be a busy month with 18 missions mounted for the loss of 21 aircraft. The heaviest loss was sustained on the 18th when the principal targets were aircraft factories at Brandenburg and Rathenow in central Germany. The Pathfinder aircraft, which was leading the 4th Wing, was shot down not far from the target area and unfortunately the Groups became rather isolated from the main bomber formation. The Luftwaffe always tried to take full advantage of such a situation, and on this day they attacked in strength and with a vengeance, with the result that eight B-17s from the Group failed to return. It was a hard introduction for the Group's new Commanding Officer – Colonel Charles Dougher – who had only taken over the previous day, when the very popular Colonel Castle had gained well-earned promotion to command of the 4th Bomb Wing, which also had its headquarters at the airfield.

Like many Bomb Groups the 94th flew their last operational mission on 21st April to Ingolstadt, and sad to relate the only aircraft lost by the Third Air Division on that day came from the Group. However, right up to VE Day and beyond the crews were active dropping leaflets over formerly occupied countries as well as ferrying displaced persons from Germany. There were plans to transfer the Group to serve in Germany and most of the aircraft were transferred to other Groups and B-17s equipped with H2X were received in return. By September plans were changed and it now seemed likely that the personnel would be back in the United States for Christmas. Indeed, most had left by 20th December when the airfield was handed over to the RAF.

The 94th had fought a long and exhausting battle over virtually every target selected by the Eighth Air Force and it would require a book to do justice to its immense contribution to the Eighth's air offensive. No less than 153 of the Group's aircraft were lost in action with another 27 destroyed in a variety of accidents. There are plenty of memorials to the Group, not least The Flying Fortress public house which is near the old airfield. But surely the most charming and evocative is the Old English Garden in the Abbey Gardens at Bury St Edmunds. The maintenance of this garden has been helped by the royalties earned from a delightful book, *Suffolk Summer*, written by John Appelby, who served as a Technical Sergeant with the 94th during 1945, and which has been reprinted countless times. The site of the old airfield is about a mile or so east of Bury St Edmunds and just off the main A45 road. Part of the site has been turned into a large industrial estate but the odd hangar and some other buildings can still be seen.

6
CHEDBURGH

The village sign of Chedburgh proudly recalls the presence of the RAF in the village during the five years when the airfield was active. The sign depicts a Lancaster bomber flying over a horse-drawn plough, an image which could well epitomise most of the wartime airfields in Suffolk. Near this sign is a plain and simple brick memorial to all the personnel who served at this Bomber Command station; one of a precious few RAF memorials in Suffolk.

Chedburgh was one of the earliest wartime airfields to come into operational use in the county. It was built during 1941/2 by John Laing & Co just to the south of the village and opened for business on 7th September 1942 as a satellite for nearby RAF Stradishall. As its parent station was under the control of No 3 Group of Bomber Command, it seemed only a matter of time before the first heavy bombers would make their appearance at Chedburgh.

It was just a month later when the first Short Stirlings landed at the airfield. The Stirling was one of the series of heavy bombers designed to the famous specification B12/36, which had such a major effect on the bombing offensive and really dictated the format of Bomber Command's strike force. Unfortunately this specification also limited the wing span of the aircraft to that of the standard width of a RAF hangar (100 feet), thus directly affecting the operational qualities of this famous bomber. It was the first of the four-engined bombers to come into service, flying its first operation in February 1941. Although the aircraft had certain limitations – notably its ceiling height (because of its 99 foot wing span) and its cruising speed – the Stirling proved to be a most sturdy aircraft that could sustain and survive considerable damage. At the time it was the first RAF bomber

The village sign at Chedburgh.

with the range and bomb capacity to be capable of delivering what Winston Churchill called 'the shattering strikes of retributive justice'!

When Chedburgh became operational in October 1942, it was at a time when the fortunes of Bomber Command were beginning to recover after the grim doubts of the winter of 1941/2. Under the leadership of Air Chief Marshal Harris it was beginning to assert itself as a powerful bomber force; the operations against Lübeck and Rostock, allied to the 1,000 bomber raids to Cologne, Essen and Bremen in May and June, had greatly restored the confidence and morale of the crews. However, the Command's losses were slowly creeping towards an unacceptable level. During the summer of 1942 over 500 aircraft had been lost (4.3%) and by the end of the year this figure had risen to 4.7% overall. It was accepted that if losses should continue at this level they would eventually lead to the demise of the Bomber Command as a strike force. Airmen selected for aircrew were expected to complete a tour of 30 missions, they were then rested for a period before being called back for another tour of 20 missions, and if they survived they were usually placed in training units and could not be forced to return to operations; although of course many did volunteer for a third tour. However, when losses hovered round the 4% mark, crews had about a 13% chance of surviving 50 missions!

The Stirlings that came to Chedburgh belonged to No 214 squadron, which had spent most of the early war years at Stradishall. The crews were soon active on some of the major bombing operations of late 1942 – Kiel, Essen, Mannheim, Genoa, Turin and Hamburg, as well as mine laying. Mine laying had become an increasingly important task for Bomber Command, and it was now committed to dropping at least 1,000 mines a month. The crews called it 'gardening' because each sea area was given a code-name, for instance Lorient was known as 'Artichoke' and the west Baltic as 'Sweet peas'! The Admiralty later claimed that for every mine dropped, 50 tons of enemy shipping was sunk on average. Mine laying was never an easy mission as *Bomber Command*, an official paperback published in 1941, explained. 'It is not unusual for the mine laying aircraft to fly around and round for a considerable time in order to make quite sure that the mine is laid exactly in the correct place. It calls for great skill and resolution. Moreover the crew do not have the satisfaction of seeing even the partial results of their work. There is no coloured explosion, no burgeoning fire to report on their return home. At least, all they see is a splash on the surface of a darkened and inhospitable sea.' However, the loss rate was lower than operating over Germany, and more especially from 1943 when the Command discovered the means of dropping mines from a greater height – 6,000 instead of 2-3,000 feet – which greatly reduced the casualty rate.

In 1943 Bomber Command launched its first major bombing offensive, which has become known as the Battle of the Ruhr – effectively 43 attacks on targets in the Ruhr conducted from 5th March to 14th July. This massive assault caused considerable damage to the heartland of German heavy industry but at a very high cost – 640 aircraft lost with almost 3,000 aircrew killed and another 760 made prisoners of war. The Ruhr had, of course, been a favourite hunting ground for Bomber Command since 1940 and had become known to its crews variously as The Happy Valley, The Land of No Return or The Graveyard of the RAF. The British war cemeteries at Rheinberg and Reichswald Forest contain the graves of many RAF airmen who were lost over the Ruhr.

Bomber Command had two new devices to aid navigation and blind bombing – Oboe and H2S. Oboe was a blind bombing device based on pulses received from two ground transmitting stations in

England, which was first trialled on 20/21st December 1942. However, the system had certain operational limits. Only one aircraft could use the two stations at one time and even by July, when three pairs of stations were operating, they could only cope with 18 aircraft in an hour. It was also limited by the curvature of the earth – its range was up to 270 miles. Furthermore aircraft using Oboe were required to fly level and straight for several minutes thus making them ideal targets for both enemy flak and fighters. Some of these problems were resolved by using Mosquitos as marker aircraft as their speed and operational ceiling nullified some of the disadvantages. One of the major advantages of Oboe was that the Germans were unable to produce a jamming device. 'Oboe' Mosquitos were employed on all of the Ruhr raids.

The second device, H2S, was an airborne radar navigational and bomb aiming aid, which was used by Pathfinder aircraft during the battle and came into general use with the main bomber force late in 1943. The name of the device is said to have originated with Lord Cherwell, one of Churchill's scientific advisers, who commented early in its development that 'it stinks', hence the chemical equation for hydrogen sulphide was used as its code-name. Unfortunately, on one of the early trials a Stirling with H2S on board was captured intact and within about six months the Germans had devised a system called Naxos, which could home in onto H2S transmissions, thus making the leading aircraft very vulnerable to enemy attack.

The first operation of the Battle of the Ruhr was mounted on the night of 5/6th March and was directed at Essen with the Krupps munitions complex being the particular target. This city proved to be the hardest hit during the war, suffering no less than 186 full-scale raids. On this first operation No 214 squadron lost one Stirling, which crashed into the sea near Texel with all of the seven-man crew being killed. The thought of ditching was one of the greatest fears for most aircrews mainly because the chances of survival were rather slim at this period of the war. Most squadrons undertook considerable training in escape drill procedures, though few crews felt it was worth the effort.

The squadron suffered further losses over Mannheim, Dortmund, Bochum, Mülheim, Wuppertal, Gelsenkirchen and Essen once again. Their worst night was on 23/24th May when the target was Dortmund. This proved to be the biggest raid of the battle with 826 aircraft taking part and over 2,240 tons of bombs being dropped. Large areas of the city were devastated. Four aircraft failed to return to Chedburgh with 23 airmen killed and another five made prisoners of war.

During June a new squadron – No 620 – was formed out of 'C' flight of 214 squadron and it too was soon active over the Ruhr. In four missions the new squadron lost nine aircraft compared with eleven lost by its 'parent' squadron. The end of the Battle of the Ruhr came with a raid on Remscheid, which had hitherto escaped Bomber Command's attentions. This proved to be the most successful and effective operation of the whole battle with almost 80% of the town being destroyed resulting in a severe loss to its industrial production. No 620 lost two aircraft, one to flak and the other shot down by a Junkers 88 night fighter near Brussels. On this operation the Stirlings suffered the heaviest losses – over 10%. Both squadrons were engaged in the four heavy raids on Hamburg during the last week of July and early August. No 620 mounted 37 sorties without a single casualty. However, the other Chedburgh squadron fared worse, it lost three aircraft. Certainly the Stirling squadrons were paying a heavy price for the Command's almost continuous nightly assault on Germany.

Then on the night of 23/24 August 1943 what has become known as the Battle of Berlin opened with a total force of 719 aircraft – including 124 Stirlings – attacking this major target. The Berlin battle turned out to be a long, harsh and very costly offensive but it was the

Short Stirling I: Chedburgh was greatly involved in operations and conversion training with these famous bombers.

target that most aircrews wanted to enter in their log-books. As one crew member recalled, 'This was different. If we could handle this one, then we could handle anything.' On the first raid No 214 squadron lost two aircraft, both of which had senior and experienced crews, each on their 24th mission. The squadron sent 32 Stirlings out on the first three raids losing five aircraft (15%), whereas No 620 squadron despatched just twelve aircraft on two raids losing two (16%) in the process. Such a heavy loss rate by the Stirling squadrons when multiplied throughout the Command could not be tolerated for very long.

The third Berlin raid on 22/23rd November saw the demise of the Stirling as a main front-line bomber. There was no doubt that the Stirling squadrons had suffered disproportionately compared with the Lancaster and Halifax squadrons. In the three raids the loss rate overall was over 16% and this was sufficient evidence for Harris to decide that the Stirlings had become a spent force. Already No 620 squadron had been transferred out to No 38 Group, which largely served the Airborne forces in providing transport aircraft and glider towers as well as flying special operations. On 10th December No 214 squadron left for Downham Market in Norfolk and ultimate service in No 100 Group, to be engaged in a variety of radio-counter measures operating with Flying Fortresses. The squadron had flown a long and meritorious campaign with its Wellingtons and Stirlings – a total of 315 bombing and 89 mine laying missions for the loss of 99 aircraft.

Like its parent station – Stradishall – the airfield now became largely engaged in the training of aircrews on four-engined aircraft and it was not until almost one year later that Chedburgh became once again a fully operational airfield when No 218 arrived from Methwold in Norfolk bringing its Lancasters. This squadron was also known as 'The Gold Coast' squadron from late 1941 when the people of that colony had officially adopted the squadron.

Since October 1944, Air Vice-Marshal Harrison, the AOC of No 3 Group had been given a relatively free hand in operating his Lancaster force. He had about 60 G-H equipped Lancasters, which were spread throughout the Group's squadrons, and they were frequently used independently of the main bomber force, acting as a rather specialised force to strike at small strategic targets, especially when the weather conditions precluded visual bombing. This new radar aid, G-H, had been first suggested at the same time as GEE but development work did not begin until 1942 and the first operational trial did not take place until November 1943. The radar set in the aircraft originated the emissions, which alerted two ground stations who responded with signals, then by measuring the time-interval between the signals and aware of his distance from the ground stations the navigator could precisely fix his position. In fact G-H really embodied the principle of GEE navigation and the H part gave an accurate position.

The squadron became involved in many of the Group's operations to a variety of targets in the Ruhr which were mounted during January to March and the majority of these were conducted in daylight. The main bombing objectives, of what has been called the Second Battle of the Ruhr, were oil installations and refineries and railway yards. Although by the end of 1944 Bomber Command's rate of losses had been reduced to about 1%, there were still occasional operations when relatively high losses were sustained. For instance, on 12th December, when Witten, just south of Dortmund, received its first major raid of the war conducted by 140 Lancasters, eight aircraft failed to return – 5.7% loss.

As the weather began to improve somewhat during February 1945, No 3 Group launched a number of daylight raids on oil and benzol plants at Dortmund, Gelsenkirchen, Datteln and Wanne-Eickel. Most of these operations were very effective and were achieved with the minimum of casualties. On 11/12th March Bomber Command mounted one of its last major operations of the war with over 1,000 bombers being directed against Essen and Dortmund. These missions showed the devastating power of Bomber Command; both cities were virtually left in ruins and with life almost completely paralysed until captured by the Allied forces some weeks later. However, the operational life of the squadron came to an end on 24th April when 18 Lancasters left Chedburgh to bomb the rail··ay yards at Bad Oldersloe. Unfortunately this final mission was marred when one Lancaster crashed on take-off killing all the crew – a very sad conclusion to the story of this wartime airfield, of which very little has survived.

7
DEBACH

Although nature has swallowed up much of the remains of this wartime airfield, which had such a brief operational life, nevertheless a search will reveal a ruined control tower. It is rather difficult to appreciate that when this building throbbed with life and rang to the sounds of wartime activity, the Eighth Air Force was at the pinnacle of its power and strength – certainly meriting the prefix of Mighty. Indeed the Bomb Group that found a home in this quiet and secluded corner of Suffolk became the fortieth and last combat unit to join the Mighty Eighth in England.

The site of the airfield, which nestled between the small villages of Debach and Clopton, had been earmarked for the USAAF as early as August 1942 and the period of gestation to full operational status turned out to be rather prolonged. It was built during 1942/3 by personnel of Nos 820 and 829 Engineer Battalions (Aviation) of the US Army with, of course, the assistance of a number of British sub-contractors. Like all heavy bomber stations constructed at this stage of the war, it was provided with three concrete runways – one at 2,000 and two at 1,400 yards – 50 loop dispersals or hardstandings and two T2 hangars. The headquarters, technical and living accommodation (for almost 2,900 personnel) were built on the farmland towards Clopton to the west of the airfield. However, Debach was slightly different to other airfields of the time in that within its perimeter was a large and rather fine house – Thistleton Hall; this was situated to the south-west of the main runway. The Hall, quite naturally, was utilised for additional billets but unfortunately it suffered so much damage after the end of the war that it had to be demolished.

It was one of the five B-24 groups that were allocated to the Third

Division in late 1943 that finally arrived at Debach in April 1944, although the aircraft did not appear until the following month. The 493rd Bomb Group, along with other tyro airmen at Eye and Mendlesham, completed the 93rd Combat Bomb Wing. Like many groups in the Eighth, the men of the 493rd decided they needed a catchy name to establish a positive Group identity instead of the anonymity of being just another number. The sobriquet they chose was 'Helton's Hellcats', after their Commanding Officer, Colonel Elbert Helton. They were equipped with B-24Js, the latest variation of this most prolific aircraft. This model was not new to England as some had been arriving since the previous November as replacement aircraft. There was little difference in performance, but it did have wing de-icing refinements and the most noticeable change was the hydraulically operated nose turret.

The Group's first mission was mounted on a most historic day – Tuesday 6th June 1944 (D-Day). In fact the introduction of a new Group was almost lost in the massive formations of heavy bombers that were despatched on that day; the Eighth had no less than 2,362 bombers airborne. Unfortunately it was not a particularly auspicious start for the Group as two of its aircraft were lost in a collision, a fatal error that perhaps betrayed the inexperience of their crews.

In the first month the crews of the 493rd spent most of their time

A winter's scene at Debach. (USAF)

77

attacking rail targets and airfields in France as well as tackling V1 rocket sites in the Pas de Calais. The first time they ventured over Germany was on 20th June when they took part in the major operation launched against oil plants, aircraft factories and a ball-bearing factory. Compared with the relatively short hauls across to France the crews found this deep penetrative mission into southern Germany a vastly different type of air warfare. On this day it was said that the bomber formations formed a stream over 200 miles long and rather fortunately the Luftwaffe's fighters were conspicuous by their absence. Colonel Helton could reflect that his Hellcats had made a satisfactory entry into the war, having lost just seven aircraft in their first month of operations.

However, shortly the Group would be required to exchange their B-24s for B-17s like the other Groups in the Third Division. Irrespective of the relative merits of the two heavy bombers, the Division's chiefs had found the problems of operating both types of aircraft increasingly difficult. Differences in range, cruising speeds, bomb loads and more especially operating altitudes had made the already complex task of mounting operations that much more complicated. The change-over started in late August and was not fully completed until October. At first there was some natural resentment over the change of aircraft, but the crews were quick to establish a loyalty to their 'ships' and soon most acknowledged, even if somewhat reluctantly, that the B-17 was easier to handle and more comfortable to operate in, with more elbow room and better heating.

The Group's last and 47th mission with B-24s came on 24th August – a fact which emphasised the hectic rate of operations during the summer of 1944. It says much for the professionalism of the crews and their Commanding Officer that in less than two weeks (3rd September) they were ready to go out on their first mission with their new aircraft. The first three missions passed without incident and in retrospect they might be considered no more than additional flying practice before they became engaged in the Eighth's major offensive against the German oil industry.

On 11th September over 1,100 bombers were sent to a variety of targets. The 493rd was despatched to Ruhland and all their aircraft returned safely but one was so badly damaged that it was considered a write-off. The following day the Group's target was Magdeburg and they were flying the 'low-box' of the formation — quite a vulnerable place. Suddenly they found themselves engaged by a large number of Me109s, which attacked singly both to the nose and tail of the

B-17G of the 493rd Bomb Group. (USAF)

bombers, and within a matter of minutes seven B-17s were shot down. This was really the Group's first taste of sustained enemy fighter attacks and they suffered grievously. Ultimately nine aircraft were lost on this mission with another one written-off; this proved to be their heaviest loss of the war in a single mission. By the end of September the Group had completed 14 missions with B-17s and in the process had lost a total of 16 aircraft. Despite the one disastrous day this was a most noteworthy initiation into B-17 operations.

On 12th December there was a clear example of the quite horrifying results that could be caused by crews having to abort missions and return to their bases still fully loaded with bombs and aviation fuel. The normal and accepted sign of an aircraft aborting was to lower the undercarriage, this informed the Group leader and the other crews to close up the formation. It was on a mission to Darmstadt that *Devil's Own* experienced engine trouble, which decided the pilot, Lt John De Witt, to abort and try to land at Debach. Suddenly the faulty engine burst into flames and although he dived the aircraft in an attempt to put out the fire it continued to blaze furiously. Returning at barely 2,000 feet, with great skill de Witt managed to make a belly landing and only just missed a parked B-17 and an army truck. Before the aircraft came to a shuddering halt the burning wing folded back over the fuselage. The crew managed to scramble out and within seconds of De Witt escaping, the aircraft blew up with a terrific explosion that rocked the surrounding countryside. The blast of the explosion took a 30 foot high hangar door off its rollers and deposited it several yards away! The rest of the crews arrived home safely but only to be greeted by a scene of utter devastation with bits of B-17 strewn all over the airfield.

A major and important milestone for the Group came on 10th January 1945 – their 100th mission. The exceptionally bad weather that was experienced during the winter of 1944/5 – icy conditions, freezing fog and heavy snowfalls – added to the problems of mounting missions. As the Group's records state, '. . . It is sincerely hoped that no future mission will be as difficult to get airborne as was this Group's hundredth mission . . . It had snowed [some six inches] immediately before take-off, making taxiing in the darkness even more tricky than usual with the result that several aircraft got stuck off the hardstands . . .' Matters were not improved when one aircraft crashed and exploded shortly after take-off, killing four of the crew. Eventually 30 aircraft managed to get airborne and bombed the Hohenzollern railway bridge near Cologne. All returned and landed safely.

Two major changes occurred in February. On the first of the month the Group lost one of its squadrons – 862 – to become the 3rd Scouting Force based at Wormingford in Essex. In August 1944 each Bomb Division had established its own Scouting Force to provide weather information over specific target areas. The early missions had been conducted by Mosquitos but P-51s were later found to be more suitable. However, in January the Third Division decided to extend this weather service to the bomber assembly points and the North Sea and for this purpose they used stripped down B-17s, hence the loss of the No 862 squadron.

The other change affected all the personnel at Debach. On the 15th the very popular Commanding Officer – Colonel Helton – left for a desk job. He had been in charge of the Group since it had been first formed in November 1943, seen it through its training and eight months of operations. The 'Old Man' would be sorely missed. His replacement was Colonel Robert Landry, who had previously commanded the very successful 56th Fighter Group whilst it was stationed at Halesworth. Colonel Landry became the only officer to command both a bomber and fighter group in the Eighth Air Force.

On 22nd February 1945, the Allied air forces launched Operation Clarion – an all-out onslaught on road, rail and canal communications in Germany, in an attempt to wipe out every means of transport available to the enemy, all within a space of 24 hours. Nearly 9,000 Allied aircraft from airfields in England, France, Holland, Belgium and Italy were engaged in this massive bombardment. Many of the targets had not previously been bombed and the orders for the operation were that the crews should attain a high degree of accuracy in order that civilian casualties be kept to a minimum.

The 493rd was just part of over 1,400 bombers that were operating on the 22nd; their specific target was Bamberg in south-central Germany and the following day they were sent to Ansbach, even further south. On both occasions all the Group's aircraft returned safely. In fact in this two days of operations over 2,700 bombers were despatched for the loss of a 'mere' eight aircraft – a demonstration of the awesome might of the Eighth Air Force.

During March the runways at Debach were closed to flying, in need of urgent repair due to subsidence. The aircraft and crews moved to Little Walden in north Essex. This was the home of the 361st Fighter Group, which had been temporarily transferred to a captured airfield in Belgium. However, by the end of the month the 493rd was able to return home and continued their operations from Debach until 7th May when they had completed the last of their food-dropping missions over Holland. Their final tally amounted to 162 missions.

With the war now over many of the personnel at Debach could safely reflect on the highlights of their twelve months in Suffolk. Perhaps for many their minds would go back to the occasion in October 1944 when one of the hangars at the airfield was converted

The ruined control tower.

to a cinema and used by MGM for the world premiere of Lana Turner's new film *Marriage is a Private Affair*! This had come about when MGM had heard that the crew of a B-17 of 862 squadron had named it *Tempest Turner* after the famous Hollywood star.

By the first week of August all the Americans had gone. Perhaps somewhat ironically the airfield buildings were used by German prisoners of war and later for displaced persons before it was finally closed down in 1948. What little remains of the airfield can be reached by taking the B1079 from the A12 at Woodbridge, through the villages of Grundisburgh and Clopton and then right onto the B1078 at Clopton Corner, where the entrance to the old airfield may be seen on the right. It must be pointed out that the old control tower is sited on private land and permission is needed to search for it.

8

EYE

For several centuries the site of this airfield had been part of the Cornwallis estate, owned by a family that became deeply involved in American affairs. Therefore it would seem rather appropriate that in September 1942 it was American soldiers of the 827th and 859th Engineer Battalions that came to prepare the site for its ultimate use as an airfield. During its construction it was known as Brome but later it took the name of Eye, from the small market town about half a mile south-east of its perimeter. The rather splendid 100 foot tower of the church of St Peter and St Paul, which so dominates the landscape along this stretch of the Dove valley, was very close to the flight path of one of the three runways and almost constituted a hazard to flying, though thankfully no accident befell the tower during the twelve months or so that the airfield was active.

Another unusual feature of the airfield was that eight of the hardstandings were sited to the west of the main A140 road, which entailed erecting a gate and a permanent guard to control the traffic when the aircraft were being moved to and from these standings.

By February 1944 the airfield was just about ready for occupation. All the American airmen, who trained with the 490th Bomb Group in Idaho during the early months of 1944, were imbued with a strong sense of purpose and determination and were utterly confident of their superiority. This attitude can partly be attributed to the inherent self-confidence and almost brashness of American servicemen generally, but it was mainly fostered by all the publicity in the American press about the Eighth Air Force successes in Europe. Many American servicemen were convinced that they were over here 'to win the war for you British', which when expressed in such bold terms did not go down too well with the locals or British servicemen! The American public were hardly made aware of the terrible losses to men and aircraft that the Eighth had suffered over Germany, particularly in the previous six months. The same could be said of the British public, who were equally kept in the dark about Bomber Command's mounting losses.

However, these young American airmen were not to know that their chances of surviving a tour of operations – now raised from 30 to 35 missions – were infinitely improved compared with the 'veterans' of 1943, when it was estimated that the average operational life of aircrews was barely 15 missions. Furthermore, as the number of missions increased dramatically from the summer of 1944, a fortunate airman could complete a tour in about three months or so. He would then return home with his 'lucky bastard' certificate, which was unofficially issued by all Bomb Groups, to prove the fact. Quite naturally these certificates became treasured possessions and most had pride of place on the walls of homes or offices.

After their arrival in England, during April 1944, the Group took their place in the 93rd Combat Bomb Wing of the Third Division, along with the other two B-24 Groups – the 34th at Mendlesham and 493rd at Debach. Their first operation was called on 31st May to attack rail targets in Belgium. However, on that day there were particularly heavy cloud formations and as the crews were ordered to climb above the cloud, the inexperienced pilots lost their formation and it was decided to abandon the mission. One 490th pilot did not hear the recall message and grimly ploughed on alone, unloading the bombs on an airfield near Rotterdam before returning to Eye about two hours later.

The Group's first successful mission was completed on 4th June when airfields in the Paris area were attacked without a single loss. D-Day saw it suffer its first casualty when one of the B-24s, returning from the Normandy beach-head, crashed on Chesil Beach in Dorset with seven of the crew managing to make their escape. Unfortunately the following day, after a rather unsatisfactory trip to Angers, where heavy cloud had made effective bombing rather difficult, two damaged aircraft landed at RAF Feltwell in Norfolk and collided on the runway with the result that they were both written off. By the time the Group were ready to exchange their B-24s for B-17s, they had lost more aircraft to accidental causes than to enemy action! Indeed, 29th July was a particularly unfortunate day as one aircraft crashed on take-off, landing at Yaxley at the south-east corner of the

The lych gate at Brome in memory of the 490th Bomb Group at Eye.

airfield. Then when the Group returned from their mission one B-24 crashed almost directly on the A140 at Brome narrowly missing the local pub, no doubt to the great relief of all the base personnel! By the end of the war the Group had lost 32 aircraft due to accidental causes, which really was about average for the Eighth Air Force.

The 490th was no different to any other combat group in the Eighth in that most crews and fighter pilots not only gave their aircraft personal names but also illustrated these names on the noses of their aircraft. This 'nose art' of the Eighth has rightly become famous. Obviously the most notable and eye-catching examples were those of scantily clothed young ladies in a variety of poses, some of which were sexually quite explicit; how much so largely depended on the attitude taken by the Group's Commanding Officer. Many of the paintings were of a very high standard, their quality depending on the artistic talent available at each airfield. The 490th did employ the services of a talented local artist – Anne Hayward. Some of the aircraft at Eye had been given such names as *Bobby Sox, Carolina Moon, $5 with breakfast* and *Alice Blue Gown,* most of the illustrations for these names inspired by the famous American artist Vargas, who was noted for his drawings of calendar girls. Of course, many of Bomber Command's aircraft were also named and there were examples of RAF nose art but these paintings tended to be far more decorous!

Unseasonable weather greatly affected the Group's first operation with its new B-17s on 27th August 1944. The targets were enemy airfields at Flensburg, almost on the border between Germany and Denmark, which incidentally was one of the last areas to surrender to the Allied forces in May 1945. Very heavy cloud over Denmark and northern Germany resulted in the mission being recalled, which was always frustrating for the crews especially in this instance as they had progressed so close to the target area. Similar poor weather conditions prevailed on 1st September but this time over France, with only six Groups (including the 490th) claiming a credit sortie. Two of the Group's aircraft collided in the heavy cloud and crashed in liberated France with the loss of 17 lives. Their first 'real' B-17 mission was launched two days later when the Division sent a 400 strong bomber force to attack German gun batteries in the Brest area, which were staunchly holding out against the Allied land forces. This proved to be a rather successful air-strike with almost all the crews claiming to have bombed the primary targets effectively. Then on four successive days, from the 10th to 13th, the 490th attacked tank factories at Nuremberg and oil targets at Ruhland, Magdeburg and Stuttgart. In these long and harrowing missions into central and southern Germany the 490th lost only two aircraft despite encountering heavy flak and some stern fighter opposition – both aircraft were lost on the last operation. During these four days the Group's crews certainly can be said to have come of age.

In almost three weeks from 17th September, the 490th undertook eleven missions without losing a single aircraft to enemy action and when one considers that the crews operated over such targets as Ludwigshafen, Kassel, Merseburg, Münster and Coblenz, this was no mean feat, and probably accounts for the fact that on 3rd October the crews were given a rare day off operations. However, 'Big B' or Berlin beckoned and on 6th October the Group was detailed for the Third Division's operation to the Elkett factories at Spandau on the outskirts of the city. This large munitions complex was thought to produce over 50% of the Wehrmacht's artillery guns. It proved to be a rather formidable mission for the Division, as 18 aircraft were lost with well over half the force returning with flak damage. One of the Combat Wings – the 4th – suffered from a sustained fighter attack, but the 490th returned home to Eye with just one aircraft missing. It would be another two months (5th December) before the crews returned to Berlin – the Tegel tanks works – and this time they went one better, they made the trip without a single loss!

In April 1945 when it was felt that the war was rapidly coming to a close, the Group found out to their cost that the Luftwaffe had certainly not yet given up the fight. On the 7th the Eighth launched a large operation to a wide variety of targets in northern Germany – fighter airfields, oil depots and railway yards. One of the main targets for the Third Division was the jet-fighter airfield at Kaltenkirchen, which was some 20 miles north of Hamburg. On this day the Luftwaffe was out in strength and their force included some Me262s – the famed and feared turbo jet-fighters. The escorting P-51s had quite a field day but what deeply concerned the crews of the 490th was that they had been attacked by a gruppe of Fw190s, who seemed hell-bent on bringing down the B-17s by any means including ramming them. One of the Group's aircraft was a victim of these suicide attacks and although the B-17 was severely damaged the pilot managed to land it on an airfield in liberated territory.

At the various de-briefings after the operation the official view was that the so-called 'ramming' was nothing more than the enemy fighters pressing their attacks too closely and then losing control. But most of the American aircrews thought otherwise and were convinced that they had faced a suicide force, which was a most daunting and frightening thought. Intelligence reports later confirmed this view. It would appear that in March, Goering had called for volunteers for 'special operations', which turned out to be a suicide force known as Sonderkommando Elbe, which was possibly about 120 strong. The Luftwaffe pilots were ordered to make a diving attack on the bombers and if that failed they were to ram the bomber's fuselage just forward of the tail, which should break the B-17 in half. However, the mission of 7th April was the only known time that these tactics were employed by the Luftwaffe, quite probably because of the 60 enemy fighters claimed to have been shot down on that day, many must have come from this 'suicide force'.

The Group's penultimate mission of the war (19th April) was to rail targets in southern Germany – Pirna and Aussig, both south of Dresden. As the 490th was approaching the marshalling yards at Aussig, a Me262 suddenly appeared and shot down a B-17 in the leading formation. This solitary fighter was quickly joined by another two, both climbed swiftly out of clouds and swept through the formation, claiming another three of the Group's aircraft. Before they could do even more damage they were shot down by two Groups of

B-17 parked in snow outside the hangars at Eye – January 1945. (USAF)

P-51s from Honington and Leiston (357th and 364th). It was a particularly harsh blow for the 490th to suffer their biggest single loss on a mission – 36 airmen would not be returning with the rest of the Group to the United States. This proved to be the last aerial battle of the war between the Eighth Air Force and the Luftwaffe.

In their eleven months of operations the Group had lost 22 aircraft whilst mounting no less than 158 missions, and considering that four of these had fallen on 19th April, it was a quite amazing performance. During the early days of May the Group was engaged on five food missions to occupied northern Holland dropping some 384 tons of food and medical supplies. However, by the second week of July all the B-17s had departed from Eye. Much later British Gas moved in and now has established a large pumping station on the site of the airfield, although much of the main runway has survived. A fine lych-gate reminds the local people of the contribution made by the 490th during their relatively short stay at Eye, and it is an acknowledgement of the 'friendship and co-operation' between the local people and the American airmen.

9
FELIXSTOWE

For almost 50 years Felixstowe was an air station, which saw all the famous, and many not so well known, flying boats of those years use its waters and facilities. They ranged from the early Sopwiths through to Felixstowes, Southamptons, Singapores, Londons, Lerwicks, Stranraers, Catalinas, Sunderlands, Walruses and Sea Otters.

It was in 1910 that the Admiralty built oil storage tanks at the small port, which were thought to be the first bulk storage tanks ever to be erected in the country. Therefore when the Naval Wing of the Royal Flying Corps (which was formed in May 1912) was seeking a base for its hydro-planes, the eastern banks of the river Orwell seemed an ideal site. In April 1913 it was announced that a Naval Air Station would be constructed in Harwich harbour. Just three months later the term hydro-plane was replaced by seaplane, and on 5th August 1913 the new air station came into being under the name 'Seaplanes – Felixstowe'. Almost a year later (1st July) the Royal Naval Air Service was formed and Felixstowe, with its three large hangars and slipways and jetties, became one of its premier stations.

In March 1924 the Marine Aircraft Experimental Unit moved from its base at the Isle of Grain and from 1st April became known as the MAEE (Establishment), echoing its near neighbour at Martlesham Heath. For the next 15 years Felixstowe would be fully engaged in the testing and trialling of all the seaplanes or flying boats of the pre-war years. From 1935 to August 1939 No 209 squadron operated its Short Singapore flying boats from the station.

At the outbreak of the war Felixstowe was considered to be in the front line and a rather too vulnerable spot for an experimental base,

Short Sunderlands – the famous flying boats – a stalwart with Coastal Command, could be seen at Felixstowe during the war years.

so the MAEE was moved north to Helensburgh in Scotland. Flying in the vicinity was also a rather risky occupation, mainly because of the balloon barrage that was in place to guard the port of Harwich, which had already taken a toll of several RAF aircraft. The air station was never really operational during the war and a Maintenance Unit moved in to undertake major repairs or overhauls on Short Sunderlands. These impressive and majestic flying boats operated with conspicuous success with RAF Coastal Command throughout the war. There was also the odd Supermarine Walrus helping out on air-sea rescue duties.

At the end of November 1940, just three Fokker TVIIIs of No 320 (Dutch) squadron of Coastal Command arrived at Felixstowe from Pembroke Dock. These small twin-engined floatplanes had belonged to the Netherlands Marine Air Force and had managed to escape, via France, from the German occupation. The aircraft stayed at Felixstowe until June 1941 when they were scrapped.

During October 1942 another Fokker floatplane from No 320 squadron arrived at the station to undertake a special operation to a lake in occupied Holland in order to pick up four secret agents. However, the first flight was abortive because of the mist covering the lake and also the agreed signal was not evident, so the crew returned to Felixstowe. The following night (16th) the crew made a second attempt, this time the correct signal was displayed and just after the

90

aircraft had landed, it immediately came under fire so the pilot took off without delay. When the aircraft arrived back to Felixstowe in the early hours of the morning, it came under fire once again, this time from a Home Guard patrol, which had assumed that it was an enemy aircraft!

From the summer of 1940 the fast motor torpedo boats of the Royal Navy used Felixstowe as one of its bases for operations in the North Sea. Also the high speed launches of No 26 Air Sea Rescue (Marine Craft) squadron operated from the station, and the brave and daring exploits of these flotillas were splendidly captured by John Harris's novel *The Sea Shall Not Have Them*, which indeed was the motto of the Service.

With the return of the MAEE in May 1945 the evaluation and trialling of a variety of flying boats continued, including several captured enemy aircraft. By March 1956 the MAEE ceased to exist with much of its experimental work being conducted at RAE at Farnborough, although the days of large flying boats were coming to an end. For the next five years the Westland Whirlwind helicopters of No 22 squadron used the base for air-sea rescue duties. In May 1961 the squadron moved to RAF Tangmere and the RAF Regiment used the base for almost twelve months, until May 1962 when the airmen's long association with Felixstowe came to an end.

10
FRAMLINGHAM

It would be fair to say that no Bomb Group in the 4th Bomb Wing had as stern a baptism of fire as the 390th. Within just five days of becoming operational, and with only two missions under their belts, the crews found themselves engaged in that most torrid operation – Regensburg. However, the story of the 390th goes back to January 1943 when it was first activated under the command of Colonel Edgar Wittan, and it was from his surname that the Group acquired its name 'Wittan's Wallopers'.

By June the crews were going through the School of Applied Tactics in Orlando, Florida, which was a new training programme intended to give the crews a more practical idea of what they were likely to experience on operations with the Eighth. In fact they were the first of the new Groups to pass through the school and their subsequent performances with the Eighth showed the value of this type of advanced training.

By the middle of July the first B-17Fs began to arrive at Framlingham although the airfield was still lacking in some facilities. The airfield, which was about three miles south-east of the historic town, had also been known as Parham from the nearby small village. It had already been occupied by a Bomb Group – the 95th – who stayed for about a month and mounted a couple of operations before moving to their permanent base at Horham about ten miles further to the north-east.

Within a month or so of their arrival the crews (or at least 21) were thought to be sufficiently prepared to be sent out on their first mission to Bonn on 12th August. The 390th became the seventh Group to join the 4th Bomb Wing, which was rapidly growing in size, almost as large as the veteran 1st Bomb Wing. Unfortunately the first operational take-off was marred by an accident to one B-17 that crashed. Just three days later 21 of the Group's crews were operating over enemy airfields in northern France. On this second mission, two of the Group's aircraft collided over Dunkirk; one crashed but the other managed to make it back to Framlingham.

The early morning briefing on 17th August confirmed the worst fears of the 20 crews that had been detailed for the day's mission. It was going to be the deepest penetration raid yet made by the Eighth – to Regensburg and its Messerschmitt factories. Then when they were told to pack an overnight bag they knew for certain that they were in for a long and harrowing day. The Group was in the leading formation and suffered almost as heavily as the 100th. Six aircraft and 60 airmen were lost but despite this the Group's crews gained the best bombing results of the whole force; over half the bombs fell within 1,000 feet of the target area and the rest within 2,000 feet – an admirable achievement for the most junior Group.

Whilst most of the Group was away in North Africa, two missions were sent from Framlingham. Only seven aircraft were available and one of these was lost on the 24th August when it ditched in the North Sea on return from a raid on Conches airfield. By the evening the surviving ten aircraft arrived back from North Africa. However, three days later when the Eighth launched its first operation against the V1 rocket sites at Watten, the 390th was only able to put up a token force of just seven B-17s.

Temporary bomb dump at Framlingham, B-17 of 390th Bomb Group in the distance. (USAF)

On 8th October 1943 the Third Division (as it had become known in September) despatched 170 aircraft as part of a three-pronged attack – almost 400 strong – on Bremen. All three Divisions met heavy fighter opposition and for the first time the leading Groups of the Third used Carpet, a British radio device intended to block the German radar used by the flak batteries. However, it was the Luftwaffe who inflicted the most damage; the Group lost three aircraft but claimed 32 of the 84 enemy aircraft destroyed, the Eighth suffered a loss of 30 aircraft (7.5%). The accuracy of the bombing was somewhat impaired by the rather effective smoke screen put up by the defences; by now most of the German ports employed smoke defences.

The following day just five of the Division's Groups went out on a long mission to Marienburg, which resulted in a 1,500 mile round trip with some ten hours flying time. This operation was an overwhelming success, excellent bombing with only two losses in total. Really a demonstration of daylight strategic bombing at its finest, which received very full publicity. Next day it was a vastly different matter. The primary target was Münster – its railway junction and the canal – although, on this occasion, the crews were directed to bomb the city centre; the first time the Eighth Air Force had resorted to 'area' bombing. The day proved to be the heaviest air battle with the Luftwaffe of the whole war, and the 390th suffered grievously in losing eight aircraft. One of its pilots who went missing over Münster was Lt John Winant, the son of the American Ambassador to Britain. However, he managed to bale out and spent the rest of the war as a POW. The ferocity of the Luftwaffe's onslaught can be gauged by the claims of enemy aircraft destroyed – 177; of this total the gunners of the 390th bagged 60, which was to prove to be the highest total on a single mission by any Bomb Group during the war.

The slaughter had not ceased, four days later the Eighth would receive a cataclysmic body blow equalling their losses of 17th August. The second mission to the ball-bearing plants at Schweinfurt resulted in 60 aircraft missing in action, another five crash-landing in England and twelve so badly damaged that they were written off. Unlike Münster it was the turn of First Division to bear the brunt of the attacks, losing 45 B-17s. The Third Division Groups bombed very successfully and suffered most of their losses on withdrawal from the target area. All 15 aircraft of the 390th were effective and only one aircraft was lost. Their performance on 'Black Thursday', as it

94

Damaged B-17 of 390th Bomb Group on return from Regensburg. (USAF)

became known, led to the Group's second Distinguished Unit Citation.

Group Captain 'Johnnie' Johnson, was leading a Spitfire formation sent out to escort the bombers back across the Channel and he described the aftermath of this great air battle. '. . . As we closed the gap we could see that they had taken a terrible mauling, for there were gaping holes in their precise formations. Some Fortresses were gradually losing height, and a few stragglers, lagging well behind, were struggling to get home on three engines . . . what a fight it must have been, because more than half the bombers we nursed across the North Sea were shot up. One or two ditched in the sea, and many others, carrying dead and badly injured crew members, had to make crash-landings . . .'

In November (16th) the Eighth decided to have another go at Norwegian targets – they had previously mounted an inconclusive operation back in July. This time the Third Division's Groups were sent to seek out a generating station at Rjukan, which was about 90 miles west of Oslo. According to Allied intelligence sources, this plant was thought to be involved in the German nuclear experiments. It was another long and tiring mission, especially as the crews spent up to one and a half hours trying to locate the target, which was deeply hidden in the mountains of the Telemark province. Little opposition was encountered either from ground fire or enemy fighters. However, the 390th lost one aircraft when it caught fire and ditched in the sea off the Norwegian coast. This loss was additional to a B-17 that crashed shortly after taking off.

The following month when the weather conditions allowed, the 390th were quite active in the run-up to their first Christmas in England and managed to mount seven missions. The north German ports of Emden, Kiel and Bremen figured large in the schedule. On 11th December the Group despatched over 40 aircraft to Emden, which had been a favourite target for the Eighth Air Force since the outset, although RAF Bomber Command had not bombed the port since June 1942. On this occasion the 390th suffered the heaviest losses of the Division; they lost five aircraft. Five days later the first of two Bremen operations went relatively smoothly with just a single casualty, however when the Eighth returned to the target on the 20th, the Group suffered at the hands of the Luftwaffe and especially from Me410s. These twin-engined heavy fighters were not often encountered by the Eighth Air Force and on this day the crews reported that they were attacked by time-fused air to air rockets. Three B-17s failed to return to Framlingham – almost half of the Division's loss – though the Group had the largest number of aircraft taking part, no less than 35 B-17s, and their gunners claimed the lion's share of the enemy fighters destroyed in the massive air battle.

Unlike most Bomb Groups the first of the Eighth's operations to Berlin in March 1944 passed without any serious mishaps for the 390th and even the missions to the German capital in May were again successfully negotiated by the crews. Indeed, in seven missions to 'Big B', the Group lost only eight aircraft in total, which probably constituted the safest record of any Group in the Division, if not in the whole of the Eighth. However, when the Eighth launched its biggest operation of the war so far against German oil targets – over 1,300 heavy bombers – some of the formations encountered very strong fighter opposition. The 390th lost five aircraft, only the 401st Group from the First Division suffered more heavily.

After all the hectic operations leading up to D-Day and all the tactical support missions flown after the big day, the Eighth returned to German targets. On 21st June the RAF Bomber Command and the Eighth planned a large combined operation – a rare occasion – but the RAF had to reluctantly pull out because of insufficient fighter support for their slower and less heavily armed heavy bombers. The Eighth continued on their own with a force of over 1,200 bombers escorted by almost the same number of fighters (a mixture of P-38s, 47s and 51s) to Berlin and Ruhland. Two Bomb Wings of the Third Division (13th and 45th) were diverted to the Schwarzheide synthetic oil plants about 90 miles south-east of Berlin. The six Bomb Groups after bombing would swing eastward to land at three Russian airfields – Poltava, Mirgorod and Piryatin – all to the east of Kiev. This was the first of the so-called 'Frantic' missions – largely mounted to placate Stalin and also to enable the Eighth to attack targets in Poland. This would be the first operation mounted by the Third Division since its change of Commander, now Major General Earle Partridge.

The 390th with the other members of 13th Wing arrived at Mirgorod late in the afternoon, with only one loss. However, the other Wing that landed at Poltava suffered from a heavy Luftwaffe strike on the Russian airfield later in the evening and within half an hour 44 of the 72 aircraft that were sent out had been destroyed and another 26 were badly damaged. A very harsh blow and perhaps the only consolation was that the aircraft had been destroyed on the ground and thus valuable experienced crews had not been lost as well. On the 26th, 73 B-17s, escorted by P-51s, took off from Russian airfields to bomb targets in Hungary whilst en route to Italy and their ultimate return to England.

On 6th August the 390th, along with the 95th at Horham, were despatched to bomb the Rahmel aircraft factories at Gdynia, from thence carrying on to land in Russia. The following day the crews attacked an oil refinery at Trzebinia in eastern Poland. Then on the next day (8th) the two Groups, comprising the original 78 B-17s, were on their way home, but they did bomb two airfields in Rumania en route! The Group's third and final Frantic shuttle mission took place on 18th September when supplies of arms were dropped to the Polish resistance fighters engaged in the famous Warsaw uprising and the 390th lost just one crew. This was their final Russian shuttle, indeed

B-17s of 390th Bomb Group in action. (USAF)

certain problems had been encountered with the Russians and the Eighth Air Force decided to abandon the project. Really the effort involved and the losses sustained, allied to rather mediocre effective bombing, made these missions wasteful in resources. However, these facts did not detract from the determination and bravery of all the crews taking part in these long and exhausting flights.

As has already been noted, of all the priority targets listed in the 'Pointblank' directions, the planned destruction of the German oil industry caused the greatest losses sustained by the Eighth throughout the war. Certainly no Third Division Bomb Group was immune from losses. On 30th November during the large operation that was mounted to Merseburg, the Group lost seven aircraft, including two B-17s that were badly damaged and forced to land in France. But unfortunately the Group would suffer more heavily in the New Year.

On 14th January 1945 the weather forecast was favourable with clear skies expected over most of northern Europe, and the Eighth's chiefs took the opportunity to launch a large strike at oil refineries and plants in central Germany. The three Divisions took part with over 550 B-17s and 350 B-24s airborne, escorted by almost the same number of fighters. The main targets for the Third's B-17s were

Magdeburg and Derben, which was about 70 miles west of Berlin. One echelon of the Group's aircraft – only seven in number – was flying in the low box of a formation and struggling to maintain the overall speed of the rest of the Group. The Luftwaffe fighter pilots were never slow to capitalise on such situations and within barely half an hour the seven B-17s had been annihilated. Another two aircraft were also lost during the operation, thus making it the most costly single mission for the 390th for the whole of the war.

Towards the end of 1944 many crews had been confidently betting that the war would be over and by Christmas they would be back home in the States. Although this was never a realistic view, the German counter-offensive in the Ardennes put paid to such hopes and furthermore ensured that Christmas 1944 would be one of the busiest periods of the war for most of the Groups. On Christmas Eve, over 2,000 heavy bombers took to the air – the mightiest air armada yet seen. Only twelve aircraft failed to return, although there had been many accidents due to the freezing conditions, and unfortunately the Group lost two aircraft. On Christmas Day the Third Division put up a token force of 174 aircraft to attack railway bridges to the west of the Rhine and the 13th Bomb Wing along with

The control tower at Framlingham has been turned into a memorial museum for the 390th Bomb Group.

two other Groups had drawn the short straw. The only casualty in the Third Division came from the 390th. Boxing Day was a day off from operations for the Group. The following day the freezing conditions at most of the airfields made the conditions for take-off and landing most hazardous. The weather caused one of the Group's aircraft to crash shortly after take off and it landed in the village of Parham, destroying the chapel. It was later said that 'the village resembled a battlefield' – nine of the crew were killed and the sad incident made the front pages of the daily newspapers. But life at the base had to go on and operations were mounted on the two following days as well as the 30th and 31st when the 390th lost another three aircraft. In the seven days seven aircraft had been lost, a rather unfortunate Christmas for the base – although despite all the sadness the Group still managed to put on a splendid Christmas party for over 270 local children.

With their very last mission, on 20th April 1945, the Group achieved a momentous milestone – 300 missions completed for the loss of 144 aircraft missing in action. Only six Bomb Groups in the Division managed to achieve this magical figure, though no member of the Eighth Air Force would better the record of Master Sergeant Hewitt Dunn, a gunner, who completed an amazing 104 missions with the Group, including no less than nine trips to Berlin – talk about a charmed life! The Group Operations Officer, Lt Colonel Robert Waltz, who was responsible for working out the complicated missions and the make-up of formations, had been with the 390th since its arrival in England; by the end of the war he had 43 missions to his credit, as well as being one of the Group's most highly decorated officers.

The 390th is well remembered by a group of dedicated local people, who have renovated the old control tower and established a fine museum to Group, which is open on Sundays and Bank Holidays from early March to November from 1 pm to 6 pm. The museum and the site of the airfield is best gained from the A12 past Wickham Market; turn off to Marlesford and then follow the museum signs.

11
GREAT ASHFIELD

The young American airmen who came to this airfield, which was situated on some relatively high land about a mile and a half from the village, would have little realised that some 25 years earlier the pioneer flyers of the Royal Flying Corps had been there before them. The small grass landing strip had become the home of the rather fragile BE2cs – 'BE' stood for Bleriot Experimental – a far cry from the massive B-17s that thundered in during June 1943. These were 'Van's Valiants' – after their Commanding Officer, Colonel Elliott Vandevanter, who would lead the 385th until August 1944.

Before the American airmen arrived at Great Ashfield during the last week of June, the airfield had been used by Short Stirlings of two RAF Conversion Units for perfecting circuit and landing techniques. Any completed airfield laying empty during 1943 would be used by the RAF because of the intense pressure placed on their operational stations. Previously in November, when John Laing & Co were in the throes of constructing the airfield, a B-24 'dropped in'; the navigator had lost his bearings in heavy cloud whilst returning to his home base at Hardwick in Norfolk. Unfortunately for him Brigadier General James Hodge, the Commander of the Second Bomb Division, was also on board as a passenger.

After about three weeks of operational training at Great Ashfield the Colonel felt sufficiently confident to inform the Wing Headquarters (4th) that his boys were ready to go. Thus, on 17th July 1943, 21 aircraft left Great Ashfield on the Group's first operation. The lucky crews joined another 20 aircraft from Knettishall, where another novice Group – the 388th – was also beginning its war, for the Fokker aircraft factory at Amsterdam. The inexperienced crews encountered very heavy cloud over the target area which greatly hampered the bombing and just five crews from the 385th claimed to have bombed the target, but nevertheless all made it home safely.

Earlier in the month the Eighth Air Force had decided to introduce clearly identifiable markings for each Bomb Group. The 4th Wing's aircraft carried a large white letter emblazoned in a blue square on the tail-fin of the B-17s. Each Group was given a letter, the 385th thus became known as the Square G and the 388th as Square H and so on. These prominent markings were retained until February 1945 when the 93rd Combat Bomb Wing was formed and the letters were replaced by red chequer-board markings.

Within the space of nine days and three operations the Group lost four aircraft, but this figure was doubled on 28th July when the Wing was sent to the aircraft factories at Oschersleben. Once again bad weather frustrated the operation and only 37 out of the original force of 120 B-17s bombed the target. The Group suffered from air-launched rockets, one of which made a direct hit on a B-17 and as it broke up it crashed into another two aircraft in the formation. This was the first time that the Luftwaffe had employed such weapons, which were really ground artillery rockets that had been adapted to fit under the wings of the fighters and were launched outside the range of the B-17 guns. With another aircraft lost on the return home, the surviving crews returned to Great Ashfield fully aware that it was going to be a long and very hard war.

As indeed they found out on the famous Regensburg mission. On the way out three were lost to enemy fighters and on their return from North Africa another two failed to get home to Suffolk. One of these, *Lulu Belle*, piloted by Major Piper, who had led the Group into Regensburg, ditched into the sea near Land's End and rather fortunately eight of the crew were saved by the RAF ASR services. Nevertheless just two days later (27th) the Group was able to send twelve aircraft to Watten in the Pas de Calais, which was the Eighth's first operation against the V1 rocket sites, although the crews were told that the targets were 'special aeronautical facilities'! Of course, like the rest of the Bomb Groups involved in the Regensburg shuttle operation the 385th was awarded its first Distinguished Unit Citation.

There were several days free from operations which enabled damaged aircraft to be repaired and new replacement aircraft to arrive before the next major operation. This proved to be the 'blood bath'

102

You have been warned! (USAF)

over Stuttgart and despite the heavy losses sustained on this operation all of the 23 crews survived.

The increasing heavy losses suffered by the Eighth did in fact lead to a consideration of night flying. Three Groups in Third Division (95, 96 and 385th) were instructed to begin night flying training and to modify some of their aircraft for this purpose. This involved installing flame dampers, gun flash eliminators and some form of blackout for the cabins and turrets. On the night of 27/28th September two B-17s joined a force of Lancasters of RAF Bomber Command on a night raid to Hanover; it was not a particularly successful operation because of fierce head winds and of the 39 aircraft missing on the night, one was a B-17.

The very successful Marienburg operation mounted on 9th October amply justified the Eighth Air Force's perseverance and faith in precision daylight bombing. The Third Division was led by Colonel Russell Wilson, the Commander of the 4th Bomb Wing, in one of the Group's B-17s. This most spectacular bombing operation did credit to all the crews that took part in it. The only blemish as far as the Group was concerned was that one of its aircraft had engine trouble and crash-landed in Denmark. The following day 19 crews were in action over Münster, another harsh operation for the Eighth with 29 B-17s lost, two of which came from the 385th, although the Group's gunners gave a very good account of themselves in the fierce air battle with the Luftwaffe – they claimed 34 enemy fighters destroyed. Four days later (14th) the Group was engaged in the second Schweinfurt operation, a day which has gone into USAAF folklore as 'Black Thursday'. Only three of the 16 Groups taking part in this very costly operation (60 aircraft destroyed) managed to survive unscathed and the 20 aircraft from Great Ashfield arrived back in England safely, although one crash-landed in Hertfordshire.

Some of the extreme conditions suffered by American aircrews can be seen on an operation to Düren, some 30 or so miles south-west of Cologne, on 20th October. The cloud base found over the target was over 29,000 feet, which compelled the B-17s to bomb from 30,000 feet. Besides the intense cold experienced at such altitudes, the safety of the crews relied on their oxygen equipment. Unfortunately on this mission three gunners from one of the 385th's aircraft died because of a failure in their equipment. Another tragic accident happened on 21st February 1944 when two aircraft returning from an operation over Brunswick collided in low cloud at about 3,000 feet. Both aircraft crashed into Reedham Marshes and 21 men were killed.

Like all Bomb Groups Berlin featured large in the 385th's history and the Group was one of the nine from the Third Division despatched on 4th March 1944 to make the Eighth's first attack on this major target. However, most of the Groups were recalled because of the weather. It is interesting to note in passing that during the whole of the war 25% of the operational days were cancelled on account of adverse weather conditions. Two days later the 385th was selected to lead the Division's formation into Berlin, with Brigadier General Russ Wilson, the Wing's chief, in the lead aircraft. This aircraft was equipped with H2X, the American development of the RAF's H2S or ground scanning equipment. It was known as 'Mickey' to the American crews and was the major blind bombing and navigational aid used by the Eighth for the rest of the war. The lead aircraft was hit by heavy flak but despite that the pilot – Major Fred Rabo – continued his bomb run. When one of the engines caught fire and the aircraft lost height, Major Rabo ordered the crew to bale out but within seconds the aircraft exploded and only three of the twelve crewmen managed to escape. One of these was 1/Lt John Morgan, who in July 1943 had been awarded the Congressional Medal of

Memorial altar at All Saints' church, Great Ashfield: in memory of 385th Bomb Group.

Honor when flying with the 92nd Group. On this day the Group escaped relatively lightly considering the Division lost 35 out of 242 aircraft (14%).

Then came a particularly torrid time during April when the Group mounted 17 missions for the loss of 15 aircraft, which in truth was relatively light compared with some other Groups in the Division. The Group's hardest day was on the 29th during a mission to Berlin when the lead aircraft made a slight navigational error taking one formation some 40 miles south of the main bomber force. Whilst near Magdeburg a strong force of Fw190s struck with speed and venom, downing 17 B-17s in almost as many minutes. The Group was in the lead formation and it suffered heavily, losing seven aircraft.

Despite the April losses the Eighth Air Force launched a massive offensive against the German oil industry on 12th May, which was their first 'oil operation'. The Third Division was allocated targets in the Leipzig area – Zwickau, Brux and Chemnitz. Almost as soon as the 4th Bomb Wing, being led on this day by the 385th and Colonel Vandevanter, was over Belgium it came under attack from a strong Luftwaffe force, which lasted for almost half an hour. This brutal onslaught had rather shattered the bomber formation and Vandevanter ordered the speed to be reduced in order that the stragglers could reform. During the whole mission the Wing sustained no less than four separate attacks from enemy fighters; as one survivor later admitted, '. . . it was the roughest trip of the war . . . they [enemy fighters] were everywhere you looked . . .' Forty one B-17s were shot down and amazingly the Group lost only two aircraft, one of which was so badly damaged that the crew abandoned it over the Thames Estuary near Southend. Photographic evidence later showed that the bombing had been of a very high standard and accuracy, almost 100% of the bombs falling within 2,000 feet of the aiming point. For this arduous but successful operation the 385th received its second Distinguished Unit Citation.

Ten days later it seemed as if the Luftwaffe had specially targeted the airfield in retaliation for the Zwickau mission. Just before dawn on 22nd May a solitary intruder – Junkers 88 – came in and dropped about seven small bombs on the airfield. One of the two hangars was hit and a B-17 was destroyed. It is surprising to discover that this was the only B-17 to be destroyed on the ground during the whole of the war – that is, in England. Almost at the end of the war the airfield was strafed by another intruder but on this occasion very little damage was sustained.

Despite some hard and rugged missions during the summer, especially the 'Frantic' shuttle to Russian, Berlin remained firmly engrained in the collective memory of the Group; although by October there were not many crews remaining at Great Ashfield who remembered the Berlin missions of April and May. On 6th October the Group was detailed for the Spandau armaments complex which was situated in the western suburbs of the German capital. The 385th was in the last formation and at Nauen, about 15 miles from the target, the Group was forced to drop about 1,000 feet below a heavy cloud formation. Lurking above the clouds was a strong force of enemy fighters and they dived down and surprised the Group. Unfortunately just one of the Group's squadrons (549th) bore the brunt of the attack and in minutes 14 B-17s were destroyed. At the end of the day the Group had lost ten aircraft, which proved to be their heaviest loss of the whole war.

During the winter of 1944/5 the Group was involved in all the major operations mounted by the Division – Merseburg, Bremen, Ludwigshafen, Berlin, Kassel, Derben, Augsburg and Chemnitz – and most of these were conducted with very minimal losses, indeed on several of them no aircraft went missing at all. However, the first two days of March 1945 proved to be unusually expensive for the Group, especially as by now the Eighth's bombers were ranging far and wide over Germany with only isolated but still very spirited opposition from the Luftwaffe. On 1st March over 1,200 bombers were despatched to a variety of rail targets in central and southern Germany. The Third Division was detailed to attack the marshalling yards at Ulm, about 40 miles south-east of Stuttgart. Unfortunately two of the Group's B-17s never made the target, they collided in heavy cloud over Belgium with 16 of the crew being killed. On this large operation not a single bomber was lost to enemy action, though six of the escorting fighters failed to return. The following day the synthetic oil plants in southern Germany were the targets and the Group, along with other Groups in the Division, were given the Ruhland as their primary target. This happened to be a day when the Luftwaffe made a concentrated attack on the formations, so much so that it was decided by the leader to change the attack to a secondary target – Dresden. This was of course after the RAF's and the Eighth's heavy raids in the middle of February. Of the eight B-17s that were destroyed on this mission, four came from the 385th – a sharp and painful reminder that the Luftwaffe was not quite a spent force.

This fact was further emphasised just over two weeks later (18th)

B-17s of 385th Bomb Group, showing 'Square G' on tail fins. (USAF)

when Berlin was the target once again. The Luftwaffe launched a most concentrated attack on the large bomber formations, mainly using their Me262 jet fighters. The 385th lost two aircraft, although one badly damaged B-17 managed to crash-land behind the Soviet front lines – it was just one of ten that managed to 'escape east'! On the following day the Group was over the other favourite target – Zwickau – and survived with just one casualty. In the following month another 26 missions were flown by the Group for the loss of four aircraft. This brought their total missions mounted to 296, or over 8,200 individual sorties for the loss of 129 B-17s to enemy action, with another 40 destroyed in accidents, and over 280 enemy fighters accounted for.

However, the Group's flying days were not yet completely finished because for six days in the first week of May many of the Third Division's Groups were occupied in dropping food supplies to the starving Dutch people. On 2nd May four of the Group's aircraft were damaged by ground fire when they inadvertently flew into a flak area. All the crews who took part in Operation Chowhound were agreed that they were the most pleasant missions of the whole war. By the end of June all of the B-17s had departed from the airfield, followed a week later by the ground crews.

In All Saints church at Great Ashfield can be found a splendid memorial altar in honour of the 385th Bomb Group. The parchment Roll of Honour records the names of over 400 airmen who lost their lives whilst operating from here.

12
HALESWORTH

Halesworth was just one of a small clutch of airfields clustered in the north-east corner of the county. It was constructed during 1942/3, the building work being shared by Richard Costain Ltd and John Laing & Son, and was situated about two miles north-east of the market town from which it took its name. However, much of the hutted accommodation was dispersed around the small village of Holton just to the south of the airfield and some of the old buildings can still be seen.

It was those early and trusty work-horses of the Eighth Fighter Command that arrived in July 1943 to christen the new airfield. These were Republic P-47Ds or Thunderbolts. The P-47 was one of the most famous American single-seat fighters of the Second World War and was built in larger numbers than any other American fighter. It was variously described as the 'Jug' (short for Juggernaut), the 'Flying Milk Bottle' or according to the RAF fighter pilots, 'The Flying Barrel'!

The first prototype had flown in May 1941 and yet it was in service with USAAF by September 1942, one of the quickest design and production programmes ever achieved. The aircraft was noticeably different from contemporary fighters; it was very heavy, almost twice the weight of the Spitfire, but it was very rugged and proved capable of sustaining and surviving heavy damage. Despite its bulk it was very fast, especially at high altitudes and was probably the heaviest armed fighter of its time with a quite devastating amount of fire-power.

However, the 56th Fighter Group was the only Group to retain P-47s for the whole of the war and indeed, in the process, demonstrated just how effective the fighter could be in the hands of experienced and dedicated pilots. The Group arrived from their rather comfortable billets at Horsham St Faith, which had been a RAF permanent station, on 8th July and found the basic accommodation at Halesworth to be far less luxurious, to say the least! The Group was led by Colonel Hubert Zemke, who proved not only to be a very fine fighter pilot but also became an acknowledged expert in fighter tactics as well as a superb leader. It was largely due to his inspiration and example that the 56th became one of the finest Fighter Groups in the Eighth Air Force.

Often fighters were bought by American towns and cities which had subscribed enough war bonds for a P-47, about $100,000, and some of the Group's fighters acknowledged this fact, eg *Spirit of Atlantic City*, which was flown by one of the leading pilots, Major Walker Maharin. Besides the normal Group markings, the P-47s were given white nose colourings to identify them as friendly aircraft as they did bear a certain resemblance to Fw190s and had been mistaken for them by several over-zealous air gunners!

By the time the Group arrived at Halesworth its pilots were at least a little experienced in air combat, having been in action since the middle of April. Although considering their later outstanding successes – more enemy aircraft destroyed than any other Eighth Group as well as having more fighter aces – the Group's pilots found victories hard to come by in their first few months of operations. Of course this was a period when there were only three Fighter Groups flying operations and it was the end of July before the P-47s were provided with extra jettisonable fuel tanks that enabled them, at long last, to penetrate the German skies. It was not until the 30th of the month that the Group opened their score from Halesworth – three enemy aircraft destroyed for the loss of two P-47s, whilst on an escort mission to Kassel.

The Group's fortunes changed with the famous Schweinfurt and Regensburg operation. In the morning the Group acted as escort for the Regensburg force and, of course, it was after they had retired at the limit of their range that the Luftwaffe attacked the bombers with such ferocity. Later on that day the pilots were out to escort the Schweinfurt force on its return home. The Group had accounted for 17 enemy fighters for the loss of three pilots, when they were relieved by RAF Spitfires near Antwerp. Captain Gerald Johnson claimed two Me109s and a Me110, and a young pilot on his very first combat mission also claimed three victories. Just two days later whilst again giving withdrawal support for B-17s, the 56th made its presence felt by downing nine enemy aircraft with Captain Johnson again scoring; indeed on this mission he became the first 'ace' of the Group and only the second in the Eighth Fighter Command.

The term 'ace' was a relic of the early flying days of the First World War. The French had first used the term and it was quickly taken up by both the British and Germans. Despite the fact that a 1920 policy statement by the Director of USAAF maintained, '. . . the USA Air Service does not use the title "ace" . . . as it is not the policy of the Air Service to glorify one particular branch of aeronautics . . .', both the Americans and Germans used the term during the Second World War. The American aces required five positive victories in air combat, whereas the Luftwaffe pilots needed ten. The Americans were particularly speedy to appreciate the promotional and propaganda value of their expert fighter pilots. On the other hand the RAF officially refused to acknowledge aces as such, because it considered the system was bad for team or squadron morale. The Service was quite happy to publicise the victories of their most successful fighter pilots, without actually calling them 'aces'!

During the month of October the Group's pilots were taking an increasing and heavy toll of the Luftwaffe, either led by the brilliant Zemke or his deputy, Major Schilling, another fine pilot and leader. It was said that the Group's pilots 'hunted like a pack of wolves' – hence their name, 'The Wolfpack'! By 5th November the Group was credited with 100 victories, almost double that of their nearest rivals – the 'Eagles' of 4th Group. However, Colonel Zemke had departed and in his place came another admirable Commander – Colonel Robert Landry – who later became the only officer to command both a Fighter and Bomb Group.

Under Landry's guidance the pilots continued their successful onslaught on the Luftwaffe, and with a marked effect on 26th November when they accounted for 23 kills for the loss of just one aircraft. The previous day the Group became engaged on the first dive-bombing operation. Fifty aircraft each loaded with 500 pound bombs attacked St Omer airfield, although it was not a particularly successful mission; not a single aircraft was lost but many returned with flak damage. As will be seen later, this type of operation became a feature of P-47 missions.

General Arnold's New Year's message to the Eighth Air Force ended with the stirring words: 'Destroy the enemy Air Force where you find them, in the air, on the ground and in the factories' – though, in truth, the Group's pilots did not require such

111

One of the greatest American fighter pilots of the war – Colonel Hubert Zemke of 56th Fighter Group. (USAF)

exhortations. By the end of January they had passed their 200th victory and had another leading ace in Captain Walker Maharin with 16 claims to his credit. During the following month under the command of Colonel Zemke, who had returned to Halesworth in January, the pilots made a ground-strafing attack on Juvincourt airfield near Rheims and made the first claim for enemy aircraft destroyed on the ground. Another initiative which later became such a feature of all the Eighth's Fighter Groups.

The speed and efficiency by which the Group added to its total of victories was really quite astonishing and demonstrated what an outstanding combat unit it had become; its very obvious success proved to be a potent incentive to the other Fighter Groups. On 17th February one of its three squadrons – 61st – became the first squadron in the Eighth to notch up 100 victories in its own right. Certainly one of their most successful months was March, which included the several Berlin missions, when the pilots shot down 85 enemy aircraft for the loss of 17 pilots. The Group was awarded its first Distinguished Unit Citation for its performance during the period from 20th February to 9th March when in 18 days it claimed 98 enemy aircraft destroyed.

Indeed, the Group was almost embarrassed by the number of aces in its ranks; besides those already noted, 1/Lt Robert Johnson (21), Lt Colonel Francis Gabreski (14), Lt Colonel David Schilling (10) and Major Le Roy Schreiber (10) were some of the more famous names. However, by the end of March the Group lost two of its leading aces – Major Gerald Johnson and Walker Maharin. Both managed to survive, Johnson was taken prisoner of war, whereas Maharin evaded capture and arrived back in England in May. In fact, Maharin was picked up on the night of 6/7th May by a RAF Lysander of No 138 squadron operating on special duties from Tempsford. He had been hidden by the French underground for almost six weeks. The Major returned in due course to the USA, later serving in the Pacific and in the Korean war when he was taken prisoner.

By the middle of April the Group found themselves once again on the move, this time they were forced to leave Halesworth to make room for a new Bomb Group that was taking over and joining the Second Bomb Division. On 18th April the P-47s left for their new home in Essex at Boxted, but it would be another two weeks or so before the first B-24Hs of 489th Bomb Group flew into Halesworth. During their rather brief stay they would operate closely with the 491st stationed at nearby Metfield, and together they formed the 95th Combat Bomb Wing.

Colonel Ezekiel Napier, the Group's Commanding Officer, was satisfied that his men were ready for their first mission, and on 30th May the 489th became part of the Division's 389-strong force attacking two aircraft depôts in northern Germany – Oldenburg, north of Lübeck and Rotenburg, east of Bremen. Unfortunately the Group crossed the Dutch border about ten miles south of the planned route and as a result wandered into a heavy flak area, but with a fair slice of beginner's luck the inexperienced crews managed to escape relatively unscathed. The only loss of the whole operation fell to the 489th, when one of its B-24s ditched in the North Sea on return because of fuel shortage, but eight of the crew were saved.

The following day proved to be a slightly easier operation – rail targets in France and Belgium, and this was again negotiated without loss to enemy action. However, on 2nd June the Group's crews were sent out on two missions. In the morning to 'Noball' targets on the Pas de Calais, then in the afternoon, along with the 491st, the crews attacked some airfields that were clustered around Paris. The new Wing encountered quite severe flak opposition and five B-24s were shot down, four of them from the 489th. As if this was not bad enough, another two of the Group's aircraft crashed on return to England – one at Leiston airfield. This proved to be the blackest day in the Group's short stay at Halesworth.

On the eve of D-Day the Eighth Air Force mounted a major offensive on the enemy's coastal defences along the Channel coast from Cherbourg to the Pas de Calais. Lt Colonel Leon Vance, the Group's Deputy Commanding Officer, was leading the 489th in a PFF (Pathfinder) B-24 belonging to 44th Group at Shipdham. Close to the target area – Wimereaux, just north of Boulogne, the aircraft was hit by flak which killed the co-pilot and badly damaged Vance's foot. Nevertheless, he ordered the pilot to continue the attack. By now the B-24 was seriously damaged and as it neared the English coast Vance ordered the crew to bale out whilst he remained in control of the aircraft. He was informed that there was an injured rear gunner who could not bale out. Vance managed to ditch the B-24 and the explosion as the aircraft hit the water blew Vance clear of the aircraft but also severed his foot. He clung to some wreckage and attempted to locate the injured crewman. When he realised that nobody was left he began swimming and some 50 minutes later he was rescued by an air-sea rescue launch. Whilst he was in hospital he was awarded the Congressional Medal of Honor – the highest American award for gallantry. During late July when he was being transported back to the United States for further hospital treatment the transport aircraft was lost on the Iceland to Newfoundland leg of the journey – a sad end for such a brave airman.

Sixteen days later (21st) when operating over the rocket sites in the

Pas de Calais, the Group had a rather important passenger, who went along as an interested observer – Prince Bernhard of the Netherlands. Four days later after returning, once again, from attacking airfields in the Paris area, sadly two of its B-24s crash-landed at Halesworth killing ten crewmen – the Group had suffered from the enemy flak batteries that surrounded the French capital. The Group's crews operated very effectively over a wide variety of targets – oil, aircraft factories, V1 rocket sites, airfields, railways and bridges – frequently without loss or just a single casualty.

On 6th August the Group was engaged in a mission to oil refineries in Hamburg and the crews were even more delighted than usual to land safely at Halesworth – although one crew did not make it. The reason for their eagerness to return was the appearance in the evening of Glenn Miller and his famous AEF band. Miller and his band had flown in from Boxted and this was just another stop on his hectic tour of American bases in England, which lasted from 14th July to 3rd October. These concerts proved to be one of the most lasting wartime memories for both the GIs and those local people who were fortunate enough to see the legendary Miller.

November came and with it the Group's final mission; the 489th had been selected for B-29 training and an ultimate posting to the Pacific. During the month most of the aircraft and personnel were

B-24s of the Second Air Division.

115

transferred to other Groups in the Second Bomb Division and by the end of the month the airfield was virtually inactive.

It was not until the New Year that two new American units moved into Halesworth. The first to arrive was 1st Gunnery and Tow Target Flight from Little Walden and on 10th January the first Vultee A-35B (known in the RAF as the Vengeance) landed at Halesworth. This aircraft had been originally designed for the RAF as a dive-bomber to be used in close support for land troops but it had not proved particularly successful in such operations as it needed a heavy fighter support, though it did operate quite successfully with the RAF in Burma and India. The Eighth had used the Vengeance as a target tower by removing all the armament and installing a light wire cable at the rear of the fuselage for the sleeve target. These aircraft along with some P-47Ds and the odd A-20B (Havoc) were used to give firing practice for the Fighter Groups in the Second Division.

About two weeks later (16th) the Air Sea Rescue squadron, which had originally been formed at Boxted in May 1944 and had latterly shared the airfield with the illustrious 56th Group, was transferred to Halesworth. The unit had been originally formed to supplement the RAF services. The squadron was equipped with 'war weary' P-47s – aircraft with high operational flying hours, which were really due for retirement. In any case P-47s were not the most suitable aircraft for this type of operation because of their lack of operational range but at the time the Eighth Air Force had very little choice. Within days of the squadron's arrival at Halesworth it was formally redesignated the 5th Emergency Rescue Squadron.

It was not until the end of the month that the squadron's most unusual aircraft arrived at Halesworth – the Consolidated OA-10A. This most distinctive twin-engined amphibian aircraft had originally been designed for the US Navy and had come into service in 1936. RAF Coastal Command had well over 600 of these aircraft, which they had christened 'Catalinas'. The USAAF had used OA-10As on air-sea rescue patrols in the Mediterranean with some success and therefore General Arnold asked for some of these aircraft for use in European waters. The aircraft had a range of 2,500 miles with a cruising speed of about 120 mph and was manned by a crew of six. One went out on its first ASR patrol on 3rd February.

The squadron's aircraft were out on patrol almost every day but March proved to be its busiest month of the war. During the month the OA-10As had rescued several American and RAF crews as well as a German pilot. However, two of the aircraft were lost during the

116

P-47s of No 62 Squadron of 56th Fighter Group. (USAF)

month. The first failed to take off from the sea after making a successful rescue of some crewmen from a ditched B-24; the unlucky amphibian sank whilst being taken in tow by a launch. Then on the 31st one of the aircraft was on the sea when it was attacked by a Me262 and it quickly sank. The six man crew managed to get away in a lifeboat but they were not finally picked up for another five days. Also during March the squadron received some old B-17s, which had been converted to carry the US designed airborne lifeboat and one was successfully dropped over the Danish coast on the last day of the month.

April proved to be another hectic month for the squadron but it was marred by a tragic accident when two of the squadron's P-47s collided and crashed near Fritton Lake, unfortunately killing both pilots. The squadron worked closely with the RAF ASR units that operated from Beccles. The last operational patrol from Halesworth was mounted on 7th May when five Catalinas were active over the North Sea to ensure that the bomber crews that were returning from dropping food supplies to the Dutch people arrived back safely.

During the last few months of the war Halesworth was a veritable hive of activity with the different aircraft coming and going at

The tank memorial to all the American units that served at Halesworth.

frequent intervals. In February the 496th Flying Training Squadron had also moved in with its P-51Ds which were used to provide operational training for replacement pilots for the Second Division's Fighter Groups. Previously this squadron had operated from Goxhill, which since 1942 had been responsible for all the induction training of fighter pilots into the Eighth. However, by the end of May all these units had been disbanded and the airfield was handed over to the RAF, although it was the Fleet Air Arm who used the airfield until it was closed for flying early in 1946.

The various and diverse units that served at Halesworth are remembered by a most unusual memorial, a large fuel tank on a grass bank at the roadside near the site of the old airfield. Close by is a memorial stone of polished marble to the specific memory of those men of the 489th Bomb Group '. . . who gave their lives in the cause of freedom and human dignity'.

13
HONINGTON

When it opened in May 1937 Honington became only the third RAF airfield in Suffolk and almost 60 years later it still remains a RAF station. The airfield was first designed and constructed in those heady days of the expansion of the RAF during the mid 1930s and many of the early buildings still survive. It was designated as a heavy bomber station and as was usual at the time it was purely a grass airfield and not provided with concrete runways. As it was placed under the control of No 3 Group of the newly formed Bomber Command most of the rather obsolete bombers of the pre-war Service – Vickers Wellesleys, Hampden Page Heyfords and Harrows – appeared at the airfield over the next few years. However, by the outbreak of the war, Honington had a squadron of the Command's newest heavy bomber – the Vickers Armstrong Wellington.

These admirable aircraft formed the backbone of Bomber Command for the early war years; during the winter of 1941/2 there were no less than 22 squadrons of Wellingtons in the Command. The aircraft had experienced a very long period of gestation. The first specification had been issued in September 1932, but it did not make its maiden flight until June 1936 and another two years passed before the aircraft finally came into service in October 1938. The Wellington had been designed by Barnes Wallis, of the bouncing bomb fame, and it proved to be one of the most successful bombers of the Second World War, its thunder only stolen by the famous Avro Lancaster. Over 11,000 Wellingtons were produced in 18 different marks, far greater than any other RAF bomber. Furthermore it proved to be a most versatile aircraft, being adapted for a wide range of operational duties within Bomber Command, and also used very successfully as a U-boat seeker with Coastal Command. It also doubled as a freight and troop carrier, and was often engaged in experimental and developmental flying. The aircraft was universally popular with all its crews – both flying and ground – who fondly dubbed it the 'Wimpy' after J Wellington Wimpy, a character in the early Popeye cartoons. The aircraft was featured in the early war documentary film *Target for Tonight*, which ensured its lasting fame and affection with the British public. Its unique geodetic design – metal lattices covered with fabric – quickly proved that the aircraft was immensely strong and durable, and able to sustain considerable damage and still fly, an attribute that saved the lives of many a wartime crew.

The Wellingtons belonged to No 9 Squadron, which had moved into Honington from Stradishall in July 1939 and was led by Wing Commander Hugh Lloyd, who after the war became Air Chief Marshal and was AOC of Bomber Command from 1950 to 1953. This squadron became one of the most illustrious in Bomber Command. Its origins went back to 1914 and the days of the Royal Flying Corps when it was formed as a wireless squadron. During the Second World War it developed into a highly trained and very effective force, often called upon to mount special operations, frequently in tandem with No 617 'Dambusters' squadron, but unfortunately without gaining the latter's fame. Indeed its badge, which featured a bat and the motto *Per noctem volames* – 'Throughout the night we fly' – became one of the most famous in the whole of the RAF. The 9th took part in the first bombing operation of the war and flew operationally throughout the whole of the conflict. Perhaps it was only right and proper that the Squadron should have been ultimately reformed at Honington in October 1982 and became the first unit to use Tornado GR1s operationally.

On 4th September the squadron's Wellingtons were sent out on the first bombing mission of the war – to seek out and attack two enemy warships off Brunsbüttel near the entrance to the Kiel Canal. Four of the crews felt that they had found some targets to bomb but unfortunately it was later discovered that the Danish town of Esjberg had been bombed – some 110 miles off target. The Wellingtons were attacked by Me109s and two were shot down.

During December three operations were launched, which proved to be significant for the whole course of the bombing offensive. On the 3rd, 24 Wellingtons took off from East Anglian bases to bomb two warships near Heligoland and they all managed to return safely – but without bombing – despite a concentrated attack by enemy fighters. This mission gave Bomber Command's chiefs an encouraging but false sense of security. So, on 14th December, a further twelve Wellingtons were ordered to attack the German cruisers *Nurnberg* and *Leipzig*. This second operation was a complete disaster, no damage was inflicted and five aircraft were shot down with another crash-landing at Newmarket. But even this abortive and costly mission did little to dent the Command's confidence in unescorted daylight operations. Indeed, they felt that the losses had been due to flak rather than enemy fighter action although the Wellingtons' gunners had been furiously engaged in fighting off repeated attacks by Me109s!

So next Monday (18th) orders came through for yet another operation and No 9 squadron would be involved. The briefing for this raid was very precise, ' . . . to attack enemy warships in the Schillig Roads at a height of at least 10,000 feet [believed to be beyond the range of effective flak!]. Great care is to be taken that no bombs fall on the shore, and no merchant ships are to be attacked. Formations shall not loiter in the target areas and all aircraft are to complete bombing as soon as possible after the sighting signal has been made.'

At precisely 9.30 am nine Wellingtons left Honington and joined another 15 from Feltwell and Mildenhall, but soon two from No 149 squadron at Mildenhall turned back because of engine trouble, leaving just 22 to drone over the North Sea at a steady speed of 190 mph. By 12.30 pm they were in sight of the German coast; it was a clear and cloudless day, perfect for the bombing mission. However, already the formation had been picked up by the two German experimental 'Freya' radar stations on Heligoland and at Wangerooge. About 45 minutes later the warships were sighted but as they were considered too close to the land, the crews were ordered not to bomb. The whole operation was beginning to assume the mantle of a tragic farce. The formation flew the gauntlet of a quite severe flak attack and the aircraft were returning home when they were set upon by a large formation of Me109s and 110s. This became the first real air battle of the war and was tragically quite short, barely lasting 30 minutes, and resulting in ten Wellingtons being destroyed. As the ragged remnants returned to East Anglia, two ditched in the sea and another three crash-landed at various airfields along the coast. At Honington only two of the original nine returned; four had been lost, two had crash-landed and one ditched off Grimsby – though all the crew were saved.

This operation clearly showed the vulnerability of the Wellington,

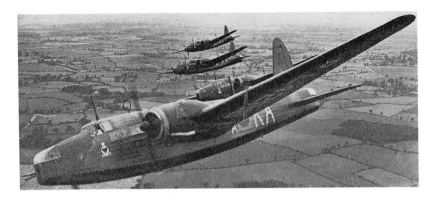

Wellington Is of No 9 Squadron.

mainly because of its lack of armour and self-sealing fuel tanks. Most of the Wellingtons lost on the 18th had gone down in flames. The December operations virtually brought to a halt daylight operations by heavy bombers without a fighter escort, and it only took another disastrous daylight operation in April 1940 to mark the demise of the pre-war bombing policy; from now on No 9 squadron along with the other heavy bomber squadrons would be solely devoted to night operations.

At the end of July a new squadron was formed at Honington. This was No 311 and was largely composed of airmen from the Czech Air Force, who had managed to escape from their homeland when it was overrun in March 1939 and had arrived in England via France. Over 40 of its officers had been granted RAF commissions but had a British commanding officer, Wing Commander Griffiths, who worked closely with the senior Czech officer, Wing Commander Toman. Much of the Czech airmen's training was conducted from East Wretham in Norfolk, which was then Honington's satellite airfield. In fact in September the squadron took up permanent residence at East Wretham and launched their first operation from there in that month. No 311 became the first Allied squadron to fly operationally in Bomber Command and was the only Czech squadron to serve in the Command.

The first strategic bombing of German industries took place on the night of 15/16th May 1940. Sixteen different targets in the Ruhr were selected for this major operation in which 99 aircraft took part with the loss of just a single plane, but not to enemy action as it unfortunately crashed in France. One German report from Münster suggested that, 'This bombing created a sensation . . . with thousands coming to see the damage . . . '! The rather successful operation was a clear indication to Bomber Command chiefs that night raids were the correct way forward.

However satisfactory such figures were, the accuracy of night bombing certainly left much to be desired. One navigator/bomb aimer with No 9 squadron recalled a raid to Hamm in November 1940: ' . . . in the end I persuaded myself that a concentration of lights below could be the marshalling yards, but the evidence was meagre – a first practical lesson in realising that better methods and equipment would be needed before an accurate bombing campaign could be mounted.' The marshalling yards that Pilot Officer (later Group Captain) Sam Hall referred to were at one of the Command's favourite targets, and it cropped up on so many BBC news reports that the raids were jokingly called 'Ham and Eggs'.

During January 1941 eleven Wellingtons from No 9 squadron were sent to attack Turin and one of the aircraft, which was badly damaged by flak, was forced to crash-land in Vichy France; the crew were careful to destroy their aircraft before being captured and interned. It was not the first time that the squadron had made the long trip to Italy, as in the previous month the crews were in action over Milan. On the night of 27/28th March the squadron was out over Cologne and one of its Wellingtons was shot down and the crew taken prisoner. The pilot – F/Lt Shore – later escaped from prison and finally arrived back to England via Sweden. He was just one of ten airmen from the squadron who managed to evade capture after being shot down during 1940/1. In fact during the whole of the war, no less than 1,975 RAF airmen managed to evade capture and get back to England with the assistance of underground workers in the occupied countries. This figure compares with just 156 RAF men who successfully escaped from prison camps. Another member of Shore's crew on this night, P/O Long was taken prisoner. He was ultimately involved in 'The Great Escape' of 1944, and after being caught was executed by the German SS.

On the night of 16/17th May 1941 a badly damaged Wellington, after a mission to Boulogne, made an emergency landing at the airfield but unfortunately crashed quite close to the bomb dump and burst into flames. The Station Commander, Group Captain J.A. Gray, along with the Medical Officer, Sqn/Ldr J. McCarty rushed to the scene and without a thought for their own safety, entered the blazing aircraft and managed to extricate two of the crew. For their

B-17s of Third Air Division at the air depot at Troston. (USAF)

bravery the two officers were awarded George Medals. Less than a month later No 9 squadron received quite a set-back. On 9th June two Wellingtons failed to return from a daylight reconnaissance mission off the French and Belgian coasts. One of them had been piloted by the Squadron Commander, Wing Commander R. G. Arnold, and both had been destroyed by Me109s off Zeebrugge. It was later disclosed that W/Cdr Arnold had remained at the controls of the aircraft long enough to allow his five crewmen to bale out before the aircraft crashed into the sea. He was killed but his crew survived as prisoners of war.

Towards the end of the summer the squadron became one of the first to be supplied with Wellington IIIs, which were equipped with the more powerful Bristol Hercules XI engines. One of these new aircraft was lost in late September, after a trip to Emden, when it crashed near Thetford. As the year was coming to a close the squadron's aircraft began to be supplied with the new GEE boxes. This revolutionary radio navigational device enabled navigators to fix their position by receiving pulse signals from three ground stations situated some distance apart in England. The first time it was used on a major operation was in early March to Essen and it made a considerable impact on Bomber Command's performance.

During 1942 the squadron was involved in most of the Command's major raids, especially the 'fire-storm' operations in March and April against Lübeck and Rostock. Then on 30/31st May the squadron was in the leading formation over Cologne – the first 1,000 bomber operation of the war. No 9 were part of the 'Incendiary Force' and the crews' briefing was very precise: ' . . . Don't drop your incendiaries unless you are absolutely sure you have identified the aiming point correctly. If these bombing runs are not accurate, a thousand other aircraft will come along and be off target as well.'

It was a devastating onslaught, which resulted in almost 13,000 buildings being destroyed or severely damaged. The effect on the German High Command was profoundly disturbing as they had no idea that the RAF could mount such a massive operation. Out of the main force of 1,047 bombers, 41 (3.9%) were missing in action – the Command's highest loss of the war so far. The first wave suffered the worst with 29 Wellingtons lost, of which two came from No 9 squadron – one to flak over the target and another to enemy fighters near Eindhoven.

The airfield was shortly due to be handed over to the USAAF and the squadron launched its final Wellington operation from Honington on the night of 31st July/1st August 1942 to Düsseldorf. During almost three years of operations in No 3 Group it had mounted 272 bombing missions in which it had lost 66 aircraft, an overall 2.8% loss rate, which was more than respectable considering that for this period it had been involved in all the major missions mounted by Bomber Command. Within days the squadron had moved out and further north to RAF Waddington to gain even greater fame with its Lancasters, and soon the Stars and Stripes would be flying over Honington.

The USAAF planned to provide an advanced air depot for each of the Eighth's Bomb Wings, so the first US personnel to arrive in September was the advance party to set up such a depot. The function of the air depots was to undertake the repair of damaged aircraft, as well as all the major overhauls and any modifications that were necessary to the aircraft. In the first instance the depot served all the Bomb Groups but by April 1943 it tended to specialise in B-17s mainly from the 4th Bomb Wing, which later became the Third Division, and from about this time also a representative of the aircraft company – Boeing – was in permanent attendance to help out and give assistance on technical matters. The depot, which later became known as Troston, largely to avoid any confusion with other combat units that might use the airfield, was mainly established on the north-western side of the airfield, although three of the four existing hangars were used by the air depot. In August 1943 it was designated the 1st Strategic Air Depot.

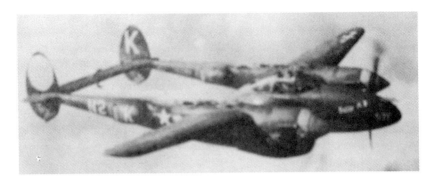

P-38 of 364 Fighter Group. (IWM)

There had been plans to provide all of the Eighth's grass airfields with concrete runways but by June 1943 these plans had changed and a steel mat runway, some 2,000 yards long and 40 yards wide was laid in addition to taxi-ways and over 70 hardstandings. The airfield would now be able to accommodate a Fighter Group and on 10th February 1944 the 364th Group arrived with their P-38Js (Lightnings).

The Lockheed P-38 was a brilliant aircraft in concept and a very advanced design for its time. The idea of a large twin-boomed and twin-engined fighter was quite revolutionary for 1937 when the aircraft was first designed as a high-altitude pursuit fighter. The first aircraft appeared two years later and its performance showed such considerable promise that after service trials in September 1940 the USAAF decided to place an order. However, its subsequent development by Lockheeds became rather protracted and the first P-38Fs did not come into service until 1942. It had been first christened the 'Atlanta' but soon 'Lightning' was considered a more appropriate name! Perhaps its major attraction for the USAAF was its operational range, indeed some of the early aircraft that came to England were actually flown across the Atlantic – a quite amazing flight for a fighter in those days!

The 364th was only the third Fighter Group to operate with the Eighth and even before their first operational mission, it suffered a rather severe setback. Their Commanding Officer, Lt Colonel Frederick Grambo, was killed in action on 29th February 1944 when accompanying the 20th Fighter Group from King's Cliffe. Three days later the Group was sent out on their first mission under their new CO – Colonel Roy Osborn. This was to escort a force of B-24s from the Second Division that were attacking Frankfurt; it was quite a coincidence because almost nine months later the Group would gain its only Distinguished Unit Citation in defence of bombers over the very same target.

In their first full month of operations the Group had anything but success. It lost 16 aircraft for the claim of just five enemy aircraft destroyed. However, many of the missing aircraft were due to engine failures, weather conditions and the sheer inexperience of its pilots. Worse was to befall the Group. On 15th April it took part in Operation Jackpot, which was a large fighter operation mounted to attack and strafe enemy airfields in central and western Germany. Over 610 aircraft were engaged in the operation and although over 40 enemy aircraft were claimed to have been destroyed on the ground with another 18 in the air, the Eighth Fighter Command lost 33 fighters, a third of them P-38s, of which no less than eight were from Honington. Although once again bad weather and heavy cloud accounted for many of the American losses rather than enemy action, nevertheless it was a heavy price to pay. By now however, the P-51s were beginning to appear in England in greater numbers and the Eighth Fighter Command had decided to convert even its P-38 Groups to P-51s. The last P-38 sorties flown by the Group took place on 29th July and the mission passed without either a loss or indeed a victory. In the five months of operations with their P-38s the Group's losses were higher than their victories – a situation the pilots hoped to change with their new fighters.

On 7th October whilst escorting a large bomber force to oil targets in eastern Germany, about 25 enemy jet-fighters appeared and three pilots from the Group managed to account for one Me163 – quite a kudos for the young pilots. Almost one month later (2nd November) whilst again in the same area, the Luftwaffe put up its strongest force for over three months when it was estimated that almost 400 enemy fighters were airborne. There was a massive air combat and the Eighth's fighter groups claimed over 100 aircraft shot down with another 30 seriously damaged. Against those figures, a total of 16 American fighters failed to return. The pilots of the 364th claimed 13 victories for just the loss of one pilot – their best performance of the war so far.

However, their finest hour was yet to come – 27th December – when the Group was led by Lt Colonel John Lowell. The 364th had been assigned the task of sweeping ahead of the bomber formations, which were attacking targets in the Rhineland. They met strong fighter opposition near Bonn and the Group's pilots accounted for 29 aircraft, with Captain Ernest Bankey becoming 'an ace in a day'. It was for this operation that the Group received its only Distinguished Unit Citation. Then four days later another 25 victories were chalked up for the loss of a single P-51; Major George Ceullers had four kills on the day. Things had certainly improved for the Honington Group!

In February one of the Group's pilots shot down the first Arado Ar234 – a new German twin-jet reconnaissance/bomber – to fall to the Eighth Air Force. Just over a month later (4th April) the Group's pilots managed to disturb two flights of Me262s that were attacking a bomber formation not far from Hamburg. Major Ceullers chased one for about 180 miles before he managed to shoot it down – quite a determined character! The Group's last victories came on 19th April when, escorting bombers in eastern Germany, they claimed five enemy aircraft destroyed (four Fw190s and a Do217). On this occasion the Group lost two aircraft, one of which was unfortunately shot down by Russian fighters and the other crash-landed in liberated territory. Their last mission was flown on 6th May and many of the personnel remained at Honington until November as the station had now become the headquarters of the Eighth Fighter Command. In any case four Bomb Groups (94th, 96th, 100th and 306th) were still in England and would not depart until towards the end of the year.

It was not until 26th February 1946 that Brigadier General Emil Kiel, the Commander of the Eighth Fighter Command, handed over the keys of the airfield to Air Chief Marshal Sir James Robb of RAF Fighter Command. Honington was the last of the 122 American air stations in England to be handed back to the RAF. As the Stars and Stripes was pulled down for the last time, it signalled the end of the Eighth Air Force presence, not only in East Anglia but in the whole of the United Kingdom – a historic event indeed. To the very end the English weather, that had so bedevilled many of the Eighth's operations over the previous three years, had its final say; the last remaining B-17 could not take off because of the low clouds. A US official was heard to remark that the only major activity left for the US forces in the United Kingdom was 'the shipment of war brides'!

Since that rainswept day the RAF has almost continuously used the airfield with a variety of aircraft from Dakotas, Valiant and Victor 'V' Bombers to Tornados, and at the time of writing it is the home of No 2 RAF Regiment.

14
HORHAM

During the war every serving member of a Bomb Group was utterly convinced that his own Group was 'the damn'd finest fighting unit in the whole of the Eighth'. Probably the members of the 95th Bomb Group felt that they had more justification than most in maintaining that their Group was indeed *the* best outfit in the Eighth. Over 300 missions completed to all the Eighth Air Force's famous or infamous targets. Two squadrons of the Group were the first to bomb Berlin. It also ended the war with the highest number of enemy aircraft destroyed. Finally the 95th was awarded three Distinguished Unit Citations – the only Group to receive three such honours. It must be admitted that it was a most remarkable war record.

This singular Bomb Group found a permanent home in a quiet and very rural part of the county near the village of Horham, from which 'Station 119' took its name; though most of the living quarters and the hospital were about a mile or so to the west clustered around the village of Denham. These rather secluded Suffolk villages were amongst the first to suffer the noise and inconvenience of construction work as the airfield was built during late 1941 and virtually completed by the following September. It was originally designated for RAF use but was allocated to the USAAF shortly before it was completed.

However, it was not until October that the first American aircraft appeared at Horham and they proved to be Douglas A-20Bs (Havocs) of the 47th Bomb Group. This Group and their light bombers were not destined to serve with the Eighth Air Force and were merely birds of passage en route to warmer activities in North Africa. Towards the end of the year they began to move away and it would

129

The unusual tail fin memorial to 95th Bomb Group.

be another four months before the roar of aircraft engines was once again heard over the airfield. It was the sound of the twin Pratt and Whitney engines of the B-26Bs of the 323rd Bomb Group. These Martin Marauders were also not fated to stay very long – barely a month – before moving to an airfield at Earls Colne in Essex during the middle of June 1943.

Almost immediately their place was taken by the B-17Fs of 95th Bomb Group, which since its arrival in England in April had been briefly based at Bovingdon in Hertfordshire, the reception centre for all bomber crews arriving to join the Eighth. Then they had moved to Alconbury, from whence the crews flew their first mission, on to Framlingham and now, at last, Horham, which was to be their permanent home for the rest of the war.

It was a most dispirited Group. After just nine missions, over half the original aircrews had been lost and morale was at a low ebb. Indeed, the whole of the 4th Wing (94th, 95th and 96th) had experienced a most traumatic and debilitating introduction into the air war. The Eighth's Commander – Lieutenant General Eaker – decided that changes might make a difference and on 22nd June, after a week at the new airfield, Colonel Kessler, who was a flyer from the days of the First World War and was known as 'Uncle Aaron', was replaced by Colonel John Gerhart – a very highly rated officer who had been appointed to the Eighth Air Force when it was first formed in January 1942, and was one of Eaker's valued backroom officers.

In these early days there was a very marked contrast between the senior officers of the Eighth and their crews. Most of the Group's commanders were long serving Army officers, many, like Kessler, had served in the previous war and others had been trained at West Point. The majority of the crewmen were very young, many of whom had never flown before they had volunteered for service with the Army Air Service. This situation did change quite quickly when younger men who had proved themselves in combat were promoted to positions of authority.

The first mission that was flown from Horham took place on 22nd June when the Eighth Air Force conducted their first major raid on the Ruhr, which of course until then had been the sole preserve of RAF Bomber Command, and soon the American aircrews would learn to their cost why the RAF called it 'Happy Valley'. The target this day was the synthetic rubber plants at Huls, which were thought to produce about one-third of Germany's needs. Although the Eighth claimed excellent bombing results with an estimated three months' loss of production, in fact the factories were back in full production well within a month. It was not a particularly costly operation (7% loss) and the 95th lost just one aircraft.

Six days later the 4th Bomb Wing was detailed to attack the lock gates at St Nazaire. The Wing, which would later become the Third Division, had been enlarged with the entry of a new Group – the 100th at Thorpe Abbots. The mission to St Nazaire was to be the longest trip so far and was only possible because the four Groups were equipped with late production B-17Fs which had extra fuel tanks in the wing tips, carrying another 1,080 gallons, greatly improving the B-17's range. These tanks were called 'Tokyo Tanks' from the erroneous belief that they would enable the B-17s to bomb Tokyo from mainland America. The only losses on this long mission were three of the Group's aircraft which ditched in the English Channel but the crews were saved by the air-sea rescue services. Six days later (4th July) the Wing went on a similar mission but a bit further south – to La Pallice, and returned with all its aircraft intact.

General Eaker felt it was time to really test the mettle of his growing

Crew of 'I'll be Around' after first raid on Berlin – March 1944. Lt Col Harvey Mumford on the right. (USAF via T. Moore)

force, as well as to demonstrate what concentrated daylight bombing could achieve; he would later dub this the 'Blitz Week'. In the process of mounting seven days of frantic operations almost 100 aircraft (about one-third of his total force) and 90 crews were lost in action. On 25th July the 95th went to Warnemünde and its Heinkel assembly plant, near Rostock. This was followed the next day by Hanover and its synthetic rubber works, where the Group lost four aircraft. Without a respite the Group took part in the costly operation to Oschersleben and its Fw190 assembly factories when 12½% loss was experienced; three aircraft failed to return to Horham, although one nearly made it, crash-landing at Framlingham. Because the earlier mission to Warnemünde was not a success, the 4th Wing was sent back on the 29th with much improved results. The week ended with an operation to Kassel and the only loss to the Group was one of their B-17s that ditched in the North Sea. Fortunately the remaining crew members were rescued, though five had already baled out over Holland and they ended up as prisoners of war. Although it had been a very hard week of operations, the outcome for the Group could have been far worse. By the end of the last mission it had lost a total of nine aircraft but the 94th's gunners claimed 38 enemy fighters destroyed, with another 15 probables and 22 damaged.

Perhaps there was no more emotive matter in the Eighth Air Force than bomber gunners' claims of enemy aircraft destroyed. Despite careful analysis of the claims it is generally accepted that on average they were about treble the number of actual enemy losses. Unlike the American fighter pilots the gunners did not have photographic evidence to substantiate their claims. The normal procedure to justify a claim was either to see the aircraft crash, burst in pieces, or see the pilot bale out. However, in the heat of battle this was not possible and several gunners claimed the same aircraft destroyed. Also the sheer speed and stress of air combat rendered later recall of incidents inaccurate. However, high claims of enemy fighters destroyed proved to be good for morale because the crews felt that at least they were inflicting great damage whilst suffering losses themselves. By May 1945 the Group had a total of 425 claims of aircraft destroyed with another 100 or so probables. Even if it is accepted that all claims were inflated, it is still a reasonable recompense for the 157 B-17s the Group lost in operations.

The Group's first Distinguished Unit Citation came with the famed Regensburg operation on which it lost four aircraft, although only eight out of the original 21 were able to make it back from North Africa. Within days of its return to Horham the Group was only able to muster seven B-17s for the Eighth's first attack on the V1 rocket sites at Watten in northern France. Within two weeks the Group was back to full strength, in time to send out 23 B-17s to the disaster of Stuttgart when the Eighth lost 45 aircraft, of which four came from Horham. It would be another month before the crews were fully tested again.

On 9th October the 94th took part in the famous and successful operation on Marienburg, which provided such excellent bombing results. The next day turned out to be a vicious mission for the leading formation (95th, 100th and 390th). The target was the railway yards at Münster, which was a major junction handling much of the traffic into the Ruhr. However, the crews were directed to bomb the city itself to cause maximum confusion to workers. The P-47s of 56th Fighter Group were planned to meet the lead formation near the target area but were slightly late, with the result that the Luftwaffe fighters struck at the bomber formation. The 100th Group and 390th suffered heavily in this first attack. The 95th went in to bomb the target and despite fierce flak opposition managed to bomb accurately. On leaving Münster the enemy fighters returned and by the time the P-47s appeared the leading Groups had lost 25 aircraft to what had been the most intense and concentrated Luftwaffe assault on an Eighth Bomb Wing of the war. The 95th had lost five aircraft and later were awarded their second Unit Citation for their successful bombing in the face of such severe opposition. Just four days later the Group despatched 18 aircraft on the second Schweinfurt operation and the crews managed to survive this torrid mission with the loss of a single aircraft, though claiming 18 enemy fighters in a just riposte.

The Group had now been ensconced at Horham for four months and although it had been a most difficult time, there were plenty of opportunities for sports at the base – soft ball, baseball, table-tennis and basketball. In the latter sport the Group's team became the Eighth's champions. There was a theatre for showing films and the occasional variety show. The Red Feather club for NCOs (a red feather featured on the Group's badge) and an officers' club provided in-base facilities, although The Grapes at Hoxne, The Green Man at Denham and The Green Dragon at Horham were all regularly used by the Americans. The men's spiritual needs were catered for by a multi-faith chapel on the site, although many preferred to use the local church at nearby Stradbroke, and before the Group left Horham they presented the church with a Stars and Stripes flag. Of course the major milestones were celebrated in fine style, with dinners and dances and many local people were invited to join in the celebrations. The Group chalked up its 100th mission in March 1944, the 200th in August, which was marked in a great manner when Glenn Miller and his AEF band arrived on 10th September. The 300th mission was celebrated by a splendid party on 21st April 1945 followed by a variety show on the following Sunday afternoon.

During the early months of 1944, when the bleak weather conditions allowed, the Eighth mounted maximum operations but in the process the crews found themselves facing a rejuvenated Luftwaffe, now greatly increased in strength. On 10th February the 95th experienced their stern and determined opposition whilst on a raid to Brunswick. The Third Division was solely operating on that day and some 160 B-17s were despatched, to be escorted by a strong force of P-47s and P-38s. However, two of the Fighter Groups failed to get airborne because of the weather conditions, another Group was late, with another two Groups arriving so late as to be of no use. The Luftwaffe fighters were always quick to seize the advantage and by the end of the day's operations 29 B-17s had been destroyed, almost one-third (seven) came from the 95th. It was almost like the bad old days of some six months ago. Nevertheless, two weeks later the Eighth still had the courage to mount an operation against Regensburg and managed to get away

134

Flak damaged B-17 lands at Horham after a mission to Bremen – December 1943. (USAF)

at small cost (4%); the Group returned from this notorious target without a single loss.

Berlin as a priority target had been pencilled into the Eighth's operational schedule since the end of the previous November but for a variety of reasons the date with destiny was postponed. However, the Eighth's chiefs were very conscious of the RAF's long offensive against the German capital and were eager to take their share. The first favourable date was 3rd March 1944 and a 748-strong force was briefed for various targets in and around Berlin. The heavy cloud formations caused considerable problems with assembling such a large force and when it was finally close to the German coast the operation was recalled because it was thought that the fuel situation would become critical.

The following day the Third Division was briefed once again for Berlin targets, but again the severe weather caused assembly problems and when the bomber formation was near German territory, the mission was abandoned. However, two squadrons of the 95th and one squadron of the 100th did not receive the message and carried on. Lt Colonel Harvey Mumford, the Group's Executive Officer, was in the leading aircraft *I'll be Around*, and he later recalled that, '. . . Going in wasn't tough, the weather was pretty bad, clouds were broken. And it was cold – damn cold – down to 55 degrees below zero...the bombing was done through clouds. I'm sure we hit the place . . .'! In point of fact 30 B-17s managed to bomb – the first American bombs to fall on Berlin. The Group lost five aircraft with the

135

The airfield at Horham resembling a battlefield after a B-17 exploded killing 18 men. (USAF via T. Moore)

100th losing just one. This first daylight raid by the Eighth received maximum publicity, especially as it was completed by a 'lone' formation. The crews at Horham and Thorpe Abbots were delighted that their Groups had been the first to bomb 'Big B'. For their leadership and performance on this historic Berlin mission the Group received its third Distinguished Unit Citation.

The exploits of the 95th were still not finished. On 21st June, along with the other Groups in 13th and 45th Bomb Wings, they went to attack oil targets in eastern Germany, then flying to land in the Soviet Union. In August a second Russian shuttle was undertaken. One of the most difficult missions during this period came on 25th August when the Division was detailed to attack the Rechlin Experimental Station on the Baltic coast and oil targets at Pölitz. Of the 380 B-17s despatched, eight were lost in action and half of these came from the 95th and another six, including one from the Group, were forced to land in Sweden. Then in September, perhaps because of their vast experience in long-distance flights the 94th became part of a 110-strong B-17 force sent to drop valuable supplies to the Polish Resistance workers in Warsaw, which had risen against the German occupation.

The Group's long battle against German targets came to a close on 20th April 1945 with their last and 320th mission, which was the third highest total in the Third Division. However, during the first week of May the crews became actively involved in dropping food supplies to

B-26 Marauder.

the Dutch people and on the last supply operation on 7th May, one of the Group's B-17s was shot at by German troops and the aircraft ditched in the North Sea after an engine caught fire; unfortunately only two of the crew were rescued. This was the final American aircraft to be lost in the European air war and the last American airmen to be missing in action. Not a particularly happy ending for a Group that had contributed so much to the Eighth Air Force's bitter campaign.

A month later the aircraft had left Horham and the ground crews had departed by the beginning of August. For several years the RAF used the airfield as a satellite for two Maintenance Units. Nowadays the villages and countryside show little sign of the old airfield. There is however an attractive and unique memorial to the Group close to the church at Horham, in the shape of a tail-fin of a B-17.

15

IPSWICH

Ipswich was formally opened in June 1930 by HRH the Prince of Wales; a rather apt choice as the Prince had obtained a Gypsy Moth the previous year and his very public enthusiasm for flying 'had done as much as any single factor to popularize air travel in Great Britain' according to the *Air* magazine. The Suffolk Aero Club used the small aerodrome and in July 1935 it hosted its first Air Day, followed three years later by the first Suffolk Air Show, which was attended by about 30,000 people, as well as the Under Secretary of the Air who opened some new buildings.

Like many other civil airfields Ipswich was used to train pilots for the Volunteer Reserve, a scheme which produced so many fine pilots for the Service. During August 1939 the Air Ministry requisitioned all such commercial airfields, which by now numbered almost 50, although not many of them were further developed during the war, mainly because they were sited too close to built-up areas. However, Ipswich was allocated as a satellite airfield for Wattisham, which had only opened as a full RAF station the previous March. Like its parent station Ipswich was placed in No 2 Group of Bomber Command. On 2nd September the first aircraft from Wattisham were dispersed to Ipswich and they were Blenheim Is and IVs of No 110 squadron.

This policy of dispersal of aircraft away from the operational stations clearly showed that the Service had quickly learnt from the bitter experience of the Polish Air Force. In the first two days of September much of the small Polish Air Force had been destroyed on the ground as a result of the Luftwaffe's bombing attacks on its airfields.

On 3rd September there were no less than 20 Blenheims (two Mark

Airspeed Oxford I – not only used for training but also target towing. (Via J. Adams)

Is and the rest Mark IVs) spread around the grass airfield at Ipswich. The Mark IV was a twin-engined light/medium bomber and the first of the new generation of monoplanes designed and developed under the pre-war expansion schemes. It was, at the time, a revolutionary aircraft and was the military version of an already proven civil aircraft, which had been produced by the Bristol Aeroplane Company for Lord Rothermere. He, rather generously, donated the aircraft to the nation and it was named *Britain First*. The Blenheim was the first stressed-skin metal monoplane complete with a retractable undercarriage to be built in Britain. The first prototype flew in June 1936 and with a speed of about 260 mph it was faster than any fighter in the Service. Great hopes lay in this fast day-bomber. It came into service during March 1938 but by the end of the year the company was producing the Mark IV. This had improved crew accommodation, a longer range, was better armed and was slightly faster at a maximum speed of 266 mph with its full bomb load of 1,000 pounds. However, the essential and marked difference was in appearance, the Mark I was short-nosed whereas the Mark IV was long-nosed; it was this mark that served with such distinction in No 2 Group as well as Coastal Command, and over 3,200 were finally produced. The first Mark IVs entered the Service with No 90 squadron in March 1939 and the Mark Ifs took up fighter duties.

Both of the Blenheim squadrons at Wattisham – Nos 107 and 110 – had their aircraft outhoused at Ipswich but it was not until the spring of 1941 that any of them flew operationally from the airfield. On 12th August when No 2 Group launched their famous and memorable low-level attack on the two Cologne power stations – Knapsack and Quadreth – a Blenheim from No 226 squadron (it had replaced No 107 squadron) left Ipswich along with several squadrons of Spitfires to act as their navigation leader on their escort duties for the Blenheim main force. Unfortunately the aircraft was shot down by a Me109 over Holland, as indeed was the other Blenheim navigator, also from No 226 squadron, which had taken off from Martlesham Heath. On this brave and valiant operation twelve of the original 56 Blenheims were destroyed – just another example of the stirring deeds accomplished by these Blenheim squadrons.

Like many other small wartime airfields that had not been enhanced with concrete runways or other improvements, Ipswich's wartime activities were confined to rather mundane and unspectacular duties, which nevertheless were very necessary to any operational Command – blind approach training and target practice both for air gunners and ground batteries. However, before the Blenheims finally bowed out of operations with No 2 Group, they were joined, in July 1942, by a squadron of Spitfires – No 340 – which had come for armament training at the Air Gunnery School at Hornchurch. This was a Free French squadron, which had been formed in November 1940, and the pilots proudly displayed the Cross of Lorraine on their aircraft just below the cockpit. For a short time they brought a bit of excitement and foreign colour to the airfield. They were the precursors of other Spitfires that appeared later in the year when the airfield was transferred to the control of Martlesham Heath and thus Fighter Command – Wattisham had been transferred to the USAAF in September 1942.

On 1st March 1943 Ipswich received full station status and within days a target towing Flight – No 1616 – arrived from Martlesham Heath. This Flight became the forerunner of similar units flying mainly Miles Martinet TTIs and Airspeed Oxfords. The Martinet had been specially developed for airborne target work from the Master trainer, and was the first RAF aircraft to be ordered for such duties; previously target towers were obsolescent aircraft. On the other hand, the Oxford was a twin-engined trainer that was used in many advanced training schools. It entered the Service in 1937 and was quickly dubbed the 'Ox-box', but nevertheless it remained in the RAF until 1954. Then towards the end of the year some Auster IIIs arrived; these very light aircraft had been used by the Army Co-operation Command as artillery spotters, or at least until the Command was disbanded in the summer of 1943.

Almost at the end of 1943 more Martinets and Oxfords appeared at Ipswich. They belonged to No 679 squadron and were largely used on anti-aircraft and searchlight co-ordination duties, as well as providing target facilities for coast batteries, especially those sited

Ipswich airfield as it is now.

around Harwich. During the spring of 1944 some Hurricanes and Spitfires of the Bomber Defence Training Flight came to the airfield and they were destined to see out the rest of the war at Ipswich.

The airfield was used, at times, as a refuge for badly damaged aircraft that could not make it back to their home station. On 4th November 1943 a B-17 of the 351st Group at Polebrook managed to make an emergency landing. However, later in January 1945 a P-51 from the 479th Group was not quite so lucky and it crashed close to the airfield. During September 1944 the airfield had some near misses from V1 rockets. The first landed close to the perimeter and killed one RAF man as well as injuring another two. Eighteen days later (19th) a V1 landed on a residential area close by and several civilians were injured.

On 30th June 1945 No 679 squadron was disbanded and the RAF decided to place the airfield on a care and maintenance basis, at least until the following April when they relinquished it. Before the year was out, pleasure flying had returned once again to the airfield.

16

KNETTISHALL

Coney Weston is a small and little known Suffolk village set on the eastern edge of the Breckland and close to the boundary with Norfolk. A quiet and tranquil place with a village green bounded by quaint and old houses, in late 1942 its peace and tranquillity were shattered when W & G French – the famous construction company – arrived with their large and cumbersome machines, heavy lorries and hordes of itinerant workers to build an airfield almost on the villagers' doorstep. By the time the airfield was finally completed many of the huts and living quarters were actually situated in the village itself, one right next door to the village school. After the contractors left during the summer of 1943, the 300 or so villagers would soon be swamped by an massive influx of over 2,800 young American servicemen, who brought with them all the noisy paraphernalia of war – B-17s, lorries, ambulances and jeeps.

The American airmen belonged to the 388th Bomb Group. They settled in at Knettishall during June and quite soon established a good rapport not only with their close neighbours, with whom they were living cheek by jowl, but also with the residents of the nearest town – Thetford – which was about six miles to the north-west of the airfield. Thetford, of course, was the birthplace of Thomas Paine, whose ideas and words did much to influence the Americans' fight for their independence and their written constitution. Sometime later one of the Group's replacement B-17Gs was named *Thomas Paine*, with all due civic ceremony, to acknowledge the town's long and historic links with America. This aircraft survived many missions, including a dramatic emergency landing at RAF Beccles during April 1944 when returning from a mission to Pölitz. It overshot the runway

'Thomas Paine' – the B-17 named after the famous son of Thetford. (Smithsonian)

and finally ended up in a field; although badly damaged it was repaired but shortly afterwards was finally retired from active service.

The Group had become a most welcome addition to the 4th Bomb Wing, and now with a growing force at his command Lieutenant General Eaker felt able and ready to launch a major offensive during the last week of July 1943. The Group, along with another new outfit, the 385th at Great Ashfield, became operational on the 17th of the month and within days both were engaged in a long flight to Bergen in Norway, which was about 750 miles distant. The B-17s were forced to fly at about 2,500 feet over the North Sea in order to save fuel, and all the aircraft returned safely from an operation which tested the navigators' expertise and nerve, as well as the crews' endurance. The Group returned to Norway in November with the task of locating and bombing a power station at Rjukan. It was not an easy task as the target was set deep in the mountains. However, most of the force managed to bomb and all 19 of the Group's aircraft arrived back safely.

The next day provided a much shorter haul to the submarine yards at Kiel, when the Group lost their first aircraft to enemy action. However, it was on the 26th July that the Group's first day of reckoning came whilst on a mission to the Continental Gummi-werke at Hanover, a large synthetic rubber plant. Out of the 21 B-17s sent out from Knettishall, five failed to return. Four days later the target was the Waldan Fieseler works at Kassel and another three aircraft were lost. It had proved to be a hard week for the new and inexperienced Group as well as the Eighth Air Force in general – almost 100 B-17s and nearly 900 airmen had been lost in this 'Blitz Week'. The 388th ended the week with ten aircraft missing in action, 24 damaged, and 100 airmen lost – a most stern and exacting introduction into operations.

On 6th September, came the infamous Stuttgart raid, which gave such a body blow to the Eighth Air Force. The weather had deteriorated so much that in truth the operation should have been aborted as the chances of accurate bombing had become so slight. On this day it was the 388th's turn to be in the low box of the formation, a notoriously vulnerable position, which experienced crews called 'Purple Heart Corner' with much justification. As the Group approached the target area, it was attacked by a large force of Me109s and Fw190s. The enemy fighters came head-on into the formation in a mad frenzy of strikes, it was later estimated that one enemy fighter struck every 30 seconds. In this quite vicious and overwhelming onslaught 17 B-17s went down in flames, of which the Group lost eleven aircraft. The whole of one bomb squadron (No 563) disappeared without trace, a grievous blow to the 388th which severely dented the crews' morale. This ill-conceived and calamitous mission proved to be the Group's heaviest loss of the whole war.

Ten days later the Third Bomb Division was detailed for targets in south-west France – La Pallice, La Rochelle and Cognac. It was fully acknowledged that this would be another long and exhausting mission, probably involving well over ten hours' flying most of which would be undertaken over enemy territory. Because of a heavy cloud formation over Bordeaux, the primary target, the force turned their attention to the U-boat pens at La Pallice and Cognac airfield with the loss of just one B-17 from the Group. However, on their return the crews experienced considerable difficulties because of the increasing darkness and a quite severe weather front that had settled over Britain. One of the Group's aircraft crashed in north Devon, another into a hill in mid-Wales and a third, which had radio failure, eventually ditched in the North Sea off Northumberland, hopelessly lost and out of fuel, when the crew had been airborne for over twelve hours! Unfortunately 14 airmen were killed in these three tragic accidents.

During October the 388th was in action over Emden, Saarbrücken,

Bremen, Münster, Gdynia (in Poland) and Schweinfurt. It was on the 14th of the month the Eighth decided to take their second tilt at this famous ball-bearing target. The USAAF claimed this operation as a great success. Their press notice said, 'Our initial estimate is that we destroyed at least half of Schweinfurt's ball-bearing plants. This raid will undoubtedly cause a decrease in the production of German tanks, aircraft and guns, and the construction of U-boat submarines will also be affected.' This was more a matter of putting a very brave face on what was in reality a very costly operation. In such a fierce operation it was quite amazing that the crews of the 388th would return to Knettishall completely intact. The two operations to Schweinfurt and Regensburg had resulted in 120 aircraft being lost and such a horrendous blood-bath completely destroyed the myth of the self-defensive bomber formation.

Like most Bomb Groups, Berlin was to feature large in the 388th's operations during 1944 and the Group undertook no less than ten missions to the 'Big B', none more shattering than that which was launched on 6th March – this was 'a real rough one', as one pilot later recalled. The Luftwaffe fighters turned out in great strength and they pursued their attacks with determination. But as well as contending with the Me109s and Fw190s the crews had also to face the heavy flak defences that surrounded the city, then considered the heaviest in all Germany. The Group suffered quite heavily on this mission – seven aircraft were lost. Two days later the crews were back over Berlin, this time five aircraft were lost. Only the 'jinx' Group – the 'Bloody 100th' at Thorpe Abbots – had suffered heavier losses on the two operations. Thankfully matters greatly improved and in the next eight Berlin missions the 388th lost only four aircraft.

Before the month was out (23rd) the Group suffered heavily over Brunswick when the 45th Bomb Wing, of which they were now part, arrived early when there was no fighter escort to save them from the renowned Luftwaffe units that were stationed in the area. In a matter of moments the Wing lost eleven B-17s, five of which came from the 388th. Another rather long mission was undertaken on 9th April, a 1,800 mile round trip to the Fw190 component plant at Poznan, which was just inside the Polish border. Heavy cloud formations caused most of the 151-strong force to seek alternative targets at Rostock. However, along with the 96th and 452nd Groups, a box of the Group's aircraft carried on regardless to the primary target despite worsening weather conditions. They found the target area clear and were able to bomb visually and accurately. The Group

Memorial to 388th Bomb Group.

returned from what was recognised as a most successful operation with just two aircraft missing.

But perhaps the Group's finest hour came on 12th May when the Eighth launched its first major operation against German oil targets. The Third Division attacked targets at Zwickau and Brux. The crews of the 388th bombed the oil plant at Brux very effectively causing considerable damage. On their return home the Bomb Wing was attacked by Me410s (Zestorers) and 41 B-17s were destroyed, but once again the crews arrived back at Knettishall without a single loss. The Group was awarded its second Distinguished Unit Citation for this mission, as well as the earlier operation to Hanover and the later shuttle mission to Russia.

The first German V1 rocket (flying bomb) was launched on 13th June 1944 and this event was to have quite an effect on the Group activities as well as life at the airfield. The appearance of these doodle-bugs decided the USAAF to activate their own 'guided weapon'. This meant using battle-worn B-17s, removing all the extraneous material before filling them with radio receiving sets, and then packing the aircraft with ten tons of explosives. The method of operation was for the 'robot' aircraft to be flown manually by a two-man crew until radio contact was ensured with the guide aircraft; the two men would then bale out to allow the robot to be directed onto the target by control from the guide aircraft. The whole project was code-named Aphrodite and was authorised for action on 23rd June.

Pilots and auto-pilots were recruited from volunteers and they were put through an intensive flight training programme at Bovingdon; everything, of course, was cloaked in great secrecy. Lt Colonel James Turner, who was put in charge of the project, moved into RAF Woodbridge early in July with ten B-17s, a couple of B-24s and eight P-47s to act as fighter escorts. However, because this airfield was used as an emergency landing ground and there was a risk of one of the badly damaged aircraft colliding with one of the lethal 'flying bombs', it was wisely felt that it would be much safer to move this secret project elsewhere. An unused airfield at Fersfield in Norfolk, which had been allocated to the Eighth, was thought to fit the bill. It was rather secluded and thus quite appropriate for this secret project, and because Knettishall was so close, it was furthermore decided that the Fersfield establishment would be operated under the aegis of the 388th with its 560th squadron supplying much of the manpower; thus the Squadron's Commanding Officer, Lt Colonel Roy Forrest, took over command of the satellite base.

The US Navy had also been working on their own rocket projectile and they decided to take a slice of the action. Their Special Unit No 1 also moved into Fersfield, and their operation was code-named Anvil. Perhaps their most famous officer in this Unit was Lt Joseph Kennedy, the eldest son of the ex-US Ambassador to Great Britain and brother of John F. Kennedy, the future President.

The first two Aphrodite missions were launched on 4th August and were directed to V1 rocket sites in northern France. The first went well but the second malfunctioned and the robot bomber landed in a wood near Sudbourne Park in Suffolk with a massive explosion, leaving a crater over 100 feet in diameter! Two days later another two launches were made but because of problems with the radio equipment both fell harmlessly into the sea.

The Naval unit launched their first rocket aircraft – a Liberator – on 12th August and it was piloted by Lt Kennedy. The robot headed out towards Southwold and at an altitude of 2,000 feet it exploded, killing Kennedy and his engineer. The wreckage was strewn over a wide area and the bodies were never recovered.

By November it was decided to move the project to the parent airfield – Knettishall – along with all the strict security measures that had been in place at Fersfield. However, only another four launches were made – two in December directed at the marshalling yards at Herford, both of which missed their target. The last two were sent out on New Year's Day to a power station at Oldenburg. The first one was damaged by enemy flak and landed short of the town but without exploding. The second was also hit by flak and ultimately crashed some miles away from the target. It is fair to say that the project had not been a conspicuous success and its future now became a political matter at the highest level. By this time there was a somewhat different attitude to rather indiscriminate bombing, despite the fact that V2 rockets were now falling haphazardly on both London and East Anglia. The debate continued for several months and finally the project was abandoned at the end of April when it did appear that the war in Europe was drawing to a conclusion.

Of course whilst all this secret work had been going on, the squadrons of the 388th were still actively engaged in normal operations. For instance, on 28th September, when the 388th was sent to oil targets at Merseburg it suffered its heaviest loss for several months – five aircraft. The Luftwaffe mounted a strong opposition to 1,000 or so strong bomber formations. In the resultant mayhem two of the Group's aircraft collided over the target area, another two were shot down and a fifth was so badly damaged that it was forced to crash-land near Liège in Belgium but all the crew escaped without harm.

On Christmas Eve the Group managed to establish a record for the Eighth Air Force in response to the call for 'utmost maximum effort', when no less than 71 bombers left Knettishall for airfields and oil centres in western Germany; included in this grand total were five B-17s from other Groups, which had been diverted to the airfield. This mission (No 760) proved to be the largest air strike of the war with over 2,040 heavy bombers airborne and some 850 fighters acting as escorts. Only one of the Group's aircraft failed to return; it crashed near Liège after all the crew had baled out.

During the month of February 1945 the Group was particularly active despite the fact that several days of inclement weather resulted in cancelled operations. The 388th went out on no less than 16 missions and none of them can be considered easy rides – Berlin, Chemnitz and Nuremberg twice each, with Hamm, Munich, Frankfurt and Liepzig added for good measure. During the month, sadly, five aircraft fell to enemy action but another six came to grief

B-17s of 388th Bomb Group over the Norwegian coast. (IWM)

for a variety of accidental reasons – collisions, crashing on take-off, engine failure on assembly and one suddenly bursting in flames over France whilst en route to Berlin. Sharp and timely reminders of the rather slim margins of error involved in flying a fully-loaded B-17, or B-24 for that matter.

A major milestone for the Group was reached during April – their 300th mission, becoming only the third B-17 Group in Suffolk to reach such a momentous target. On 21st April they had flown their last and 306th operation and overall had lost almost 180 aircraft to enemy action and other causes. After a two year sojourn at Knettishall, the Americans left.

Fifty years later there are few immediate signs of the old wartime airfield. The two memorials to the 388th – one at the crossroads outside the village but close to the main entrance to the airfield, and the other in the nearby small church of St Mary – record those far-off days when this quiet and delightful village hummed with excitement and drama, but was also inevitably tinged with sadness and sorrow.

17

LAKENHEATH

It is perhaps somewhat difficult to believe that Lakenheath, now a compact 'township' of some 5,000 people, was once a small and rather isolated village; but it needs an even greater stretch of the imagination to visualise just how the airfield appeared during wartime, so utterly has it been swallowed up under the massive USAF development that occurred during the days of the Cold War. Lakenheath's importance as a major NATO base has somewhat overshadowed its rather brief wartime existence when Short Stirlings left there to bomb targets in Germany and Italy.

Quite early in the war years the site was recognised as a suitable place for an airfield, being almost in the centre of the Breckland and nearly equidistant from two important pre-war RAF stations – Mildenhall and Feltwell. It first came into being as a 'decoy airfield' for Feltwell, and was just one of the many sham airfields to be found in the East Anglian countryside in the early war years. Their purpose was to confound the enemy aircraft, with the hope of drawing air attacks away from the active operational airfields. This involved the construction of dummy hangars, living quarters, and even mock model aircraft to make the sites even more realistic from the air. These 'Q' sites, as they were known, were often provided with flare path lighting to heighten the illusion. However, by late 1940, it was decided to develop Lakenheath into a proper bomber station with the provision of the usual three concrete runways and two T2 plus another B1 (Bellman) hangars.

The airfield opened in June 1941 as the earliest of all wartime airfields in Suffolk and was allocated as a satellite for Mildenhall, some five miles or so to the south-east. Although some of

Mildenhall's aircraft were dispersed there during the early months, the airfield did not really become active until November, when towards the end of the month No 20 OTU (Operational Training Unit) brought their Wellington Is from Lossiemouth in Scotland after that airfield had become somewhat waterlogged.

During the pre-war years there had been a rather relaxed system of operational training in the RAF. Crews were transferred to squadrons directly from basic flying training and it was left to the squadrons to train their new crews. However, even in 1938, it was recognised that this system was not really satisfactory, so a number of aircraft and experienced crews were placed in reserve and a reserve pool was established for each of the Command's Groups. By early 1940 these Group pools were made into Operational Training Units, where separate aircrew categories went through at least six weeks of specialised training, and then for the final two weeks they came together as a made-up crew for night navigation, formation flying, bomb aiming, firing training as well as escape drill procedures. The crews were formed mainly by friendship rather than coercion and the bonds established during this training remained firm and strong throughout their future operations. It was a system that seemed to work very well for the RAF, although the USAAF favoured an official selection of crews.

By May 1941 there were no less than 16 OTUs in Nos 6 and 7 Groups, which were specially formed to organise such training, though less than two years later there were three Groups (91 to 93) controlling 21 OTUs. Such a heavy commitment to operational training placed an enormous strain on Bomber Command's front-line bomber force with so many valuable aircraft and even more precious experienced and battle-hardened crews being involved. The politicians were continually pressing the Air Staff for these training units to become more involved in the bombing offensive; indeed, Air Chief Marshal Harris had to draft in a considerable number of 'training' aircraft to achieve his target of 1,000 bombers for the Cologne operation at the end of May 1942. No 20 OTU supplied 14 Wellingtons for this raid.

The training Wellingtons returned to Scotland in January 1942 and for about two months some Stirling Is arrived on detachment from Mildenhall but it was not until the beginning of April that Lakenheath's first permanent squadron arrived. No 149 squadron had been reformed at Mildenhall in 1937 and had remained there until its move to Lakenheath. During the previous November it had converted to Stirlings and was a very experienced squadron, which was destined to serve continuously with Bomber Command throughout the war, achieving one of the lowest loss-rates in the whole of the Command.

The squadron was involved in one of the most important operations raised by Bomber Command during the war – Operation Millenium – the 1,000 bomber attack on Cologne. Air Chief Marshal Harris later maintained, 'My own opinion is, that we would never have had a real bomber offensive if it had not been for the 1,000 bomber attack on Cologne, an irrefutable demonstration of the power of what was to all intents and purposes a new and untried weapon.'

It was during the last week of May 1942 that the crews at Lakenheath were aware that something big was in the offing. All weekend passes were cancelled, crews on leave were sent immediate recall telegrams and the ground crews were told that every available aircraft was to be prepared for a special operation. The Group Commanders were aware of what was planned: 'a maximum force of bombers directed on a single and extremely important town in Germany, with a view to wiping it out in one night or at least two.'

Gravestone of Flight Sergeant R.H. Middleton, VC at Beck Row, Mildenhall.

Hamburg or Cologne were the two targets in mind, which target would be selected depended on the weather forecast. Finally the decision was made by Harris, it would be the night of 30/31st May and Cologne was chosen; the weather conditions seemed more favourable for Cologne, which in any case was more suited because of the operational limitations of GEE.

The briefing at the 53 airfields involved in this massive operation took place at 6 pm and when the crews were informed that it was Cologne, there was considerable relief that it was not going to be a daylight mission or indeed that it was not Berlin. When they were informed that they were going to just one city with more than 1,000 aircraft taking part the reaction was quite amazing, cheering broke out and this had to be silenced for Harris's message to be read out. 'The force of which you form a part tonight is at least twice the size and has more than four times the carrying capacity of the largest air force ever before concentrated on one objective. You have the opportunity therefore, to strike a blow at the enemy which will resound, not only throughout Germany, but throughout the world . . . Press home your attack with the utmost determination and resolution in the foreknowledge that if you succeed, the most shattering and devastating blow will have been delivered against the very vitals of the enemy. Let him have it – right on the chin.'

The Wellingtons and Stirlings of Nos 1 and 3 Groups would be in the first wave. They would be loaded with incendiaries and their target was the Neumarkt – the centre of the old town. It was made clear to the crews that the whole success of the operation depended on their bombing accuracy and No 149 along with No 15 squadron from Wyton would be amongst the first bombers over the target. Of the 1,047 bombers that were despatched some 860 managed to bomb the target causing quite indescribable damage with over 12,000 buildings destroyed or severely damaged. Though 41 aircraft failed to return (4.1% of the force), 149 squadron came back to Lakenheath without a loss and one of the crews claimed a Me110 destroyed over München Gladbach on their way out. This was a most successful operation, which dealt a shattering blow to the German High Command and gave a powerful surge to the British public's morale. After suffering the severe air raids of 1940/1 the British public felt that at long last they were hitting back with a vengeance; the Cologne raid was claimed to be the first British 'victory' of the war.

During October 1942 the priority of Bomber Command's main force changed from Germany to targets in northern Italy; this was largely due to the start of the Eighth Army's offensive on the 23rd of the month and the Anglo-American invasion of North Africa 18 days later. From 22nd October to 11th December 1,646 sorties were mounted with 62 aircraft being lost. Milan, Genoa and Turin suffered a succession of raids, which had a great effect on Italian morale. Despite their long flying time and having to negotiate the Alps, the Italian missions were quite favoured by the crews as the Italian flak was much lighter than that experienced over German targets. Of the 32 VCs awarded to airmen, two were awarded for operations over Italian targets.

On the night of 28/29th November 1942 just seven Stirlings of No 149 squadron left Lakenheath for a mission to the Fiat works at Turin. Because of the severe weather conditions over the Alps only four of the aircraft carried on to the target area and one of these was piloted by Flight Sergeant Rawdon Middleton, an Australian, who was one of the most experienced pilots in the squadron; this was his 29th mission. Middleton completed no less than three bombing runs over Turin in order to identify the precise target. It was whilst the aircraft was on its third run that it was struck by flak. The fragments of the shell struck Middleton in the leg, chest and face, destroying his right eye. Middleton became unconscious and the aircraft plunged down to 800 feet before being righted by the second pilot, Flight Sergeant L. Hyder, who was also badly injured. The aircraft was hit again and at this stage Middleton regained consciousness and insisted on taking control of the aircraft despite his dreadful injuries.

The aircraft was in a sorry state, there were gaping holes in the fuselage and the windscreen was completely shattered. With supreme skill and courage Middleton managed to coax the aircraft over the Alps but over France the aircraft was hit again by flak. The front gunner, Sergeant S. Mackie, who was on his 33rd mission, was at Middleton's side to give him visual aid and just after two o'clock in the morning the aircraft crossed the French coast. The crew had been airborne for almost eight hours. By the time the Kent coast was in sight the aircraft had about five minutes of fuel left. Because of his injuries and those of his co-pilot and the state of the aircraft, Middleton felt that an emergency landing was impossible and he would not take the risk of hitting houses. So he turned to the English Channel and ordered the crew to bale out while he flew parallel with the coast for a couple of minutes. Five of the crew baled out, including Hyder, and all managed to survive. Mackie and Sergeant J. Jeffrey, the Flight Engineer, stayed to help Middleton up to the last

Stirling crews of No 149 Squadron relax after a mission. (Via J. Adams)

possible moment. They baled out but did not survive the night in the water and their bodies were found later in the afternoon. Just before three o'clock the fuel was exhausted and the aircraft crashed in the sea just off Dymchurch. On 15th January 1943 Flight Sergeant Middleton was posthumously awarded the Victoria Cross and all the surviving crew were awarded either the DFC or DFM. On 1st February 1943 Middleton's body was washed up near Dover and he was buried with full military honours at the churchyard at Beck Row near Mildenhall.

During the Battle of the Ruhr the squadron was involved in many of the raids, losing six aircraft. However, in the four operations to Hamburg during July to August 1943, 61 sorties were mounted with not a single aircraft lost. A second squadron – No 199 – had arrived from Ingram in Lincolnshire during June, and both squadrons were operational on 23/24th August, which was the opening salvo in the Command's offensive against Berlin, in which both squadrons lost just one aircraft. The Stirling of 149 squadron was one of the nine aircraft that were lost on the way out to Berlin when they strayed into a heavy flak area near Hanover. The 199 Stirling was shot down shortly after completing its bomb run, and the rear gunner, who was the only survivor, later recalled: 'We had bombed and had nearly got to the edge of the searchlight area; we thought we were over the coast. Then it was as though a giant hand took hold of us and there was a huge shuddering and shaking sensation, just like a massive dog shaking a rat . . . The next thing I knew was that I was coming down on the end of a parachute . . .' Before the Stirling squadrons were taken off German targets both Lakenheath squadrons took part in three Berlin raids losing three aircraft each.

By the end of 1943 the Stirlings were no longer directly involved in bombing operations, but in January 1944 the Stirlings of 199 squadron were being equipped with Mandrel screens. Mandrel was an electronic device that had been developed to transmit signals that effectively jammed the German early warning Freya system. It had been first used operationally in December 1942 but since then had undergone considerable modification and was now quite a sophisticated system. The intention of the Mandrel squadrons was to be present in the main bomber formation, either in the front to form an adequate screen or mingling in the centre of the main force. At the beginning of May 1944 No 199 squadron would join No 100 (Special Duties) Group, which had been formed to co-ordinate and further develop all manner of counter-devices, at North Creake in Norfolk and become greatly involved in the D-Day operations.

In the meanwhile No 149 squadron, besides being fully engaged in other operations, particularly mine laying, also became involved in dropping arms and supplies to the French Maquis resistance fighters, as well as the occasional special operation over Holland. However, it moved to Methwold in Norfolk and it was from this airfield that the last Stirling bombing operation was mounted to Le Havre on 8th September.

During the early months of 1944 the Air Ministry had decided that certain airfields would be developed into what were termed Very Heavy Bomber Stations, possibly to accommodate either the heavy Boeing B-29 or the new RAF heavy bomber that was still on the drawing board and tentatively named the Windsor, which was never produced. Thus, during May, Lakenheath's rather brief wartime existence came to an abrupt end, just when the air offensive was beginning to reach a crescendo. It was not until July 1948 that Lakenheath again became active with the rather appropriate arrival of the American B-29s, ushering in an American presence that would last for over 40 years.

18

LAVENHAM

This 'most resplendent of Suffolk wool towns', as it has been described, was to become the spiritual home for the personnel of the 487th Bomb Group, who were stationed at the nearby airfield about three miles to the north-west of Lavenham. The historic town must have resembled a Hollywood film set to most of the young Americans who arrived here in 1944, so completely did it match all their pre-conceived ideas of rural and olde worlde England!

The airfield, which had been built by John Laing & Co in 1943, first echoed to the heavy throb of the powerful Pratt and Whitney engines of the B-24Hs in April 1944. This new Eighth Air Force Group had as its Commanding Officer one of the 'old stagers' of the Eighth – Lieutenant Colonel Beirne Lay Jnr. As a mere Captain, Lay had been one of the small and select coterie of officers that General Eaker brought to England in February 1942. However, Lay was no mere backroom headquarters officer and he had always been keen to get into the action.

By 7th May, Lay felt that his crews were ready for action. However, heavy cloud over the target area – Liège marshalling yards – prevented much of the force from bombing. Two other missions to Brussels and Laon airfield took place without incident. Then on the 11th, Lay was leading the 92nd Combat Bomb Wing to Chaumont marshalling yards in eastern-central France. Due to some faulty navigation the Wing stumbled across a very heavy flak area; Lay's aircraft was shot down, as was his deputy's, a third was badly damaged and it was decided to abort the whole mission. The badly damaged aircraft was finally abandoned over the English coast and ultimately crashed near Chichester with one crew member being killed. Lay managed to escape from his aircraft, evade capture and he ultimately returned to England – but more about him later.

At the end of the month after returning from an operation over Münster, one of the Group's aircraft was forced to ditch in the North Sea not far out from Lowestoft. On this occasion the eight members of the crew were rather lucky and they were all rescued. During the war it was reckoned that over 450 heavy bombers had ditched in the sea and the survival rate for crews was about 35%.

The 487th achieved an unenviable record on 6th June – D-Day. It proved to be the only Bomb Group in the Eighth Air Force to lose an aircraft to enemy action. By 21st July they had launched their last and 46th mission with their B-24s. However, the Group was only off operations for just eleven days and on 1st August they took their new B-17Gs to Tours airfield and brought all of them back safely. It would be another five days before their first B-17 was lost in action and this was when the 487th was attacking the Krupps munitions works at Magdeburg. On the following day the crews were given their first taste of the Berlin flak. Despite the fact that the bombers were almost equalled in number by the P-51 escorts, five aircraft failed to return and one of these belonged to the 487th.

The Group's crews played a full and active part in the Eighth's massive and on-going offensive against the German oil industry. Encouraged by relatively light losses during October when the Luftwaffe had hardly challenged any of the operations, November saw a number of heavy strikes against oil targets mainly, at least as far as the Third Division was concerned, against the Leuna synthetic oil plant at Merseburg in eastern Germany. This large oil complex was one of the Eighth's favourite targets, having been attacked no less than eleven times since 12th May. It is worth noting that it was not until 6/7th December that RAF Bomber Command launched its first *major* night raid on this target when five out of the 475 Lancasters were lost. However, without doubt Merseburg ranked alongside Berlin in the unpopularity stakes with aircrews. Not only did it entail a long flight over very hostile territory but there was also a fearsome corridor of flak batteries to be faced before arriving onto the target. It was not a new experience for the 487th, the crews had been there twice before, but with four missions planned for November, it was going to prove a long and harsh month.

Perhaps the hardest Merseburg mission came on the last day of the month when due to a minor navigational error by the lead aircraft the formation were forced to fly through an even more concentrated barrage of flak, which lasted for almost 20 minutes. One gunner later recalled, '. . . It didn't seem possible for any ship to get through such a hell . . .' The early reports of the operation were quite dire; it was first thought that 56 aircraft had been lost, though this figure was later amended to 29 when it was discovered that many of the 'missing' aircraft had landed at a variety of airfields on the Continent. Nevertheless the Third Division took the brunt of the losses, 17 out of 539 aircraft despatched failed to make it back and it was said that over 80% of the surviving B-17s had suffered some form of battle damage. The Lavenham Group lost just one aircraft on this operation and only five in total for the whole month – a quite remarkable achievement in the circumstances.

For about a week before Christmas 1944 the weather was not really conducive to operational flying. It was during this period (on the 16th) that the German army launched a major offensive in the Ardennes. Most of the Eighth Air Force Groups were grounded because of fog and were thus unable to provide any tactical support for the American forces that were experiencing such a hard time. However, by the 23rd the weather showed signs of improvement and the forecast for Christmas Eve was much more promising with a strong possibility of clear visibility. Therefore the Eighth Command issued a General Order to all Groups that 'a maximum effort' was to be made – anything that could fly should be airborne on the day. As a result over 2,000 heavy bombers took to the air on Christmas Eve, making it the biggest single mission ever mounted by the Eighth Air Force.

Early that morning Brigadier General Fred Castle arrived at Lavenham from his headquarters at Bury St Edmunds, where he was the Commander of the 4th Bomb Wing, which since November had become the largest Wing in the Eighth Air Force comprising five Bomb Groups (including the 487th). It was Castle's intention to lead the Third Division's formations on this massive operation, flying as co-pilot in the Group's lead aircraft. He was an experienced officer and pilot, with 29 missions to his credit mainly gained when in command of the 94th at Bury St Edmunds.

A wide range of targets in western Germany were selected for the day's operations – airfields, road and rail communications centres and canals – with the intention of frustrating the movement of troops and supplies to support the German offensive in the Ardennes. The weather was good with clear visibility, as had been forecast, but unfortunately the first escort of P-51s were late to the rendezvous point and this, plus an unusual Luftwaffe fighter tactic, resulted in the 487th flying into deep trouble.

'Twelve O'Clock High': the classic war film, co-author Lt Col Beirne Lay Jnr (CO at Lavenham) – some of the scenes were also filmed at Lavenham. (CBS Fox)

Just over Liège in Belgium the lead bomber formation was suddenly attacked by a gruppe of Me109s. This was a most unexpected ploy as normally the Luftwaffe fighters were loath to strike whilst the bombers were over Allied held territory. Furthermore they had judged the moment exactly, attacking at a time when the bombers were completely unprotected. Already General Castle's aircraft was suffering from some loss of engine power, causing a reduction in its speed. In the initial fighter strike the aircraft was hit, and it was forced to fall back to the rear of the formation. Being in a rather isolated position made it an even better target for further fighter attacks, which set two of its engines on fire. The B-17 appeared to be in imminent danger of exploding and Castle took over control of the aircraft. Three of the crew had been wounded and Castle ordered the rest to bale out, including Lt Harriman, the pilot. Castle now took over the control of the aircraft.

What happened next was clearly stated in the citation for his award. '. . . Without regard for his personal safety, he [Castle] gallantly remained alone at the controls to afford all other crew members an opportunity to escape. Still another attack exploded gasoline tanks in the right wing, and the bomber plunged earthward, carrying General Castle to his death. His intrepidity and willing sacrifice of his life to save members of the crew were in keeping with the highest traditions of the military service.' Castle was awarded the Congressional Medal of Honor, the last such award of the war and he was the highest ranking officer in the Eighth Air Force to be so honoured. In the air battle three of the Group's aircraft were shot down and another five were so badly damaged that they had to make forced-landings in

B-24 of 487th Bomb Group taxiing past the control tower. (USAF)

Belgium and all were classified as write-offs. However, six of Castle's crew managed to escape and survive.

After such a painful and traumatic mission it was a most dismal and dispirited Christmas at Lavenham although the crews had three blessed days free of operations; but by the 28th they were back in business flying to Coblenz and on the following day to Frankfurt, where yet another crew was lost. Despite the severe weather that was experienced in January 1945, which played such havoc with the Eighth's schedule of operations, the Group lost four aircraft on the 18th whilst engaged on a mission to Derben oil installations, about 60 miles due west of Berlin. This part of Germany seemed to hold a fatal attraction for the 487th because almost three months later (10th April) another four B-17s fell foul of flak at Brandenburg, which was about 20 miles from Derben. However, during 1945 the Group led the whole of the Third Division in the accuracy of their bombing. Photographic evidence had shown that a greater percentage of their bombs fell within 1,000 feet of the MPI (Mean Point of Impact). By the time of their last mission (No 195) the Group had paid a relatively high cost for their eleven months of war, with 48 aircraft lost in action.

By August 1945 all of the Americans had left and the airfield was taken over by RAF Transport Command, but by 1948 it had become inactive with virtually all the existing buildings intact. However, by now Beirne Lay Jnr, the one-time Commanding Officer, along with another Eighth Air Force officer, Sy Bartlett had written a novel about an American Bomb Group stationed in England called *Twelve O'Clock High*. They also wrote the screenplay for the film, which was produced by Darryl Zanuck for Twentieth Century Fox. The film, starring Gregory Peck, was released in 1949 and became an instant success. This classic war film was partly filmed at the old airfield at Lavenham.

The town of Lavenham, itself, holds many memories of the 487th Bomb Group. In the lovely Market Place there is a memorial plaque to the Group and at the famous Swan Hotel there are several items relating to the Group on display, as well as a portrait of Lieutenant General Castle, as the Swan was one of his favourite haunts. To reach the airfield take the A134 road out of Long Melford towards the village of Alpheton and it will then be found along a minor road to the north-east of the village.

Standing on the very edge of the old airfield, with the old control tower – now a private house – in the distance on a still and quiet spring morning, it was not too difficult to visualise a line of B-17s straining to take off, as they did so often over 50 years ago.

19

LEISTON

There is a simple plaque fixed to the Old Post Office at Leiston which lists 69 fighter pilots (it should be 68) that lost their lives whilst serving with the 357th Fighter Group at the nearby airfield, which was situated some two miles to the north-east of the town.

The men from the Air Ministry's Directorate of Works quickly recognised the potential of the farmland along this particular stretch of the Suffolk coast and requisitioned nearly 500 acres adjacent to the village of Theberton for the site of a new airfield, which was almost equi-distant between this village, Leiston and Saxmundham and at various times was called after the three places, although Leiston became its accepted name. As the site was barely three miles from the coast the location seemed ideal for RAF Fighter Command, although only days after the main contractor – John Mowlem & Co – moved in, during September 1942, the airfield had been allocated to the USAAF for their ultimate use as a fighter base. Its prime position, so close to the coast, did result in several badly damaged aircraft using the nascent airfield during its throes of construction despite all the inherent dangers of the partially completed runways.

The first fighters to use the airfield were P-47Ds of the 358th Group, who landed there at the end of November 1943 after a short flight from Goxhill in Lincolnshire. This was the main reception base for fighter units arriving in England.

The Group's Commanding Officer, Lt Colonel Cecil Wells, who was later to be killed in action when the Group were serving with the Ninth Air Force, felt confident enough to allow his young lads into action on 20th December, as part of a large fighter escort mounted for a multi-divisional mission to Bremen. It turned out to be a severe

P-51 of 357th Fighter Group landing at Leiston. (USAF)

introduction into air combat but at least the newcomers managed to escape unharmed, though without a victory. The following day the pilots were detailed to provide an escort for B-26Cs of the Ninth Air Force, which really was quite a coincidence because in just a month's time they would be transferred to the Ninth.

In all honesty the Group's short stay at Leiston was anything but impressive. It flew 17 missions in all, losing four aircraft whilst claiming four enemy destroyed. However, unbeknown to the pilots the Group had become merely a pawn in a little horse trading between the powers of the Eighth and Ninth Air Forces. The object of the exercise was for the Eighth Fighter Command to get their hands on a P-51 Group. By mutual consent the 358th was exchanged for the 357th Group, then working up to operational readiness with the Ninth Air Force at Raydon. Thus at the end of January the Group packed its bags and left for Raydon, or as one crew member succinctly put it, 'we exchanged one mudhole for another'! As can be gathered from this comment neither airfield had been completely finished and an East Anglian winter had certainly not improved living and working conditions around the two bases.

And so on the last day of January 1944 the first P-51 Group to serve with the Eighth Air Force arrived with just 15 aircraft. On paper it would appear that the Ninth had gained the better deal, it had received a fully equipped and fully operational Group in exchange for a barely equipped and largely untried Group that was still experiencing certain difficulties with its P-51Cs. It was not until 5th

February that more of the precious aircraft arrived at Leiston and then they were almost immediately grounded whilst a serious fault was investigated. However, it proved in the long run that the Eighth had done quite well out of the exchange because the 357th developed into the most successful P-51 Group in the whole of the Eighth Air Force.

On their first mission, which was mounted on 11th February 1944, the Group was led by Major James Howard of the 345th of the Ninth Air Force then at Boxted – a most experienced pilot who had only recently (11th January) been awarded the Congressional Medal of Honor. On this day he led the 41 P-51s on a sweep of Rouen in support of a force of B-24s that were bombing V1 rocket sites at Siracourt. The next two days were similar missions and one aircraft was lost when it came down in the sea near Clacton though the pilot was rescued. It was during the so-called 'Big Week' that the Group pilots came of age. In five days of operations from 20th to 25th February the pilots accounted for 22 enemy aircraft for the loss of four of their own. They were now on their way to great things.

The first ill-fated Berlin mission, on 4th March, showed the mettle of the Group's pilots; because of the quite atrocious weather, which resulted in most of the Bomb Groups being recalled, few of the fighter groups made it to the targets. However, 357th managed to complete their mission with the loss of only one aircraft on a day when 16 P-51s alone went missing. The following day things did not go so well. Whilst operating on a sweep of French airfields the Group's Commanding Officer, Colonel Henry Spicer, was shot down, although he did manage to bale out and was taken prisoner. It was probably very little compensation for the pilots that they managed to claim another seven victories.

The second of the Eighth's operations to Berlin took place on 6th March and although 48 aircraft left Leiston no less than 15 had to return with engine failure, mainly due to coolant problems. However, the rest of the Group acquitted themselves most admirably, they provided both protection over the target as well as withdrawal cover and remained over Berlin to the limit of their aircraft's endurance. On their way back not only did they escort the last returning B-24s from some miles south of Bremen but they even managed to destroy a Me109 on the ground at Ulzen airfield, which proved to be the first recorded instance of ground strafing by P-51s. Furthermore they returned to Leiston with claims of 20 enemy aircraft without a single loss. This was quite an amazing performance for a relatively novice Group, and their new Commanding Officer Donald

Me262 – the Luftwaffe's 'jet' fighter – which caused problems for all fighter groups. (Via J. Adams)

Graham must have been delighted to have taken over such a competitive bunch of pilots. In their first complete month of operations the Group had accounted for 59 enemy aircraft – they were amply justifying their 'transfer fee' from the Ninth!

By this time all of the P-51s were regularly using the British designed paper drop tanks, which extended the range of the fighters. This was very effectively shown on 13th May when the P-51s escorted a force of B-17s to western Poland – 1,470 miles – the longest mission yet undertaken by American fighters. The Group returned from this long mission with five claims and no casualties. In June the Group was given a new gyroscopic gunsight to test. It was a British designed sight for use in heavy bombers. The new sight was quickly dubbed 'No miss um' by the American pilots and ground crews. It allowed successful firing at nearly twice the previous maximum range, as well as offering deflection shooting. The ground crews at Leiston managed to fit it into the P-51Cs but ultimately the Americans built their own version – K-14 – and this was later installed in all P-51Ds.

Towards the end of June whilst on an escort mission to Leipzig, the P-51s encountered a heavy concentration of Me109s and 410s and quite a vicious and bitter air battle ensued. At the end 34 enemy fighters were shot down for the loss of three P-51s, and of this total the 357th claimed the lion's share – no less than 20 . For this mission and the earlier Berlin mission back in March, the Group was awarded its first Distinguished Unit Citation – a well-merited recognition of the continuing excellence of the Group's pilots.

In August (6th) the Group was selected to escort the B-17 force on the Frantic shuttle mission to the Soviet Union. At 9.30 am 64 aircraft took off from Leiston and by the late afternoon they had landed at a Russian airfield – a very physically demanding flight. The following day the pilots escorted the B-17s to an oil target in Poland and returned to Russia. The return flight home via Italy started the next day, but whilst in Italy they flew escort for some C-20 transports that landed in Yugoslavia to pick up wounded servicemen. On the 12th the pilots returned to England via Bordeaux. During the whole of this long round trip the Group suffered not a single loss. The handful of P-51s that had been left at Leiston managed to chalk up another three kills in the meantime.

The Group passed a major milestone on 12th October, when engaged over Bremen the pilots notched up their 400th victory – a tremendous performance considering that the Group had been operational for less than a year. On this day one of their most famous and successful pilots claimed five of the eight victories. This was Captain Charles Yeager, or 'Chuck' to his friends; indeed, Yeager had been the first fighter pilot to become 'an ace in a day'. In December, Yeager would be shot down over France but he managed to evade capture and with the help of the French underground reached Spain and ultimately came back to England. Yeager became the first fighter pilot of the Eighth Air Force to return to operations after being shot down over enemy territory. After the war he gained lasting fame as the first pilot to break the sound barrier, and he ultimately became a Brigadier General in USAF.

The Bremen mission was the first to be launched by the Group under its new Commanding Officer – Lt Colonel John Landers – who was one of the most famous American fighter pilots and leaders of the war. Landers had served in the south-west Pacific before coming to England in April 1944 to serve first with the 55th Fighter Group at Wormingford in Essex. Landers was not destined to stay long at Leiston and he later went on to command another two Fighter Groups – the 78th and 361st. It was during this period also that another unit came to share the airfield – 2nd Gunnery and Target Towing Flight. Like the Flight at Halesworth it operated with Vultee A-35B Vengeances as well as P-47s and the odd A-20B Havoc.

During 1945 the Group maintained the highest rate of victories of any Fighter Group in the Eighth Air Force. Perhaps their finest hour came on 14th January when engaged on escort duties to oil targets at Derben to the west of Berlin. The Group was led by Colonel Irwin Dregne, who had taken over from Landers. On this mission the Group's pilots found themselves ahead of the B-17s and not far from

Brandenburg where they managed to surprise a large formation of enemy fighters, thought to be in excess of 120, which were awaiting the arrival of the bombers. One squadron managed to drive off the Fw190s from the bomber formations, whilst the other squadron set about the rest of the fighters – mainly Me109s.

At the end of the air battle the pilots had claimed 56 aircraft destroyed, which was the highest total ever achieved by a Fighter Group on a single mission; and although this total was later reduced to 48, it was a really spectacular performance considering that only three of their pilots were reported as missing. Only three B-17s fell to enemy fighters and quite rightly the Group was awarded its second Distinguished Unit Citation for this operation. General Doolittle, the Commander of the Eighth, sent a personal message to Colonel Dregne, '. . . You gave the Hun the most humiliating beating he has ever taken in the air. Extend my personal admiration and congratulations to each member of your command, both ground and air, for a superb victory.'

The 'Yoxford Boys' as they had become known, made a massive contribution to the eventual defeat of the Luftwaffe. Only six days after the great air battle, one of the Group's young pilots – 1/Lt Karger – who was only 19 years of age, claimed two Me262s on a

A fine model of a P-51 at the Cakes and Ale caravan site on the old airfield at Leiston.

single mission, quite a feat for the young man and his aircraft, which was appropriately named *Bobby Socks*! In 313 missions the pilots of the 357th claimed no less than 609 aircraft downed in air combat with another 100 or so destroyed on the ground. It is not surprising to find that in such a large total there were many aces amongst the Group's pilots – almost 40! Some of the more famous names were – Captain Leonard 'Kit' Carson (18½), Captain John England (17½), Major Robert Foy (17), Major Richard Peterson (15½) and not forgetting Captain 'Chuck' Yeager. Perhaps their very success proved to be a disadvantage because instead of going back to the United States like most of the Fighter Groups, the personnel and aircraft left Leiston in July bound for Neuburg in Germany to join the Allied Occupation forces. The airfield was handed over to the RAF and it has now returned to agricultural use with part of it accommodating a smart caravan park called *Cakes and Ale*. Outside the camp's reception offices is a rather splendid model of a P-51, a fine and fitting memorial to all the pilots of this remarkable Fighter Group.

20
MARTLESHAM
HEATH

Martlesham Heath was Suffolk's oldest airfield. It came into being on 16th January 1917 when the RFC moved its testing squadron from Upavon to 'The Heath'; by the following October it became known as the Aeroplane Experimental Station with the responsibility of trialling and testing not only new aircraft but also those that had been captured. After a rather serious fire in 1922 the Royal Air Force decided to greatly enlarge the facilities at Martlesham and two years later the importance of the experimental work being undertaken there was acknowledged when the units were renamed the Aeroplane and Armament Experimental Establishment (AAEE). For the next 15 years it was at the centre of all the new developments in Service aviation. Martlesham Heath became one of the Service's most prestigious airfields, and despite the secret nature of its work, it nevertheless opened its gates to the public on the very first Empire Air Day in May 1936.

During the last peacetime summer of 1939 as the war clouds were gathering, it was considered prudent to move the AAEE from such a vulnerable airfield and, in September, the Establishment left for Boscombe Down in Wiltshire. Being only about eight miles from the coast the airfield was perfectly placed to act as a fighter station, and thus it was allocated to No 11 Group of Fighter Command. It was basically used as a satellite or advanced landing ground for two sector airfields – North Weald and Debden. Martlesham Heath was a most distinguished fighter base throughout the Second World War seeing virtually all of the famous wartime fighters – both RAF and American – mount operations from the airfield.

The first fighters to appear at Martlesham were Bristol Blenheim Ifs of No 604 'County of Middlesex' squadron then based at North Weald. The Blenheim was one of the first of the new generation of monoplane bombers ordered by the RAF under the pre-war expansion schemes. By late 1938 the light bomber had been converted to a day and night fighter. By day it operated east coast shipping patrols and stood by at night in the role of a night fighter. Soon it was recognised that the aircraft was more suited to night fighting and it was equipped with AIMkII – the rather cumbersome early radar equipment. However, early in the New Year the Blenheims departed to RAF Northolt.

More than any other fighter it was the Hawker Hurricane that became closely associated with the airfield's early wartime operations. The aircraft had been designed by Sidney Camm, the chief designer of Hawker, and the first prototype was flown in November 1935. The Air Ministry took about three months to decide whether to accept the aircraft and finally ordered 600, although later in 1938 the order was increased to 1,000 (some 14,000 were finally built). The first Hurricanes, powered by Rolls Royce Merlin II V12 engines, entered the RAF at the end of 1937 and they introduced a new and glorious era for RAF Fighter Command. Although the aircraft was slower than both the Spitfire and the Luftwaffe's Me109, it was a very sturdy and reliable fighter, accounting for more victories in the Battle of Britain than its more famous close rival. The 'Hurry' as it was fondly called, inspired great loyalty in its pilots and there was always a keen debate on which was the better aircraft – the Spitfire or the Hurricane.

The first Hurricanes flew into Martlesham during October 1939 and they were a detachment of an auxiliary squadron – No 504 'County of Nottingham' – then based at Debden. These Hurricanes stayed around until May 1940 when they were sent to France. Other Hurricanes arrived from Debden towards the end of the year, again detachments but this time from No 17 squadron and they would almost become permanent residents over the next twelve months or so.

The airfield's first permanent squadron – No 264 – also arrived towards the end of the year and it brought yet another new fighter, the Boulton Paul Defiant. This was the first squadron to be equipped with Defiants. This two-seater fighter with the unique enclosed

Hurricanes of No 151 Squadron leaving Martlesham Heath.

power-driven turret, had first flown in August 1937 and had come into service in December 1939. The squadron first saw action in the following March when a detachment was based at RAF Wittering, but they were merely engaged in coastal patrols. Although the squadron's Defiants performed well over the Dunkirk beaches, the early aerial combats of the Battle of Britain cruelly exposed their weaknesses – lack of speed and vulnerability to attack from below and directly ahead. Indeed No 264, and another Defiant squadron, suffered so heavily during August 1940 that they were quickly withdrawn from the Battle of Britain. Ultimately the Defiant was developed into a more than useful night fighter and operated valiantly during the London blitz.

The first Spitfire, that classic fighter of World War II, landed at Martlesham Heath in March 1940 when No 266 – a Rhodesian squadron – arrived for a short stay. These were, of course, Mark Is, the first of a long line of variants with well over 20,000 different models being built throughout the war. The aircraft had been designed by R.J. Mitchell , the chief designer of Supermarine, who unfortunately did not live long enough to see the outstanding success of his aircraft. Supermarine had gained its reputation with seaplanes and the Spitfire was a direct derivative of their famous S6B seaplane, which had won the Schneider Trophy in 1931. The first Spitfire

172

prototype flew in March 1936 and with a top speed of 355 mph, it was then the fastest fighter in the world. Indeed its performance was quite staggering and 310 were immediately ordered but by September 1939 the contract was increased to 4,000! Powered by a Rolls Royce Merlin II engine and armed with four (later doubled) .303 Browning machine guns, it became a most formidable fighting machine. The first Spitfires arrived in the RAF (at Duxford) in June 1938 and by the outbreak of the war Fighter Command had nine full squadrons of Spitfires. Although outnumbered by Hurricanes during the Battle of Britain (957 against 1,326), nevertheless it is forever remembered for its exploits during that historic and critical battle, which virtually created the Spitfire legend.

What had been a quiet war so far as the airfield was concerned, suddenly changed on 10th July when the airfield was bombed, but little damage was sustained. Now Hurricanes of No 85 squadron led by Sqn Ldr Peter Townsend (later Group Captain) were using the airfield, as well as a detachment of Blenheim Ifs of No 25 squadron, and these were active each night flying patrols along the Thames estuary. Contrary to later public belief the summer of 1940 was not eternally clear and sun-drenched, in fact the Luftwaffe offensive – Adlerangriff or Eagles' Attack – was postponed for several days in August because of the inclement weather. On 27th July the airfield was flooded and out of commission for almost two days.

By the time August came it was quite clear that the airfield was considered to be right in the frontline, at least judging by the number of important visitors that arrived. On the 9th, Major General Majendie came to examine the airfield's defences, the same day that Anthony Eden made a fleeting call. Then on the 10th Air Vice-Marshal Keith Park, the Air Officer Commanding No 11 Group, made an official visit. Just three days later the Luftwaffe launched its major attacks against fighter airfields and the aircraft factories. By now though, No 85 had returned to Debden and it was replaced by the Hurricanes of No 17 squadron.

The airfield was attacked on 15th August but fortunately most of the aircraft were airborne at the time, although many of the buildings and two hangars were damaged with a couple of large craters in the middle of the airfield. Five days later the Luftwaffe came back but this time only superficial damage was sustained. For the Hurricane pilots it was a long and almost continuous battle against the hordes upon hordes of Luftwaffe bombers and fighters. On 18th August, which was considered to be the hardest day of the battle, No 17 squadron lost two aircraft, one of which was destroyed on the ground at Manston when the airfield was strafed, for two kills and a couple of possibles. A sergeant pilot with the squadron recalled the chaotic state of the air combat in the battle: 'In peace time we had practised our set piece attacks, but actual combat was nothing like that. Our CO [Sqn Ldr A.G. 'Dusty' Miller] would say "Attack! Attack!" and we would follow him. Whenever we mixed it with the Germans there was no time to organise attacks or anything like that. We just went in and had a go!' During August Fighter Command lost 389 aircraft with 176 pilots killed, compared with 694 Luftwaffe aircraft destroyed. However, it was to be September that proved the critical month.

At the beginning of the month another Hurricane squadron moved into the Heath, No 257, which had already suffered rather heavily in the battle when operating mainly from Northolt and Debden. The squadron was named the 'Burma' in recognition of the financial support received from that country. The squadron's badge carried a motto in Burmese, which translated to 'Death or Glory' and the pilots had tried to live up to this motto. The squadron was also without a leader, and the officer chosen to take charge of the somewhat demoralised unit was Sqn Ldr Roland Stanford Tuck, one of the Command's most successful pilots. Sunday, 15th September, now acknowledged as Battle of Britain Day, proved to be the climax of the battle with no less than three separate and heavy waves of Luftwaffe bombers and fighters attacking London and the south-east. No 257 were in action for most of the day and although the RAF claimed to have destroyed 172 enemy aircraft for 23 losses, the true figures,

Hawker Typhoons of No 56 Squadron at Martlesham Heath.

Spitfire VB: Many squadrons at Martlesham Heath were equipped with this famous mark. (Via J. Adams)

disclosed after the war, showed 52 destroyed for 27 fighters lost – a far closer outcome. Nevertheless two days later it became known through intelligence sources that the German High Command had postponed Operation Sealion (the invasion of Britain) indefinitely. Victory had been won but at a great cost, and it had been 'a damned near run thing'!

After all the fury of the Battle of Britain, the next flurry of action for the Hurricane squadrons came on 11th November when Hurricanes from Nos 46, 249, and 257 squadrons were sent up to intercept a daylight raid on Harwich by units of the Regia Aeronautica – the Italian Air Force. Just ten Fiat BR 20 bombers, escorted by 40 Fiat CR 42 fighters took off from airfields in Belgium in a vain attempt to aid the Luftwaffe bombing offensive. Basically the Italian aircraft were no match for the Hurricanes and indeed the Italian pilots, though brave, were sadly ill-trained. On this ill-fated operation seven of the bombers were shot down as well as four fighters without a single Hurricane being lost. Later in the month there were two more small Italian raids on Harwich and Ipswich but very little damage was sustained.

Just before Christmas 1940 No 257 squadron left for Coltishall near Norwich and in its place came Hurricane IIAs of No 242 squadron. Originally this squadron had been made up of mainly Canadian pilots, and had as its CO Sqn Ldr Douglas Bader, the most charismatic fighter pilot and leader of the Second World War. This amazing pilot was known to his pilots as 'Dogsbody' from his call sign 'DB', which were, of course, his initials. Bader had led the

Duxford Wing throughout the Battle of Britain. A replica of the Hurricane he used during this time is now proudly displayed at the main gate of RAF Coltishall.

From the beginning of 1941 Fighter Command went more on the offensive; it proceeded to carry out combined operations with light and medium bombers, flew individual sweeps over northern France and the Low Countries attacking enemy airfields and transport systems, as well as patrolling the English Channel for enemy shipping. These operations for some unaccountable reason were known under a variety of strange names: Circus, Ramrod, Jim Crow, and Roadstead. The squadron made its first 'circus' on 10th January when the Hurricanes provided an escort for some Blenheim bombers from No 2 Group attacking targets in northern France. By the middle of March Bader had been promoted to Wing Commander and had left for Tangmere, from where he was shot down over St Omer airfield and taken prisoner of war. By April his old squadron had also departed.

During the next two years a vast number of fighter squadrons used the airfield, some for just a month or so and others for a little longer. For most of 1941 these squadrons were equipped with Hurricane Mark IIs, which were powered by Merlin XX engines and most had six .303 Browning guns in each wing. Perhaps the most interesting Hurricane squadron to arrive in 1941, especially considering the airfield's later American connections, was No 71. This was the very first of the three RAF 'Eagle' squadrons to be formed – so called because they were manned by American volunteer pilots. When the squadron arrived at Martlesham in April it had only been operational for about two months. It then had an American as its leader – William Taylor – a very experienced US Navy pilot. The Eagles soon became involved in fighter sweeps over France and Holland and during one of these operations Mike Kolerdorski was killed – the first Eagle pilot to be lost in action. In June the Americans moved to North Weald but returned at the end of the year, staying until May 1942 when the squadron moved to Debden.

By 1942 most of the squadrons that came to Martlesham were flying Spitfire VBs. However, there was one glaring exception and this was No 182. It was actually formed at Martlesham on 1st September as a Typhoon bomber squadron. The Hawker Typhoon, or 'Tiffy' to its pilots, had been designed in 1938 as a more powerful version of the Hurricane and first flew in February 1940. Because of the threat of the new Luftwaffe fighter – Fw190 – which outpowered the existing

RAF fighters, it was rushed into production and saw service as early as September 1941. Although the new Napier Sabre 11A engine gave it a top speed just in excess of 400 mph, there were several teething problems with the aircraft and it proved to be rather disappointing in an interceptor role. However, by late 1942, the Typhoon had proved itself to be an excellent ground attack aircraft able to carry two 1,000 pound bombs and later airborne rockets, with which it gained fame as a 'train buster', especially with the 2nd Tactical Air Force. It was not until January 1943 that the squadron became operational when it conducted a 'rhubarb' to Bruges; these were effectively low-level strike operations mounted against a variety of targets in occupied territories in cloudy conditions, which, in theory, provided the element of surprise and the best protection. However, by March the squadron had left for Middle Wallop.

By now the RAF's wartime days at Martlesham Heath were becoming numbered, and during the late summer two runways were laid down in preparation for the first USAAF unit. These runways were quite unique for the time, as they were constructed of soil which had been stabilised with tarmac, rather than the normal great slabs of concrete. When the Americans finally moved in during October 1943 there was still one RAF unit operating from the airfield – No 277 – which was involved on air-sea rescue duties.

The first P-47Ds of the 356th Fighter Group, which had been training at Goxhill in Lincolnshire, arrived on 9th October. They were led by Lt Colonel Harold Rau, who by the end of November had departed and handed over command to Colonel Einar Malstrom. The Group's first couple of missions were merely fighter sweeps over Holland and it was not until the 20th of the month that the Group acted as escorts on an operation to Düren. It would be over three weeks before the 356th opened their score and this occurred whilst escorting bombers to Bremen when 15 enemy fighters were destroyed, of which the Group claimed five but for the loss of five of their P-47s. This had been the pilots' first taste of aerial combat and it did not augur well for the future.

Subsequently the 356th gained the unenviable reputation of being a 'hard luck' Group and certainly some of its early operations seemed to bear this out. Even when other Fighter Groups were busily notching up large tallies of victories, the 356th would only have the odd kill to their credit and normally these came with a corresponding and equal loss of their own aircraft. However, on 24th January 1944 whilst over Frankfurt its pilots shot down ten enemy aircraft without loss and then in just two missions in February another 16 aircraft were accounted for with the loss of just one pilot. These three successful missions proved to be rather isolated incidents. For instance, in two missions to Berlin during early March, although 160 enemy fighters were claimed to have been destroyed, the 356th's share was only two and those were only gained at the cost of two of their P-47s.

Perhaps the Group's shining hour, at least with their P-47s, came on 4th August when they were part of a strong fighter force escorting a mission to Bremen. They 'bounced' a strong formation of Me109s from a height of 38,000 feet. The Me109s dived almost to ground level in an attempt to shake off the attack but this was the wrong tactic as the P-47 had a far greater speed than the Me109 when diving. After a short but fierce battle the 356th's pilots had accounted for 15 Me109s for the loss of one fighter – their most successful mission of the war so far.

Like most other Fighter Groups the 356th became very involved in providing air support for the US airborne landings in Holland. On 17th September they were engaged in the difficult and dangerous operation of attacking flak batteries, and on this day they lost four aircraft. The following day the Group found themselves acting as escort to B-24s dropping supplies to the airborne troops; they lost one pilot. Finally on the 23rd they were part of an almost 600-strong fighter force attacking enemy strongholds in Holland, and on this occasion all the fighters returned safely to Martlesham. For their operations over these three days the Group was awarded their only Distinguished Unit Citation.

During the early weeks of November the pilots were still getting used to their new P-51Ds and unfortunately lost one pilot on their first mission with the new aircraft. Suddenly, six days later, it would seem to them that their luck had finally changed when, whilst escorting B-24s to Hanover, the Group's pilots managed to destroy 21 enemy aircraft with a single casualty. As has already been noted, March and April were the two months when the P-51s were beginning to gain some successes against the Luftwaffe's Me262s. In March the pilots of the 356th gained a notable victory when they downed three Ar234s – Arado Blitz (Lightning) – the first jet bombers; this was no mean feat!

By the time the Group had completed their last operation, on 7th May, the pilots had accounted for 201 enemy aircraft in air combat but for the loss of 122 fighters – unfortunately a very high ratio; the

A permanent reminder of Martlesham's RAF days.

Group had experienced a most torrid time during which 72 of its pilots were killed in action. Colonel Philip Tukey Jr, who had admirably led the Group since the loss of Colonel Malstrom was no doubt pleased to leave Martlesham for the United States in the late autumn.

The airfield reverted to the RAF but by 1963 it was closed. In the last 30 years very substantial development has taken place on the site but there are ample reminders of the famous airfield's passing. Many of the roads around the estate bear names that recall its RAF days, such as Lancaster Way and Hawker Drive, and some of the old buildings have managed to survive – the hangars and the watchhouse. But perhaps the most lasting memorial to the days of Fighter Command is the public house near the few surviving remains of the old runways, which is appropriately called The Douglas Bader. Nor indeed have the American airmen been forgotten as there is a memorial to them on what was the RAF parade ground.

21

MENDLESHAM

No old and long vanished wartime airfield is so prominently indicated as is Mendlesham. The tall television tower, which is such an obvious landmark alongside the A140 road, rather conveniently and very accurately pin-points the site. The rather fine memorial to the American airmen that served here is set at the side of this busy road. Its central feature is an attractive bronze plaque, which was designed by Henry Berg, a Baltimore sculptor. It certainly provides a most impressive and fitting reminder of those airmen of the 34th Bomb Group who flew from the nearby airfield.

The airfield was built, during 1942-43, to the east of the main road and close to the hamlet of Wetherup Street, with the living quarters across the other side of the road and bordering onto the village from which it gets its name. It was completed during the last months of 1943 and destined for the Eighth Air Force, indeed the first USAAF personnel arrived in December to prepare the base for its occupants. However, the first aircraft to use the airfield were RAF Spitfires. These belonged to three Czechoslovakian squadrons – Nos 310, 312 and 313. Perhaps the most famous of the three was No 310. This squadron had the honour of being the first solely to be formed from Czech refugees. These proud and brave airmen had fought with great verve and distinction during the Battle of Britain when the squadron had claimed 37½ enemy aircraft destroyed. At the time of writing one of the founding members of No 312 – Ivo Tonder, a famous Czech fighter pilot – died at the age of 82!

The Spitfires that landed at Mendlesham were a mixture of VBs and LFIXBs. The Vs were perhaps one of the best-known marks of this much developed and splendid aircraft. Its Merlin 46 engine gave it a maximum speed of some 370 mph and the most distinctive feature of the VB was its clipped wings, which were designed to improve its performance at low-level altitudes. This mark of Spitfire had also been adapted to carry either two 250 pound or one 500 pound bombs. The LFIXs (LF for low fighter) were refinements on the Mark Vs with an increased speed of just in excess of 400 mph and they, too, had been adapted for a ground attack role with bomb attachments.

One of the main reasons for their sudden appearance at Mendlesham was for a period of training at RAF Southend, on a dive bombing and ground attack course at No 17 Armament Practice Camp, where each squadron stayed for about two weeks. Meanwhile the pilots were also regularly engaged in low-flying practice over the flat East Anglian countryside. However, the Czech pilots did manage to get some operational flying time in, acting as escort for medium bombers attacking targets in Holland. When the pilots of No 310 squadron finished at Southend on 3rd April 1944 they flew directly to their new airfield – an Advanced Landing Ground at Apuldram in West Sussex – to be nearer to the action leading up to D-Day. The following day the other two squadrons left Mendlesham to join them and the airfield awaited its new American residents.

The RAF officially handed over the airfield to the USAAF on 15th April and the first B-24Hs of the 34th Bomb Group trundled in to land just a few days later after their long and harrowing flight by the southern ferry route. This Group was the oldest in the Eighth having first been activated in January 1941 and had been engaged in flying B-17s on anti-submarine patrols along the eastern seaboard of America. However, from July 1942 it had acted as a replacement training unit providing members for other bomb groups in the Eighth and it was not until the beginning of 1944 that the Group was ordered to train on B-24s for ultimate transfer to England. The Group was placed in the 93rd Combat Wing of the Third Division with the Wing's headquarters also being based at Mendlesham.

It took Colonel Ernest Wackwitz Jr just over a month before he felt that his crews were sufficiently trained and properly prepared for their first operational mission. This came on 23rd May, when along with other B-24 groups of both Divisions, they were despatched to attack enemy airfields in the Paris area and all returned without loss. During the next ten days the crews were in action every day. The first few missions, which were directed against airfields and rail targets, passed without incident, and on each occasion the Group's aircraft arrived safely back at Mendlesham. The crews must have felt that

Detail of the fine memorial to 34th Bomb Group.

this air war was not quite as dangerous as they had been led to believe.

However, this changed on the 28th when over 1,270 B-17s and B-24s were despatched to seven primary oil targets in Germany. The Third Division's B-24s (100) bombed the Halle plant at Lutzendorf, and although three B-24s failed to return, none came from the 34th. The following day (29th) brought a long and exhausting operation to north-east Germany to the oil installations at Pölitz and the aircraft factories sited at Tutow. The Luftwaffe fighters were out in force to oppose this major operation and the 34th lost three aircraft, one of which landed in Sweden. However, the damage had been done by enemy flak rather than by the Luftwaffe. The Group would ultimately hold quite an amazing and unique record in not losing a single aircraft to enemy fighters over enemy territory – the only aircraft shot down by fighters happened over their own airfield!

On the way out to the Normandy beach-head on D-Day one of the Group's aircraft crashed at Corfe Castle in Dorset and the whole of the crew were killed in the terrible explosion. But perhaps their moment of truth came on the following day. The Group was sent out on an afternoon mission to a variety of tactical targets in central France but the operation was largely unsuccessful because of the heavy cloud cover in the target area and only one of the bomber force was lost. The Group's aircraft were approaching Mendlesham just as dusk was falling when suddenly a number of enemy intruders struck. They proved to be Me410s – the fast twin-engined fighter/bombers that were proving so effective for the Luftwaffe on such intruder raids. Within a matter of minutes four B-24s had been shot down. One crashed into the equipment store at Mendlesham, two others crashed in the vicinity of the airfield and the fourth crash-landed at nearby Eye airfield. The ground control would only allow one aircraft to land at Mendlesham so the crews found themselves landing at no less than 13 different airfields. RAF night fighters managed to account for just one of the enemy aircraft. This fateful evening would prove to be the Group's single highest operational loss of the war. It was a harsh and salutory lesson, a grim and costly reminder to the rest of the crews, and more especially the gunners, that they could not afford to relax until their aircraft had landed safely.

Along with the other five B-24 groups in the Third Division, the 34th was required to change to B-17s. Their operational record with the B-24s was particularly good and only on rare occasions did they lose an aircraft. For instance on 25th June, whilst engaged over French airfields, one of the Group's aircraft that had been heavily damaged by flak was forced to ditch just off Shoreham and only three of the crew were saved. Their last mission with the trusty B-24s took place on 24th August to Kiel and two failed to return; one landed in Sweden and the other crashed on a house at Holt in Norfolk. This was piloted by Major Joseph Garrett and whilst still over the North Sea the aircraft was thought to have only three minutes of fuel left and rather than risking ditching nine of the crew baled out; Major Garrett managed to retain control of the aircraft for sufficient time to enable him to bale out – all of the crew survived.

With this general change of aircraft there was a rumour circulating in the Third Division that B-24s were being sent to targets where the enemy flak was known to be heavy just to get rid of the aircraft 'naturally'! Certainly Kiel had a most unenviable reputation in both Bomber Command and the Eighth for the intensity of its flak batteries. However, as has already been noted, the B-24s suffered more heavily from enemy flak due to the lower altitudes at which they bombed. Most of the Group's B-24s were ultimately transferred to the 466th Group of the Second Division based at Attlebridge in Norfolk.

In just three months the Group had mounted 62 missions with their B-24s – no mean achievement. The crews became involved and fully occupied with a rather hectic round of training and familiarisation flights with their new aircraft – B-17Gs. By the 17th September the Group was back on operations – attacking flak batteries in Holland in support of the airborne landings at Nijmegen and Eindhoven. Two more missions were completed without loss, then on the 22nd when the Henschel armament factories at Kassel were the target the Group lost their first B-17, and true to form it fell to enemy flak.

For the next six months the 34th waged a most active and successful campaign with no critical losses on their operations, never losing more than a single aircraft on a mission despite the fact that the Luftwaffe's jet fighters were then making their presence felt over many German targets. Unfortunately on 26th March 1945 one of the Group's aircraft collided with a B-17 from 452nd Group at Deopham Green whilst assembling and both crews were killed. The 34th held another unique record in that it lost more aircraft (39) to accidental causes than were lost on operations (34)!

During the month of April 1945 when most crews felt, with much justification, that the war in Europe was fast coming to a close, the men of the 34th could be forgiven for thinking otherwise as they experienced a most active time. From the 1st to the 20th, the date of their last operation, they flew no less than 16 missions to oil and rail targets, enemy airfields, as well as the enemy strongholds and flak batteries in the Royan area on the French Atlantic coast; it was on this operation that the Eighth's bombers dropped 500 pound napalm tanks for the first and only time of the war – these strongholds were among the last pockets of German resistance to surrender to the

B-24H of 34th Bomb Group. (USAF)

Allied forces. The Group lost just two aircraft during this period. One of these was unfortunately a victim to an enemy flak battery still grimly holding out near Dunkirk. The unlucky B-17 came down in the English Channel and six of the crew were finally rescued from the sea on the following day.

Before the Group left Mendlesham during July and August, they had one final unusual record to notch up – they had the youngest aircrew in the whole of the Eighth Air Force, with the 2nd Lieutenant being the senior member at the ripe old age of 21 years! Once the B-17s had departed no more flying took place at the airfield, it became a storage depot for ammunition. The old technical site, which is close to the A140, has now been developed into an industrial area. The Group's memorial is certainly well worth a visit – it can be found on the eastern side of the main road shortly after passing a turning to Mickfield. There is a rather convenient lay-by to park some 300 or so yards further on.

22

METFIELD

On 9th August 1943, 16 P-47Ds took off from Metfield airfield for a fighter sweep of Abbeville and Poix in northern France. This was the introduction into the war for the pilots of the 353rd Fighter Group. For over two months they had been kicking their heels at Goxhill in Lincolnshire whilst waiting for their aircraft to arrive from the United States – there was a considerable shortage of P-47s.

The Group's Commanding Officer, Lt Colonel Joseph Morris, was also eager to get his boys blooded. He managed to bring them to operational readiness within six days of arriving at Metfield, despite the fact that the airfield was still in the throes of being completed. Furthermore the chiefs of Fighter Command were only too delighted to welcome the 353rd as it became only the fourth Fighter Group to join the Eighth Air Force. Their first mission passed without incident, the inexperienced pilots had been well shepherded by their guides and mentors – the 56th Group – which was the normal operational procedure with fledgling fighter pilots, at least at this stage of the war when American fighters were so thin on the ground, or in the air for that matter! Three days later the full Group was airborne on a high altitude sweep of the Ostend area.

Just four days later (16th) when escorting a force of B-17s to Le Bourget airfield, Lt Colonel Joe Morris was seen to dive steeply onto a single Fw190 that was heading for the bomber formation and almost immediately a strong force of yellow-nosed Fw190s appeared from nowhere, the rest of the Group's pilots immediately engaged them and a fierce and hectic dog-fight ensued. However, when the sky cleared, the CO's aircraft was nowhere to be seen. This was the Group's first tangle with the Luftwaffe and they were rather fortunate to survive with just one casualty, albeit their CO. It is perhaps not too surprising that they were unable to claim a single enemy aircraft, as they had been engaged by the famed 'Abbeville kids' – an experienced gruppe of Luftwaffe pilots. The 353rd were saved by the arrival of the very experienced 'Eagle' pilots of the 4th Fighter Group, who managed to account for no less than 18 enemy aircraft.

Soon the Group were involved as escorts on some of the Eighth's most gruelling and costly operations – Schweinfurt, Stuttgart, Nantes and Emden. It was on this last mission (27th September) that the Group came of age. It proved to be a long flight over the North Sea, for which the P-47s had been equipped with 75 gallon drop tanks. Despite quite atrocious weather, the 353rd still managed to make the rendezvous on time. On this day they were fortunate to have the advantage of height on the Luftwaffe and they were able to surprise a force of Me110s. The young pilots attacked with great gusto, especially when they realised that the Me110s were no match for the P-47Ds. The short dog-fight ended with eight Me110s being destroyed without a loss, although one of the P-47s crash-landed at Metfield on return from the mission but luckily the pilot managed to make his escape.

October and November proved to be a most hectic couple of months for the Group. In 27 missions they accounted for 35 enemy fighters all for the loss of just seven aircraft. The pilots were becoming rather expert in the killing game and none more so than Captain Walter Beckham – nicknamed 'Turk' – who had claimed six kills in just six sorties. It was during this time that the Group was instructed to investigate the feasibility of using P-47s as dive bombers. A couple of experienced pilots led by Captain Beckham went to Llanbedr in North Wales to practise their techniques. Beckham had some experience of bombing when flying P-39s (Airacobras) and P40s (Warhawks).

The first dive-bombing mission was launched on 25th November when 16 P-47s, each loaded with a 500 pound bomb, set out to attack St Omer airfield. The initial approach was made at about 14,000 feet and then the pilots dived to about 8,000 feet before releasing their bombs. The Group's Commanding Officer – Colonel Loren McCollom – was leading the attack and his aircraft received a direct hit from the heavy flak defences; this forced him to bale out and he was taken prisoner.

The pilots of the 353rd, enthusiastically led by Colonel Glenn

Flight of P-47s of 353rd Fighter Group at Metfield in June 1944. (USAF)

Duncan, the new Commanding Officer, started to ground strafe enemy airfields whilst returning home from escort duties. On 21st January, Duncan, supported by his two wingmen, shot up a Dornier 217 which was sitting on an airfield just north of Amiens. From then on the Group's pilots were encouraged to make such attacks, at least when favourable circumstances dictated. Of course, later in the year, ground strafing was to play a large part in fighter operations, especially when it was officially recognised that aircraft destroyed in this manner equalled a victory in aerial combat. It was then fully acknowledged by the Eighth Fighter Command that ground strafing could be as difficult as aerial combat and often was far more dangerous.

Quite how fraught with danger these attacks could be was clearly shown on 22nd February when the Group was returning from another escort mission. A few Junkers 88s were sighted on an airfield near Bonn; Major Beckham took his squadron (351) down to attack but they were met with heavy and concentrated ground fire. Beckham's aircraft was so badly damaged that he was forced to bale out and survived as a prisoner of war. At the time he was the leading ace of the Eighth Air Force with 18 victories to his credit from 57 missions, and had been awarded the DSC for heroism in October 1943. After the war he reached the rank of Colonel in the USAF.

The loss of Major Beckham was keenly felt in the Group and the Eighth could ill-afford to lose such a talented fighter pilot. However, Colonel Duncan was deeply concerned at the way Beckham had been lost, he was convinced that more specialised tactics should be devised

188

for this type of operation. Duncan put forward a proposal that a special squadron should be formed, manned by some of the Eighth's most experienced pilots, who would develop and perfect the techniques of this new kind of fighter warfare. Major General William 'Bill' Kepner, the Commanding Officer of the Eighth's Fighter Command from August 1943 to July 1944, finally approved Duncan's idea and duly authorised him to set up the squadron and to mount some experimental missions.

Sixteen volunteer pilots were called from four Groups – 353, 355, 359 and 361 and the squadron became known as 353rd 'C' Fighter Group, operating from Metfield under Duncan's direct control. However, these pilots quickly acquired the name of 'Bill's Buzz Boys', from, of course, Bill Kepner. The techniques were developed by using Metfield as the target airfield. Generally the pilots would dive from about 15,000 feet, levelling out within five miles of the target and then fly line abreast at a very low altitude in order to gain the element of surprise and spread the area of targets for the defending flak batteries. From 26th March to 10th April six experimental missions were flown, in all 14 enemy aircraft and 36 trains were destroyed for the loss of just three aircraft. At the end of the experiment the small Group was disbanded but it was felt that sufficient evidence had been gathered to enable Fighter Command to draw up plans for ground strafing on a large scale.

With the growing imminence of the invasion of Europe there was a realignment of some fighter groups in East Anglia. Metfield was required for a new Bomb Group, which had already been allocated to the Second Division and was due to arrive in the next month or so. Therefore, the 353rd moved to Raydon to replace another fighter group which had moved on to an Essex airfield. The fighters left Metfield on 12th April and almost a fortnight later the first personnel of the 491st Bomb Group arrived at the airfield. Quite unusually the majority of the ground crews were drawn from existing groups in England rather than coming over directly from the United States.

The first B-24Hs began to arrive during the last weeks of May after a long and exhausting flight via the southern ferry route. The new Group would complete the 95th Bomb Wing of the Second Bomb Division. It had gained the name of 'The Ringmasters' and by the end of the war had achieved the highest rate of operations of any B-24 Group. The speed with which the 491st ticked off its missions in the early months, allied to a very high safety record, probably gave its aircrews the best chance of not only staying alive but also completing their tours in a record time. So it proved for Lt Charles Griffen; he was on the Group's very first mission and when his aircraft landed at Metfield on 2nd August he had completed his 30th mission in just 62 days – almost two calendar months. He had hardly had time to get used to the English beer!

With such an excellent early performance, one could be forgiven for assuming that the Group had been fortunate in going out on a number of 'easy' missions, though in truth by the summer of 1944 there were few, if any, of these. Certainly the Pas de Calais and its sites did figure frequently in the Group's itinerary but these were no longer 'milk runs' as the Germans had greatly strengthened their defences. However, there were some formidable targets as well written up on their Operations Board – Berlin, Bernburg, Munich, Lutzendorf and the dreaded Brunswick. On the latter operation, which took place on 5th August, the 491st was selected to lead the Second Division's formation into the attack on the aero-engine and armament factories at Brunswick and managed to return from this fierce cauldron of fire without a single loss. Lady Luck must have played a part but the safety record of the 491st says much for the close and disciplined formation flying by the crews, following the Eighth's old training adage, 'the tighter you fly, the lighter you fall'.

The Group, however, was a little unlucky with some unfortunate accidents. For instance, on 8th June the mission to French airfields was delayed because of ground fog, then when clearance was given one B-24 had engine failure on take off and it 'fell straight to the ground'; the bombs exploded, blowing the aircraft into pieces. The nine man crew were killed and several aircraft in the vicinity were damaged. Another serious accident happened on 15th July when the bomb dump blew up. The terrific explosion, which was heard for miles around, killed at least five men and severely damaged several aircraft. An internal inquiry was set up to investigate the cause of the accident, which at first was thought might have been sabotage. The Group was stood down from operations for the next four days whilst the inquiry sat, but it was finally decided that the explosion was due to accidental causes.

During the middle of July the Eighth Air Force received a request to mount a support operation against the German land forces that were stubbornly resisting the American First Army's offensive near St Lô in Normandy. Although it was not a type of operation really suited to heavy bombers, on 24th July the 491st was part of a 1,500 strong bomber force. However, because of a heavy ground haze only

Fighter pilots of 353rd Fighter Group leaving dispersal areas at Metfield – note the mud and the bikes! (USAF)

about one-third of the force was able to bomb and unfortunately some of the bombs were released over Allied lines, which resulted in the loss of 20 US personnel and another 60 injured. Because of the unsatisfactory bombing results another operation was mounted the following day when over 1,500 heavies managed to bomb. Despite every care being taken to ensure the bombing was accurate some of the bombs once again fell on US servicemen causing over 100 deaths and over 300 casualties. These were perhaps the most unfortunate and saddest missions flown by the Eighth Air Force throughout the war, and the incidents were not quickly forgotten by US Army personnel.

On 14th August the Group was ordered to move from Metfield into North Pickenham airfield in Norfolk. Metfield was then passed over to the European Division of Air Transport Command and the airfield began to come alive again when a few Douglas C-47s began to appear. The C-47 was a military version of the very successful DC-3 commercial airliner and it was used by USAAF as a general transport aircraft – General Eaker and his fellow officers arrived in one in February 1942. The aircraft would take up to 24 passengers or 7,000 pounds of cargo. Of course, it was better known in RAF circles as the Dakota. The C-47 was probably the most celebrated transport aircraft in the world; one is even preserved in the RAF Museum at Hendon. However, the trusty and familiar B-24s had not completely disappeared from the scene, several arrived, stayed awhile and then left at odd intervals. They were engaged in the highly secret Sonnie project, which involved sending ground crews to Sweden to service and repair all the Eighth's aircraft that had landed in that country. They also brought back American airmen who had been interned there.

The whole question of aircraft landing in neutral Sweden had become a deep concern for the Eighth Air Force. Most of the crews that landed at Bulltofta, an airfield at the southernmost tip of Sweden where most of the aircraft landed, were genuine, their aircraft so badly damaged that there was little chance of surviving the North Sea crossing. But there were several instances of completely undamaged aircraft landing in order that their crews could seek sanctuary in neutral Sweden. In the early days the crews were under orders to fire their aircraft should they land in neutral territory; later these instructions were either changed or ignored by crews. The Swedish Government, however, were not prepared to do anything which might impinge on their neutrality and bring about some retaliatory action from Germany.

After one Berlin mission no less than 18 aircraft landed there. Already there was quite an 'American colony' established in Sweden and even a special American air-attache appointed to look after the American airmen's interests. These interned crewmen still received their full pay and were kept in fairly comfortable accommodation paid for by the US Government. Some had even married Swedish girls. Ultimately an agreement was reached whereby the aircraft could be serviced and repaired by US personnel, and then both aircraft and crews were released on the strict condition that neither would be used again in operations in Europe.

The Metfield airfield was returned to the RAF in 1945 but was not used again for flying. It was probably the most secluded wartime airfield in Suffolk and as such it is very difficult to locate, as there are so few remains of it and rather unusually there are no memorials to all the American airmen that served there. The old site may be reached by taking the B1123 from Harleston to the village of Metfield and then turning into a by-road to the east, which crosses the site of the old airfield.

23
MILDENHALL

Most people, if asked to name an airfield in Suffolk, would probably answer with little hesitation – Mildenhall. For over 60 years this airfield has managed to capture the attention and imagination of the public, perhaps most latterly for its successful and popular Air Days. When Mildenhall opened in October 1934 it was one of the RAF's most modern and prestigious stations – a showpiece for the confident and expanding Service.

Without a shadow of a doubt Mildenhall or 'Beck Row', as it was also known to generations of airmen, was a most important and very active heavy bomber station throughout the Second World War, with over 8,000 bombing sorties being made from the airfield and some 200 aircraft lost in action; few airfields could claim such a long and meritorious record of service. Several famous bomber squadrons operated from the airfield flying, at times, Wellingtons, Stirlings and the inevitable Lancasters. Furthermore the thousands upon thousands of film-goers who watched the popular wartime film *Target for Tonight* were quite unaware that Mildenhall had been the location of the documentary film. This film provided a great fillip to the public's morale at a very dark period of the war.

At the beginning of September 1939 two bomber squadrons were based at the airfield – Nos 99 and 149, but the first was quickly dispersed to Newmarket Heath leaving No 149 or the 'East India', as it was also known, squadron in residence. Its prominence as a night bomber unit dated back to 1918 and the squadron had been reformed at Mildenhall in April 1937. The crews had only recently exchanged their rather cumbersome and outmoded Handley Page Heyfords for Vickers Wellington Is. They did, however, share the airfield with

193

Wellington III of No 115 Squadron being loaded with 1,000 lb bombs.

some other doughty RAF aircraft – Gloster Gladiators. These truly remarkable little bi-planes that gave such admirable service throughout the war, were engaged in collecting weather data for use by the Met officers at Bomber Command Headquarters and the Flight stayed until October 1941.

On the afternoon of 3rd September 1939 when most people were digesting their Sunday lunches and the rather disturbing fact that the country was now at war with Germany, just three crews of No 149 squadron set out on an armed reconnaissance flight over the North Sea to search for German warships; no contact was made and all three arrived back safely. The following day eight Wellingtons were despatched to Brunsbüttel to attack two German warships. One of the crews claimed to have bombed the targets but alas, it was later discovered that they had fallen on a Danish town killing two civilians. The squadron also took part in the ill-fated operation which was mounted on 18th December 1939, in fact it was led by the squadron's Commanding Officer – Wing Commander Richard Kellett; who was a rather famous pre-war RAF officer noted for his speed records. Another illustrious bomber pilot made an unscheduled appearance at Mildenhall during May 1940 – Guy Gibson. On the night of 22/23rd he landed his badly damaged Hampden at the airfield after a mission to destroy a railway bridge in Belgium. At this stage of the war Gibson was a mere Flying Officer with No 83 squadron at Scampton in Yorkshire. Of course, his subsequent fame was gained with No 617 'Dambusters' squadron.

Right from the outset of the war No 149 squadron was in the thick of the bombing offensive and it was one of only two squadrons to serve continuously with Bomber Command throughout the war, flying almost 6,000 sorties for the loss of over 130 aircraft. As befitted such a famous bomber squadron, it took part in the Command's very first operation over Berlin, which was mounted on 25/26th August 1940 and had been approved by the War Cabinet by way of reprisal for the previous night's raid on London. Just over 80 aircraft – Wellingtons and Hampdens – attacked the city but it was anything but successful as thick cloud greatly hampered the bombing. Six aircraft, all Hampdens, were lost but the British newspapers greeted the operation with headlines like 'Great Fires in Berlin' and the raid gave the airmen of the squadron a great boost to their morale to know that they had gone to Berlin and survived without a single casualty.

During 1941 No 149 squadron was fully engaged in the bombing offensive with Cologne, Mannheim, Brest, Kiel, Bremen, Emden, Hanover, Turin, Stettin and Berlin all featuring in their operations. During the year the squadron lost 30 aircraft in action with another three lost in training flights. Any loss of aircraft and crews was hard to bear but when a returning crew was in sight of the airfield, only then to fall, it seemed to be far more tragic. On 18th March after a successful operation over Bremen one of the Wellingtons was coming in to land when it was shot down by an enemy intruder, a Junkers 88C. The Wellington crashed onto a bungalow at Beck Row killing its six man crew.

On the last night of March one of the squadron's Wellingtons dropped the first 4,000 pound bomb of the war. These blast bombs were known as 'blockbusters' or 'cookies' and they ultimately became one of the Command's main weapons. The squadron was also involved in the two rather costly operations to Berlin. The first took place on the night of 7/8th September and it resulted in an overall loss of 8% with the squadron losing one aircraft. Two months later to the very night, Bomber Command received a rather severe body blow, which almost caused the demise of the Force.

Air Chief Marshal Sir Richard Peirse was quite determined to launch a major operation against Berlin despite a weather forecast so unfavourable that the AOC No 5 Group refused to allow his squadrons (mainly Hampdens) to take part. Strong headwinds were expected over the North Sea and as Berlin was about the absolute limit of the Hampden, Air Vice-Marshal Slessor (later of Coastal Command fame) felt that many of his aircraft would run out of fuel on their return flight. The Air Staff backed Slessor and his Group's aircraft went out to the Ruhr. Because of the heavy cloud formations more than half of the 169 aircraft failed to reach the targets and those who did had great difficulty in bombing accurately with very scattered results. To make matters worse, 21 aircraft (12%) were lost, only one of which was from No 149 squadron. However, on the night's operations the Command lost 37 aircraft, which was almost double the highest loss for any previous night. Largely as a result of this disastrous mission Peirse was ordered to limit the Command's operations to only the bare essential operation, and Berlin was not seriously bombed again until January 1943.

The Berlin mission was one of the last operations mounted by the squadron with their faithful Wellingtons as it was in the process of converting to Stirling Is. The first Stirling sorties were launched on 27/28th November to Düsseldorf, although already one Stirling had been lost on a training flight. During December a new Wellington squadron was formed at Mildenhall largely comprised of airmen from the Royal Canadian Air Force. It was given the number 419 and became the third Canadian squadron in Bomber Command. Wing Commander John (Moose) Fulton, DSO, DFC, AFC was appointed its first Commanding Officer and he was one of the most able Commanders in Bomber Command, who led by example. Fulton was a Canadian by birth and the squadron was also known as 'Moose' from his nickname. The squadron's first operation came on 11th January 1942 when just two Wellingtons were sent to Brest. Like their counterparts in No 149 squadron, the Canadian crews were engaged in the three operations to Essen between 8th to 10th March when GEE was used for the first time.

After a residence of virtually five years No 149 squadron left for the new airfield just up the road at Lakenheath during the end of March and, until the middle of August, the Canadians had the airfield to themselves. The 1,000 bomber raid to Cologne at the end of March saw 16 Wellington IIIs and a single Wellington Ic from No 419 squadron take off from Mildenhall. The 'old' Wellington Ic was flown by W/Cdr Fulton as his usual aircraft was being repaired and he did

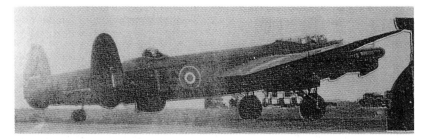

Lancaster of No 15 Squadron. (RAF Museum)

not wish to miss this very special operation! However, he was unfortunately lost on a raid to Hamburg on 28/29th July, which was bedevilled by quite atrocious weather; in this operation No 3 Group lost 25 aircraft, over 15% of those despatched. Airmen and leaders of the calibre of Fulton were difficult to replace. The squadron left for Leeming in Yorkshire during August, and ultimately to serve in No 6 Group, which was specially formed in January 1943 to house all the Canadian bomber squadrons.

Their place was taken by one of the most famous squadrons in No 3 Group. It was No 75 (New Zealand) squadron, which had become operational at Feltwell in April 1940 as the first Commonwealth squadron in the Command. At that time it was mainly made up of New Zealand airmen – hence the name. One of their New Zealand pilots, Sergeant James Ward, had received the Victoria Cross for his supreme bravery on a mission to Münster in July 1941. Unfortunately Ward was no longer with the squadron as he lost his life whilst on a raid to Hamburg in the following September. By the end of the war the squadron had flown over 8,000 sorties – the highest number in all of Bomber Command, and in the process lost 193 aircraft. It was a massive and costly contribution to the air battle over Germany.

By the middle of September 1942 they were joined by another famous bomber squadron – No 115 – which had been based at Marham and by the end of the war had achieved one of the finest records of operational service in Bomber Command; it was the only squadron to lose more than 200 aircraft during the war – an immense sacrifice. However, both squadrons were not destined to stay very long at Mildenhall; by the beginning of November No 75 had left for Newmarket Heath and No 115 went across the county boundary to East Wretham. The reason for their early departure was that the airfield was to be modernised with the provision of concrete runways. The airfield did not reopen for operational flying until April 1943 and by then it was known officially as 'No 32 Base'.

In the previous December Mildenhall was the first RAF station to be brought into the 'base' system. With the number of airfields coming into operational use a considerable strain was being placed on each Group's administration so it was decided that three airfields, each normally holding two squadrons, would be linked to form a base, usually under the command of an Air Commodore though this was not always the case. The main airfield, invariably a pre-war permanent station, would undertake all the personnel functions as well as much of the repair and overhaul work on all the aircraft. The

197

satellite airfields became known as sub-stations and the base system was generally brought into operation from March 1943.

To reopen the station came one of the oldest operational squadrons in the RAF – No 15. It had been formed in March 1915 and was re-formed in March 1924 at Martlesham Heath. During the war so far it had been equipped with Battles, Blenheims, Wellingtons and now Stirling IIIs. Since 1939 the squadron had been unofficially known as 'Oxford's Own', as certain squadrons were affiliated to cities and towns in order to foster good relations between the public and the Service. Already, C Flight of the squadron had been hived off to form a new squadron – No 622 – under the command of Wing Commander G.H.N. Gibson DFC, and both squadrons remained at Mildenhall for the duration of the war.

It was on the night of 16/17th April that No 15 started its operations from Mildenhall and considering the crews had only arrived about 24 hours earlier, it was quite remarkable that 18 Stirlings were ready to go to Mannheim as part of the Battle of the Ruhr. As one crew member recalled, 'Raids over the Ruhr were the worst. The towns were so close together they just passed you from one group of defences to the next. The bombers could therefore be under continuous fire.' Just two Stirlings failed to return from this mission and most of the surviving aircraft were damaged, including one that had no less than 300 shell holes in it as a result of a prolonged attack from two Me109s, although its gunners had managed to destroy one of them. In just ten operations to the Ruhr the squadron lost 15 aircraft; their worst night was 4/5th May over Dortmund when three aircraft failed to return.

During the early weeks of August 1943 Bomber Command mounted several operations against Turin and Milan. These missions were more for political than strategic reasons. It was an attempt to persuade the Badoglio regime, which had come to power after the

Stirling I of No 149 Squadron at Mildenhall – November 1941. (Via J. Adams)

198

downfall of Mussolini, to consider peace proposals so that valuable Allied forces in Italy could be released for other war theatres. It was on one of these operations that Wing Commander John Searby of No 83 squadron acted as 'Master of Ceremonies'; his aircraft remained over the target for the whole of the raid and he controlled the bombing by VHR R/T. Leaflets were also dropped during these operations with the message – 'The Government of Rome says the war continues. That is why our bombardment continues'. Peace terms were agreed on 3rd September! No 622 squadron had seven Stirlings operating over Turin on the nights of 12th and 16th August.

On the following night six crews (five from No 15 and one from No 622) were briefed for a secret operation to bomb 'an important radar experimental station' at Peenemunde on the Baltic coast. The briefing ended with the warning, 'If you don't knock out this important target tonight it will be laid on again tomorrow and every night until the job is done', a most uncommon occurrence. This was, of course, the famous and successful operation against the V1 and V2 rocket research station. Almost 600 aircraft attacked in three waves, each with separate targets. The Stirling squadrons were in the first wave with the living quarters of the research staff as their target. Much of the success of the operation was due to A/Group Captain John Searby, who acted as Master Bomber (the first time the term had been used), and issued instructions to all the crews as they arrived over the target and corrected any previous instructions if the progress of the raid required it. Although 41 aircraft were lost – mainly from the third wave – the operation was a complete success inasmuch that it caused several months delay in the work as well as forcing the Germans to move their operation to more distant and concealed sites. Only five Stirlings arrived back at Mildenhall, one from No 15 squadron was missing. Sadly, at the end of the month the 15th lost its Commanding Officer – W/Cdr J.D. Stephens – who was killed whilst flying a Boulton Paul Defiant on a local trip.

During December both squadrons were converted to Avro Lancasters, and most of the crews were sent to the Lancaster Finishing School at Feltwell in Norfolk. This most famous RAF bomber had been developed from the rather ill-fated and unsuccessful twin-engined Manchester; the first prototype was known as the Manchester III. The Lancasters first flew operationally in March 1942, which was merely the start of an almost non-stop offensive by these heavy bombers. The Lancaster had a magnificent war record, with the largest bomb capacity of any Allied bomber and

199

was the only aircraft capable of carrying the 22,000 pound 'Grand Slam' bomb. Lancasters took part in most of the famous bombing operations of the war – notably the 'Dambusters' raid and the attack on the *Tirpitz*.

Both Mildenhall squadrons were deeply engaged in the Battle of Berlin, which lasted from August to March 1944; each took part in nine raids operating with both Stirlings and Lancasters. No 15 squadron lost seven aircraft and No 622 just three more with over 120 airmen failing to return. As Ed Murrow, the distinguished American reporter, who survived a trip to 'Big B' in a Lancaster commented: 'Berlin was an orchestral hell, a terrible symphony of light and flames. An unpleasant form of warfare but for those brave men – just a job.' For most crews the Berlin raids were the worst experiences of their operational flying. In the large British War Cemetery in Berlin over 80% of the graves are those of Bomber Command men, many of whom lost their lives in the Battle of Berlin, when over 600 aircraft were lost and 2,690 aircrew killed with another 1,000 made prisoners of war.

On the night of 30th March 1944, 27 Lancasters (eleven from No 15 and the rest from No 622) were lined up and ready to take off, the pilots just waiting for the green flash of the controller's lamp. On most operations, at least when the weather was fair, the ground crews and other station personnel gathered to watch and wave farewell to the crews as they left. Once the signal had been given, the engines were turned up to full boost, the brakes were released and slowly each aircraft turned onto the runway, slowly gathering speed, until just over 100 mph was achieved when, if everything was working well, the heavily laden Lancasters would take off. This was the most critical time, especially as the aircraft had almost twelve tons of petrol and bombs on board.

The target on this night was Nuremberg, an important industrial town in southern Germany, which also had major political implications because of its close links with the Nazi party. Almost 780 bombers took part in what turned out to be a major disaster for Bomber Command with it suffering its heaviest loss of the war – 96 aircraft lost and 604 airmen killed. The severe weather conditions could be considered one contributory reason for the magnitude of the disaster but also the crews had to suffer heavy and fierce fighter attacks, especially on the long run home. All the aircraft from No 15 squadron arrived back safely but two Lancasters from No 622 squadron were lost – one to a night fighter and the other collided

King George V at Mildenhall July 1935 – Silver Jubilee Review of the Royal Air Force.

with a Halifax over Belgium. One of the Lancasters of No 622 squadron was brand new and on its first operation – LL885 'JIG' went on to complete 114 bombing sorties. However, this superb record was surpassed by LL806LS-J of No 15 squadron when it survived no less than 134 missions – evidence of the durability of these fine aircraft.

Much to the delight of all the station's personnel Mildenhall received a visit from HM King George VI, Queen Elizabeth and Princess Elizabeth on 5th July 1944. One of the main hangars was specially decorated for the occasion and 30 aircrew were invested with their medals – DFCs and DFMs. It was almost nine years to the very day since the King's father had visited the station, but so much had changed and happened in that relatively short period of time!

At the beginning of November Air Chief Marshal Harris was reminded by the Air Staff that he should concentrate his forces on oil targets with railway communications as a secondary priority. The operational life of the two Mildenhall squadrons during the latter stages of the war certainly reflected these priorities. Along with the rest of No 3 Group's Lancaster G-H force the crews found themselves engaged in attacking such targets, especially in the Ruhr. For instance in November no less than four operations were made to Homberg and its Meerbeck oil refinery, with the last one on the 21st being the most successful when the crews reported '..a vast yellow flame followed by black smoke rising to a great height..', which ensured the virtual end of oil production there. Dortmund, Duisburg and Castrop-Rauxel were all attacked before the end of the year. The Nordstern synthetic oil plant and the Consolidated benzol works at Gelsenkirchen came in for particularly harsh treatment with no less than eight raids up until the end of March 1945. Railway targets at Solingen, Coblenz, Hamm, Osterfeld and Cologne also became victims of the Group's onslaught. Virtually all these operations were conducted in daylight with a strong fighter escort and the majority were achieved with very light losses, or at times no casualties. The damage was quite horrendous and it was a clear demonstration of the awesome power of Bomber Command.

During the New Year the squadrons ventured further afield, notably to Munich, Dresden, Chemnitz, Potsdam and Leuna. Then for three days in March – 11th to 13th – the Command sent over 2,500 aircraft to Essen, Dortmund and Wuppertal, and over 10,650 tons of bombs were dropped through heavy cloud, an example of the technical excellence of the RAF Bomber Command at this stage of the war. All these operations were completed for the loss of 0.2% – what an amazing change in fortunes!

After a most hectic six months of operations the two squadrons completed their wartime offensive on 22nd April with a mission over Bremen and sadly one Lancaster from No 622 squadron was seen to go down in flames but six parachutes opened. Thus the last of the squadron's 51 aircraft failed to return from 268 operations, most of which had been conducted with Lancasters. However, No 15 squadron, who were the old stagers in the game, having first seen service with the Advanced Air Striking Force in France at the beginning of the war, had completed over 5,780 sorties and in the process had lost 166 aircraft, the majority of them Stirlings. The squadron motto of No 622 was 'We Wage War by Night', which was very appropriate for all the aircrews that left Mildenhall throughout the Second World War.

24

NEWMARKET
HEATH

It was the most unlikely looking airfield in the whole of East Anglia, perhaps even in the whole of the country; right until the end of the war strings of racehorses would still not have looked out of place and certainly more appropriate than the variety of aircraft that lined the edges of the racecourse, while several of the racecourse buildings (including the grandstand) were used for accommodation and mess halls. The main grass runway was very long by the standards of the time – 2,500 yards!

The Royal Flying Corps had first recognised the value of 'The Heath' in November 1917 and two squadrons – Nos 190 and 192 – used the airfield. The latter stayed until May 1919 thus establishing a link with the RAF that was renewed on 2nd September 1939 when the first Wellington Is of No 99 (Madras Presidency) Squadron flew in from Mildenhall. This was one of the premier squadrons of Bomber Command, having been reformed in 1924, and had served at Mildenhall for the last four years.

The squadron's first operation of the war took place on the night of 8/9th September 1939 when three aircraft were despatched to drop leaflets over Hanover (one aircraft aborted) as well as a reconnaissance flight over Bremen and Wilhelmshaven. However, its first trial by fire came on the disastrous operation mounted on 14th December 1939 to the Schillig Roads, just off the north German coast near Wilhelmshaven. In rather poor weather conditions twelve aircraft left Newmarket Heath and largely because of the low cloud the bombers could not get into a favourable position to bomb the

German Naval convoy. As the weather worsened the Wellingtons came down to 2,000 feet, whereupon they were immediately engaged by enemy flak and a strong force of fighters. Almost immediately five Wellingtons went down in flames, and two of them collided in mid-air. The remaining aircraft struggled back to Newmarket with their 500lb bombs; unfortunately another aircraft crashed quite close to the airfield killing three of the crew. The squadron lost no less than 33 airmen on this mission. Bomber Command's chiefs would not credit that the enemy fighters had wrought such havoc and their disbelief led to another catastrophic operation to the same area just four days later.

On 10th June 1940, Italy entered the war but this move had been foreseen as a force of Wellingtons (including six from Newmarket) had been sent on 3rd June to a hastily prepared landing field at Salon in Provence, southern France in order to launch bombing attacks on Genoa and Milan. For some unearthly reason this operation was code-named Haddock! On the afternoon of 11th June, twelve Wellingtons were made ready for the mission but were prevented from taking off by a line of French army lorries placed on the runway. It would appear that the French Government had had second thoughts, mainly because they feared retaliatory raids on the south coast of France, which was virtually defenceless. After considerable high level political debate permission was granted and eight Wellingtons were allowed to take off on the night of 15/16th June, although only one aircraft managed to bomb Genoa. The following night 22 left for targets in Genoa and Milan but encountered severe storms and only 14 were able to bomb. No losses were sustained on these rather abortive missions, and, on 17th June, the French Government surrendered to Germany. Although the aircraft were in Vichy France the crews were hastily recalled with the strict orders to destroy any aircraft that could not be flown back and two of the squadron's Wellingtons suffered this fate.

During July 1940 the squadron was engaged in a variety of night operations – bombing targets in the Ruhr, leaflet dropping and mine laying – which had really become the mainstay of the Command's air offensive. The losses were relatively slight (2%) but it was quite difficult to judge what damage was being inflicted because of the sad lack of photographic evidence. Some crews were said to be completing their 30 missions without seeing a single night fighter – they were the fortunate ones! However, on the night of 25/26th July, 166 aircraft were sent out to seven targets in the Ruhr and the

Propellor memorial to No 99 Squadron at Newmarket Heath.

squadron was detailed to bomb Dortmund. On this night some Me110s were active and one of the squadron's Wellingtons was shot down but shortly afterwards a gunner from the squadron – a Danish airman, P/O Hansen – claimed the first enemy fighter to be destroyed by a night bomber. Hansen was later awarded the DFC for his historic victory.

The propellor that forms the memorial at Newmarket Heath came from one of the squadron's Wellingtons that crashed on the night of 11/12th February 1941 a few miles south of Wisbech, after returning from a raid to Bremen (although the aircraft was only uncovered in 1982). As the aircraft returned to Newmarket Heath conditions had deteriorated with the fog far denser than had been forecast. However, eleven of the original force of twelve Wellingtons managed to land safely but the last aircraft was diverted to Mildenhall. After several unsuccessful attempts to land, and with the fuel running low the pilot, Sergeant C. Robinson, flew north of the airfield and ordered the crew to bale out. On that night no less than 22 aircraft were lost over eastern England because of the heavy fog, though most of the crews survived.

Just over a month later (18th March) the squadron moved to a new airfield at Waterbeach and it was replaced by a detachment of

Blenheim IVs from No 107 squadron at Wattisham, who barely stayed a week. They were followed, in March, by some of the new heavy bombers – Short Stirlings – of No 7 squadron, which had only recently entered into operations. The squadron's home base of Oakington had become rather waterlogged and the crews used Newmarket Heath for just under a month until conditions at their home airfield improved.

On 19th March 1941 Newmarket Heath came under the control of Stradishall as its official satelite, and this link with Stradishall led directly to the airfield's involvement with the clandestine special operations mounted on behalf of the Special Operations Executive (SOE). This involved dropping supplies and agents over enemy-occupied territories as well as picking up agents, politicians, resistance leaders, and escaping airmen. The early development of these operations undertaken by No 1419 (Special Duties) Flight will be noted under Stradishall, and when the Flight arrived at Newmarket, during the spring of 1941, it was equipped with Armstrong-Whitworth Whitleys, Westland Lysanders and a single Glenn Martin Maryland.

The Westland Lysander, which was affectionately known as the 'Lizzie', had entered the service in 1938, and was specially designed for ground support duties with the Army Co-operation units. There had been five squadrons of Lysanders serving with the British Expeditionary Force in France. However, in 1941 it had largely been withdrawn from Army duties – at least in Europe. One of its most valuable attributes was its ability of landing and taking off from small and unprepared strips, which made it ideal for this type of special duties with the Flight. The normal procedure at the agreed landing field was an exchange of identification by flashing morse letters, and then a standard pattern of torches would be switched on as a target for parachutes or a flarepath for landings. This was normally in the shape of an inverted L of three torches, 50 yards by 150 yards long, which was just sufficient for the Lysander to land and take off! Whilst on these operations the aircraft were painted entirely black with not a sign of any squadron markings or serial numbers but normally supplied with extra fuel tanks. Needless to say it was a highly dangerous type of flying and the Lysanders gained lasting fame from these secret operations, although many more of them operated in a less glamorous role, that of a target-tower.

During May 1941 the Flight was quite active operating from Newmarket Heath with several missions over France, one of which

206

resulted in a Me110 being shot down by one of the Whitley's rear gunners. It was during this month that the question of raising the Flight to squadron status was suggested by Bomber Command, with the ulterior motive that it could also be used for other special duties. However, it was not until 25th August that Air Chief Marshal Sir Charles Portal rather reluctantly agreed to the proposal and thus No 138 squadron came into being.

The squadron's first operation took place on 29/30th August when a Whitley was operating over Châteauroux. On this mission Sqn/Ldr P.C. Pickard, DSO went along for the ride, although he was said to be 'map reading'! 'Percy' Pickard was supposed to be resting after completing 65 bombing missions and had been appointed to No 3 Group Headquarters at the nearby Exning Hall, as the official pilot for high ranking officers and officials. Pickard had been the star of the famous documentary film *Target for Tonight* and later became the CO of another special duties squadron – No 161. As a Group Captain he lost his life whilst leading the famous Mosquito raid on Amiens prison in February 1944. According to Sir Basil Embry he was, '. . . in courage, devotion to duty, fighting spirit and powers of leadership . . . one of the great airmen of the war . . .'. Besides Pickard various nationalities served with the squadrons – Czechs, Poles, French and even a Russian, Sqn/Ldr Romanoff, who was a cousin of the late Tsar.

By the time No 138 squadron had moved back to Stradishall in the middle of December it had completed over 50 missions from Newmarket Heath. However, there was considerable pressure on the slim resources of the squadron and the Special Intelligence Service (SIS or better known as M16) were pressing for their own air unit to drop and pick up their agents. It was therefore decided that a new squadron – No 161 – should be formed largely from men and equipment from No 138 as well as some additions, a Wellington and Hudson, from the King's Flight. On 14th February 1942 the squadron was set up at Newmarket Heath with the main responsibility of landing and picking up agents, whereas the 'old' squadron would concentrate on dropping supplies with its Whitleys, and later on with Halifaxes.

The squadron's first Lysander mission left Newmarket on 27/28th February and the following night No 161 borrowed an Avro Anson from No 10 OTS at Abingdon to undertake a pick-up of four persons from France. Included in this party was Sqd/Ldr John Nesbitt-Defort of No 138 squadron, who had been free in France for about five weeks

Westland Lysander: painted black and supplied with an extra fuel tank, the 'Lizzies' gained their fame operating over occupied territories. (Westland)

since his Lysander had failed to return from a pick-up. His experiences on these special operations and his adventures in France have been related in his book *Black Lysander*. This flight was the first and only occasion that an Anson was used on such a mission. However, on the same day the squadron left for the new airfield, which had just been completed at Graveley in Cambridgeshire, which would prove to be only a temporary move until both squadrons settled in Tempsford in Bedfordshire.

Early in July, a very hush-hush aircraft arrived by road from the Gloster aircraft factory. This proved to be the first prototype of a twin-engined jet propelled fighter, which had been developed under the Air Ministry's Specification F9/40. After some taxiing trials it was found that the Rover turbo-jet engines were not really adequate for the aircraft. Almost a year later an improved prototype which had first flown in March 1943 arrived at Newmarket for more trials and on 28th May 1943 left Newmarket on a historic flight to a new home in Oxfordshire. The jet-fighter – Meteor I – finally came into service with the RAF in July 1944 with No 616 squadron, and whilst operating from Manston had considerable success engaging V1 rockets.

It was not until the latter months of 1942 that its next and last operational squadron arrived at Newmarket Heath. The squadron was No 75 (New Zealand), which came from Mildenhall and was in the process of converting from Wellingtons to Stirlings using the

208

facilities at Oakington, which had been a famous 'Stirling Station' since early 1941. Within a month of becoming operational the squadron ran into severe trouble just before Christmas 1942. On the night of 16/17th December a small force (eight Stirlings) were detailed to mine the river Gironde near Bordeaux. After three had successfully taken off despite a strong cross-wind, the fourth crashed just after becoming airborne, with the result that the other aircraft were grounded. The following night No 3 Group was given the Opel works at Fallersleben as its primary target, and 16 Stirlings and six Wellingtons made up the Group's small force with five of the Stirlings coming from Newmarket Heath. However, very heavy cloud was encountered throughout the flight and only three aircraft managed to bomb the target. It proved to be a most costly operation with no less than eight aircraft lost. Only one aircraft returned to Newmarket Heath and the Commanding Officer of the squadron, Wing Commander V. Mitchell, was lost on the night's mission. It was a harsh reminder of the very effective flak encountered in the 'Happy Valley'. On the night Bomber Command lost 17 out of 49 aircraft sent – 35%! Though it was shown as a 'minor operation' in official records, it was a crushing blow.

During January 1943, H2S was used for the first time on a major operation but not with particular success. On the next raid a Stirling from No 7 squadron at Oakington was shot down and the Germans obtained one of the new sets, which enabled them to develop a device to home in onto the bombers using H2S. On 3/4th February Hamburg was attacked for the second time in four days. The squadron despatched nine aircraft, although five had to abort because of adverse weather and of the remaining four, only two managed to bomb, the other two were victims of a strong enemy fighter force which, on the night, claimed 16 aircraft (6% loss). On 1st March the squadron sent eight Stirlings as part of a 300-strong force to Berlin. Although it proved to be a costly mission for Bomber Command (5.6%), No 75 squadron survived with not a single loss. In one of those strange quirks of fate the Telefunken works, which was working on the captured H2S sets, was badly damaged during the raid and the set was completely destroyed. However, on the way home a Halifax was shot down over Holland and an almost intact H2S set fell into German hands to enable them to continue their research!

From March to June the squadron took a full and active part in the Battle of the Ruhr. On 1st April the airfield had become a full RAF

209

station in its own right but as a sub-station of the main base airfield – Mildenhall. On two occasions when over targets in the Ruhr, the squadron suffered quite heavily. The Wuppertal and Mülheim missions cost four aircraft on each raid. The Mülheim operation, on 22/23rd June 1943, was particularly effective but also proved rather costly with over 6% of the force being lost. Mülheim had not been previously attacked by Bomber Command despite the fact that it contained iron foundries, furnaces, and rolling mills, and in fact the code-name for the operation was Steelhead. A large proportion of these industries were severely damaged and it was estimated that over 60% of the town had been destroyed in this single raid. By the time No 75 squadron left for a new airfield at Mepal, near Ely, towards the end of June, it had flown over 580 sorties and had lost 24 aircraft, either in action or due to accidents. With losses averaging 5% it was a clear demonstration of the immense sacrifice made by the Stirling crews during this period of the war. They paid a hard price for the Command's strategic bombing offensive.

It now became the turn of fighters to use the airfield. Hurricanes of the Air Fighting Development Unit arrived in July to undertake flying exercises with various bomber squadrons and later in 1944 some Spitfires Vbs came to mount day fighter affiliation exercises with bomber squadrons, because the Command, and more especially No 3 Group's Lancasters, was then operating during the daylight hours. However, by 25th February 1945, all the fighters had left, as had the various aircraft of the Bombing Development Unit, which had been involved in trialling a variety of new equipment and systems for Bomber Command. Thus flying ceased at Newmarket Heath and its rather interesting existence as a wartime airfield came to a close, although it was not until the end of 1947 that the airfield was returned to its owners, the Stewards of the Jockey Club.

25

RATTLESDEN

There was a strong belief held by many members of the RAF that American airmen received medals along with their rations; some even maintained that 'Purple Hearts' were given for frost-bite! This was certainly not so, although it was a fact that over 41,000 Distinguished Flying Crosses and some 122,000 Air Medals were awarded to members of the Eighth Air Force, which perhaps might suggest that the USAAF was more liberal in this respect than the Air Ministry. These two American decorations were for 'extraordinary achievement involving combat'. Above them in order of prominence were three decorations awarded for special acts of heroism and gallantry – the Congressional Medal of Honor, Distinguished Service Cross and the Silver Star. The Medal of Honor was the USAAF's highest gallantry award and was equivalent to the Victoria Cross. Whatever may be said, or thought of the American distribution of the minor awards, the Congressional Medal of Honor was certainly not bestowed lightly and only 17 were given to Eighth Air Force men throughout the Second World War, of which ten were awarded posthumously. Therefore the presentation of such a prestigious medal was a rare honour indeed.

The 447th Bomb Group at Rattlesden was therefore justifiably proud of their own hero – 2/Lt Robert Femoyer. He had served as a navigator with the 711th squadron since September 1944. On 2nd November the Group was detailed for an operation to the synthetic oil plants at Merseburg; this would be Femoyer's seventh mission, and just two days earlier he had celebrated his twenty-third birthday.

The badge of 447th Bomb Group.

During the previous month the Luftwaffe had been unusually inactive but on this mission the enemy fighters had gathered in force. Despite this it was still the tremendous flak barrage at Merseburg that created most of the problems and dangers.

Femoyer's aircraft *L-Love* sustained damage from three near misses and he was severely wounded in the back and side by shrapnel. Despite a considerable loss of blood and being in extreme pain he stoutly refused any morphine as he needed to be alert to safely navigate the aircraft around the known areas of heavy enemy flak. Unable to sit at his table, he was propped on the floor with his charts and instruments around him. Only when the aircraft was safely over the North Sea did he allow the crew to sedate him. The aircraft arrived safely back at Rattlesden but unfortunately Femoyer died shortly after he was removed from the aircraft. However, it was not until early in 1945 that his heroism was recognised by the posthumous award of the Medal of Honor.

The 447th had been operating from Rattlesden for almost one year before the ill-fated Merseburg mission in November, on which the Group had lost five aircraft. The Group joined two veteran units – 94th and 385th – to complete the 4th Bomb Wing of the Third Division. Actually the airfield had originally been designated as a satellite for Bury St Edmunds and had been alive, if not active, since the end of 1942. So when the 447th mounted its first mission to the Pas de Calais or 'Rocket Coast', as it was known to the more experienced crews, on Christmas Eve 1943, Rattlesden had taken an unusually long time to become fully operational.

It was not until the New Year that the crews got their first real taste of the Luftwaffe fighters and this was on January 11th 1944 whilst making for Brunswick. Most of the other formations responded to the recall message but the 4th Wing, led by Lt Colonel Thorup from 94th Group, continued the mission and the Wing managed to bomb the target – the Me110 plant at Waggum. Despite almost continuous fighter attacks the 447th came back home with the loss of just three aircraft. Their bombs had fallen within 1,000 feet of the target – a most commendable achievement for a novice Group. The crews of the 447th ultimately gained the reputation of being the most accurate bombing Group in the whole of the Third Division. By a strange coincidence Lt Colonel Thorup would later arrive at Rattlesden to take over command of the 447th for the last few months of the war.

In four missions to Berlin in March just four aircraft were lost in action, although on the 9th two aircraft were destroyed by flak, another ditched on the way home but all the crew were saved, and a second crashed at RAF Honington. In fact April proved to be an equally stern month of operations and none more so than the visit to the Messerschmitt works in Augsburg on the 13th. The Luftwaffe managed to mount their strongest opposition for several months. However, the B-17s had to face very heavy flak for much of the flight to southern Germany. The Third Division lost 18 aircraft (7.5%) but ten of these found sanctuary in Switzerland, including three from the 447th. One B-17 that almost made it back to Rattlesden crashed at Ham Street killing the pilot. A trip to the Hamm railway yards on the 22nd resulted in another crew not coming home. This, of course, was the evening when the Second Division's B-24s suffered heavily at the hands of enemy intruders as they returned to their home bases, losing 14 aircraft.

However, on 29th April, when the Group was leading the 4th Wing to Berlin, the operation was beset with problems from the outset. Difficulties with the assembly resulted in a rather ragged formation, heavy and overcast skies all the way over did not help either and finally a critical navigational error took the Wing some 40 miles south of the main bomber formation and thus divorced it from the fighter escorts. The Luftwaffe in the shape of the dreaded Fw190s struck quickly and with great purpose; in barely 20 minutes ten of the Group's B-17s were destroyed and another badly damaged aircraft was forced to ditch in the North Sea. This Berlin mission was to be the Group's worst disaster of the whole war. Also during the month there had been a rather serious and unfortunate accident. On the 21st whilst aircraft were being bombed up, one bomb accidentally exploded killing several ground crew as well as destroying three B-17s that were close by.

The following month proved to be a hectic time for all the Eighth's aircrews. The 447th managed to complete 19 missions and on one day (11th) two separate operations were completed. The Eighth's operational schedule for the month provided a very mixed bag of targets and they really exemplified its main bombing objectives of the war – Berlin, V1 rocket sites, oil targets, aircraft factories, U-boat

Some of the runways have survived – Rattlesden – and in the far distance is a wind sock for the gliders that now use the airfield.

pens and then, as the Eighth's contribution to the softening up
process prior to the D-Day landings, the so-called Transportation
Plans. The Group's crews were greatly involved in attacking enemy
airfields and rail targets in south-central France. But of all the
missions the one to the oil targets at Zwickau and Brux, on the 12th,
proved to be the most costly, when no less than seven aircraft failed
to return – another sad and unfortunate day for the 447th. The
Division lost no less than 41 aircraft on this mission (14%), a grim
example of the terrible cost borne by the Eighth Air Force for their oil
offensive.

During 1944 both Air Forces had stepped up their propaganda
campaigns. Besides employing a special night leaflet squadron, the
Eighth decided, in June, to use some of the operational Bomb Groups
to distribute propaganda material whilst on their normal missions.
The 447th was one of those selected in the Third Division. Eight
aircraft each mission carried no bombs, just leaflets. Special T2 leaflet
bombs had been devised, designed to burst open at about 2,500 feet
above the ground, and were then supposed to cover a 200 by 50 yard
area. After D-Day the Eighth Air Force increased its campaign and in
July more leaflets were dropped in just one month than through the
whole of 1943. The propaganda war continued well into 1945, in fact
on one Berlin raid over 1.25 million were dropped!

Towards the end of June, when the Eighth had returned once again
to German targets, the 447th became involved in their most secret
missions of the war. A message had been received by the Allied
Intelligence services that the French Maquis (partisan fighters) were
fighting a desperate battle in south-west France in a brave attempt to
prevent a SS Panzer Division from joining the Normandy battlefront.
The Maquis required arms and ammunition urgently as they were in
dire danger of being slaughtered. The Third Division was given the
task of dropping supplies to beleaguered resistance fighters. The
briefings for this mission were conducted in the utmost secrecy with
the crews given strict orders not to discuss the mission with anybody
on the base, even after the operation had been completed!
Furthermore it strongly emphasised that all the containers should be
dropped within 1,000 yards of the aiming point otherwise they would
be likely to fall into enemy hands. The B-17s were to fly in over the
dropping zones at 2,000 feet with their undercarriages lowered to
decrease their speed and help the accuracy. The crews were assured
that no serious ground opposition was likely to be encountered.

The first mission took place on 25th June and the aircraft took off

B-17G of 447th Bomb Group. (USAF)

shortly before dawn. On this first operation many Allied agents were also parachuted down, with their main task being the instruction of the French fighters in the use of the American arms. A second mission, code-named Operation Cadillac, was mounted on 14th July, when over 3,700 packages were dropped over seven different areas. The following day a message was received that 'Daylight raid very successful. Took place without a hitch.' The third drop, coded Buick, took place on 1st August when another 2,280 containers of supplies were successfully landed. The last of these missions went off on 9th September when only the 94th and 447th Groups were used in Operation Grassy. Just 180 containers of food and medical supplies were safely dropped at Besancon, which was in the Massif Central deep behind the enemy lines and close to the Swiss border. Of course these special operations were additional to the regular missions by the so-called 'Carpetbaggers' – two Bomb Groups that supplied the French Resistance as well as landing Allied agents into France.

At the beginning of October the Group had a rather unfortunate mission. On the second day of the month their target was the Henschel Armaments works at Kassel. Sadly, during the assembly procedure two of the Group's aircraft collided and crashed – one at Kettlebaston and the other at Hitcham – and 16 crewmen were killed. No other aircraft were lost over Kassel; one badly damaged aircraft crash-landed in Belgium but luckily all the crew were saved.

As we have already seen Merseburg proved costly to the 447th at the beginning of November and when they returned to the same target on the 25th of the month, its crews once again had to suffer the intense and frightening flak barrage, which had now made this area one of the most dreaded in the whole of Germany. One crewman

216

described the flak as 'so thick that you could stand on it'! Many airmen showed the classic signs of being 'flak happy' – utter fatigue, listlessness, battle nightmares or the inability to sleep. The Eighth fully acknowledged the problem and sent most combat crews to the various rest homes for a short break from operations. Needless to say these homes were quickly nick-named 'Flak Houses'. The number of aircraft that were named '*Flak* . . . ' showed just how deeply the crews worried about the dangers of enemy flak. Certainly there was ample evidence to justify their fears. It was estimated that during 1944 over 3,000 aircraft had fallen to flak, far more than had been shot down by fighters, and that is without the thousands of aircraft that arrived back to base bearing the scars of enemy shrapnel. Though most Groups could proudly show aircraft that had completed well over 50 missions despite being badly damaged by flak on a number of occasions – the 447th had one B-17 named *Milk Wagon*, which ultimately completed no less than 129 missions! Another B-17 *Scheherazade* managed to make over 100 successful sorties. The flak at Merseburg accounted for another eight B-17s in late November and a quarter of these came from Rattlesden.

February 1945 became rather a notable month for the Group. Some 14 operations were completed for the loss of just two aircraft; although on the 21st when the crews were not detailed for an operation, a B-17 exploded at the airfield, destroying another two aircraft as well as injuring six men. During the middle of the month the Group was selected to undertake three missions to attack the rail bridge at Wesel, just to the east of the Rhine. These operations were part of what was known as the Ruhr Transportation Plans, whereby the Allied Air Forces attempted to isolate the Ruhr from the rest of Germany and make it particularly difficult for the German forces to either retreat or reinforce the area in front of the Allied armies. The Group's aircraft attacked Wesel on three separate occasions – 14th, 16th and 19th – with RAF Bomber Command also making heavy attacks during the same period. With another raid by the Eighth towards the end of the month, and further RAF attacks in March, it was reckoned that Wesel was the heaviest bombed town in Germany, with over 97% of its buildings and houses destroyed.

By the following month most aircrews felt reasonably confident that the war was fast coming to a close and many began to think for the first time that a safe return to the States was now becoming a distinct probability rather than a somewhat distant possibility. Nevertheless, however quickly the Allied armies were closing on Berlin and the

Eighth's targets were reducing in number, the Eighth Air Force was operational on no less than 26 days, mounting over 30,000 individual sorties, which exceeded the previous record that had been set in June 1944. Indeed, the Eighth unloaded their heaviest tonnage of bombs for any month of the war. So it was not quite a time of relaxation for the Group . . . at least not yet.

In all this intense operational activity things seemed to be going quite well for the 447th, at least until the middle of the month. On the 15th the Third Division despatched over 600 B-17s to the marshalling yards at Oranienburg, which was about 30 miles north of Berlin. It was not a costly mission by any stretch of the imagination, just eight aircraft failed to return but half of these losses were borne by the Group – a rather unfortunate and heavy blow to sustain at such a late stage of the war.

Almost one month later, on 19th April, when the Division was engaged in attacking a variety of rail targets in south-eastern Germany, the Groups came under attack from several Me262s – the dreaded jet-fighter. These were believed to be part of the elite fighter unit JV44, which was led by the legendary General Galland. These fighters were equipped with airborne missiles, which could be launched very accurately from outside the range of the B-17s' defensive fire. In a short flurry of action the Me262s accounted for five B-17s, one of which came from Rattlesden. It was piloted by 1/Lt Robert Glazner, and rather fortunately all but one of his crew managed to bale out and they were liberated just a couple of days later. These B-17s were the last American bombers to fall to the Luftwaffe, but it did show that had the Me262s been brought into action much earlier, they could have made a significant difference to the late stages of the air war.

Just two days later the 447th went out on their final and 257th mission. During their time at Rattlesden 97 aircraft had been lost to enemy action and a further 43 in accidents.

By the end of July most of the aircraft had departed and when the airfield was finally handed over to the RAF in October peace had once again descended on this quiet backwater of the Suffolk countryside. Although part of the old airfield is still used today, the quiet solitude has not been broken, as gliders now silently use the air-space. The old control tower has been renovated and acts as a club house.

26
RAYDON

Along a quiet country road, only a mile or so from the busy and noisy A12, can be found the peaceful little village of Raydon. The very first American servicemen to disturb the even tenor of this corner of the county were men of the 833rd and 862nd Engineer Battalions. Their specific task was to build a standard bomber airfield between the villages of Great Wenham and Raydon, which were some three miles to the south-east of Hadleigh. Work started in the late summer of 1942 but during its construction the plans of the Eighth Air Force had changed somewhat. Several of the Bomb Groups that had been allocated for the Eighth were diverted to North Africa to serve with the Fifteenth Air Force. And then with the reformation in England of the Ninth Air Force during October 1943, when the airfield was nearing completion, there was quite an urgent need for airfields to accommodate the various Fighter Groups that would ultimately operate with this Tactical Air Force. So it came about that Raydon, because of its situation so close to the Essex boundary, where the majority of the Ninth's Groups were based, was allocated to the Ninth Air Force Fighter Command.

At the beginning of December 1943 the first personnel of 357th Fighter Group arrived at Raydon station after a long and tiring overnight journey from the Clydeside, where they had recently disembarked from the *Queen Elizabeth*. By no stretch of the imagination could the airfield be said to be completed, and it was quite a dismal sight that greeted the American airmen – mud, mud . . . and more mud! The 357th was only the second P-51 Mustang Group in the USAAF but because these precious aircraft were in such short supply, the Group was temporarily given ex-RAF Mustangs in order that some training could be started. However, the chiefs of the Eighth's Fighter Command had already cast covetous eyes on this P-51 Group and little did the airmen know that their stay at Raydon would be of very short duration. By the end of January a transfer had been arranged, a straight exchange with the 358th at Leiston some 40 or so miles further north.

The new Group arrived with its P-47Ds at the beginning of February. Its pilots had already been blooded in 17 missions but without a great deal of success. Within a day or so they were in action over Wilhelmshaven. For the next two months whilst the Group was stationed at Raydon it frequently operated under the Eighth's control and it was involved in most of the Eighth's major operations, including all the Berlin missions that were conducted during March. The pilots could be excused for thinking, why bother to change bases? However, in April they knew the answer to this question when it was decided that the Ninth's fighter units should be moved to airfields in south-east England to be closer to the pre-invasion action over France. Bags were packed, farewells were made and the 358th were again on the move. By the time the year was out they would have changed their base no less than five times!

By 12th April 1944 the third and last Fighter Group moved in – 353rd – which had been operating successfully from Metfield since the previous August. It was a most experienced group of fighter pilots led with great panache by Colonel Glenn Duncan in his P-47D rather inappropriately called *Dove of Peace*. Just two weeks after arriving at Raydon Colonel Duncan had a very close call. On 27th April one of the Group's squadrons was armed with bombs with the intention of attacking Florennes airfield in France, whilst the rest of the Group provided withdrawal support for the bombers. Almost immediately after take-off Duncan's aircraft suffered an engine failure, however he managed to jettison the two bombs harmlessly over farmland before crash-landing at Copdock near Ipswich. Duncan walked away unharmed, indeed he seemed to have a charmed life! The following day he was leading 31 of his pilots on a dive-bombing mission to another French airfield – Châteaudun to the north-west of Orleans. All returned safely to Raydon with one enemy aircraft destroyed on the ground; the 353rd would show a certain healthy talent for ground-strafing and their final tally of the war amounted to 414 aircraft destroyed.

It would appear that the personnel quickly settled in at Raydon, despite the muddy conditions. The living sites, which were to the south of the airfield close to the village of Great Wenham, had been given names to remind the servicemen of home – such as Dodge City, Greenwich Village, Powder River, and Alcatraz! The base had its own orchestra, as well as its own cinema, which was aptly called Thunderbolt Theater. Many of the original pilots, who had come over from the States almost twelve months earlier, had already completed their tours and were on their second. Unlike the bomber crews their tours were not based on the number of missions completed but rather on the number of combat hours flown – 200 made up a completed tour of operations.

During May the Group proved to be most active; no less than 24 missions were flown and the pilots were particularly successful on the 8th when the major bombing targets were Berlin and Brunswick. The Eighth's fighters had a most profitable day with 55 aircraft downed, of which the 353rd claimed 21 without a single loss. Then on the 21st of the month the Eighth launched its first major operation against the German railway system and rolling stock; it was code-named Chattanooga – for obvious reasons. A successful, if some-what costly operation with over 2,000 locomotives being attacked and almost half of them being destroyed. Just two of the Group's aircraft were lost, one of these came down in the sea some 20 miles from Felixstowe and the pilot was rescued.

During the first days of June most of the Eighth's endeavours were directed against the V1 rocket sites at the Pas de Calais. However, it was quite obvious to all at Raydon that the invasion of Europe was very close. All leave was cancelled and everybody was confined to the airfield. Each aircraft was carefully serviced, fully armed and fuelled ready to take off at an instant. On 5th June each aircraft was painted with broad black and white bands across the fuselage and wings and they were then covered up to ensure the 'secret' markings would not be seen. Some of the ground crew that were given this task swore that the paint tins were labelled 'for the cake walk'! These 'invasion stripes' were, of course, additional to the Group's normal markings, which in the case of the 353rd were black and yellow chequered nose cowlings – one of the most colourful Fighter Groups in the Eighth. On D-Day itself the pilots flew almost continuously and completed seven missions, the following day they went out nine times and in the two days only four pilots were lost.

However, on the 12th matters took a turn for the worse. Some 260 fighters – P-38s and P-47s – were sent on a fighter-bomber operation to several rail targets in the Paris area. The Luftwaffe had managed

353rd Fighter Group preparing to land at Raydon. (USAF)

to regroup after the terrific aerial onslaught of the previous six days, and a strong force of Me109s attacked the Group – more especially the 350th squadron led by Captain Dewey Newhart. In a fierce but rather one-sided battle, the squadron lost six aircraft, including Captain Newhart, as well as another two pilots from the 352nd squadron. Later in the day when Colonel Duncan became aware of the full enormity of the loss, he obtained clearance for another sweep of the same area. The 56th from nearby Boxted were sent out half an hour later to add support should it be needed. This revenge mission proved to be quite successful with nine Me109s claimed by the Group and another five falling to the 56th's pilots. Perhaps this was some small consolation but nevertheless the loss of eight pilots on a single mission would prove to be the Group's heaviest defeat of the war.

There was another heavy loss to bear in July when Colonel Duncan failed to return from a ground-strafing attack. His aircraft was so badly damaged that he had to force-land in Holland. Once again he managed to evade capture and nothing could repress this ebullient and enthusiastic officer as he became actively involved working with the Dutch underground. He returned to England when part of Holland was liberated and finally arrived back at Raydon in due course. At the time he was shot down he was one of the leading aces in the Eighth with 19 victories in the air and another six on the ground. His place was admirably filled by Lt Colonel Ben Rimmerman, who was the Group Executive Officer. He was well-known and well-liked by the pilots and ground crews, and he led the Group for virtually the rest of the war.

It was the rather ill-fated operation code-named Market Garden that resulted in the Group's only Distinguished Unit Citation. Market Garden was the Allied airborne forces' attempt to capture various bridges in Holland and has passed into military history for the courage and valour of those forces taking part. From 17th to 23rd September the Group's pilots were engaged on several difficult and dangerous missions. Perhaps none was more severe than that on the 17th when as a prelude to the airborne operation, the flak batteries in the dropping zones were required to be destroyed. The fighters were used almost as flak bait as a way to establish the exact location of the hidden batteries to enable the heavy bombers to come in and bomb. On the 21st whilst on a constant patrol of the skies above these torrid battlefields the Group completed its 300th mission. At the end of the week's operations – a most severe test for the pilots – the Group had claimed 15 victories for the loss of six pilots and it thoroughly deserved its Unit Citation.

During this period the pilots were also involved in changing from P-47s to P-51Ds, one of the last of the Eighth's Groups to make the change. The first mission with the new aircraft took place on 2nd October, though it would be almost another month before they scored a victory. This was not because they were particularly unskilled with the P-51s but for most of October the German skies were virtually devoid of enemy fighters. However, it was a vastly different matter on 2nd November when the Luftwaffe opposed the Eighth's major offensive against oil targets. It was thought that over 400 enemy fighters were in action on that day and over one quarter of them were claimed to have been destroyed by the fighters. In this massive air battle, one of the largest of the war, the 353rd claimed just four. However, on the 28th in another torrid combat with the Luftwaffe, 18 enemy fighters fell to the Group's guns and it would be another four months before its pilots bettered this total. This occurred on 24th March whilst giving support to the Allied forces crossing the Rhine; 23 were destroyed on this mission with Lt Colonel Wayne Bickerstaffe and Major Robert Elder both becoming 'aces in a day'.

The sudden death of President Roosevelt on 12th April 1945, which so shocked the world, brought deep and genuine sorrow to all the American bases in England, and when the operational schedules permitted memorial services were conducted at the various American bases. Fortunately both the 14th and 15th were quiet days for the majority of Fighter Groups, and most of the rather moving services took place on those days. On the 16th over 900 fighters were airborne and the 66th Wing was given the freedom to attack enemy airfields almost at will. This resulted in a massive number of enemy aircraft claimed to have been destroyed on the ground. By now, in fact, many of the Luftwaffe units were grounded because of a severe shortage of aviation fuel. The Wing claimed over 400 aircraft destroyed with the 353rd credited with 128 and another three in the air. It was almost as if the fighter pilots were on a vengeance mission on behalf of their late-lamented President.

A week later (22nd April) the Group welcomed back Colonel Duncan. Ben Kimmerman was promoted to a full Colonel when he took over the command of 55th Fighter Group at Wormingford across in Essex. Unfortunately he was killed in a flying accident some weeks later. There was just one final mission for Colonel Duncan to lead, escorting a force of Lancasters of RAF Bomber Command to Berchtesgaden, Hitler's mountain retreat in southern Germany.

The war had come to an end as far as the Group's pilots were concerned. Over 330 enemy aircraft had been destroyed in the air with over 400 on the ground. Quite appropriately the Commanding Officer led the field as far as victories were concerned, although there were another 17 air aces and 32 pilots claiming five or more kills on the ground. Although the crews were quite naturally keen to get back home, the last personnel of the Group did not leave until the end of October. Even then there were still some Americans left at Raydon – the remnants of 652nd Weather squadron – but they too had departed by the end of the year. A visit to St Mary's church will confirm the American presence with its fine vestry doors bearing the emblem of the Eighth Air Force as well as a dedication to the 353rd Fighter Group, along with a memorial book.

27

SHEPHERD'S GROVE

This rather late wartime airfield, which owed its name to a small wood situated to the west of the field, had been recognised quite early as a suitable site for a bomber station; indeed as far back as August 1942 when it was known as Hepworth from the neighbouring village. Not only did it have to wait a long time before it became operational but even longer for its brief moments of glory. It was during the dark days of the Cold War when, on 27th August 1951, F-86A Sabre jets of 81st Fighter Interceptor Wing of the USAF arrived to become the first foreign aircraft to be assigned to the air defence of Great Britain. For the next seven years Shepherd's Grove would be the home of American jet fighters, but unlike the other Suffolk airfields – Bentwaters, Lakenheath and Woodbridge – which also were American bases, the airfield was not further developed and its existence has now been largely forgotten.

It was perhaps most appropriate that American airmen would ultimately be based at Shepherd's Grove because when the airfield was constructed in 1943 it was with the express purpose of being used by the Eighth Air Force. However, by the time it was completed in early 1944 the USAAF had sufficient airfields and it was superfluous to their requirements. The Air Ministry, who then were also not particularly short of airfields, decided to allocate it to No 3 Group of Bomber Command, and it came into being as a satellite for No 31 Base at Stradishall.

When the airfield opened during the first days of April, its parent station was almost solely involved in advanced aircrew training for

No 3 Group and so within days No 1657 Heavy Conversion Unit arrived equipped with Stirlings and for the rest of the war Shepherd's Grove would become essentially a Stirling base.

Towards the end of the year when the Base station returned once again to bomber operations, Shepherd's Grove was transferred out of No 3 Group to No 38 Group Transport Command. This Command was relatively new having been formed in March 1943 and 38 Group came into being on 10th October as the air support for the Army airborne forces, which involved dropping supplies and troops as well as towing gliders. The Group was mostly equipped with Stirlings and Halifaxes. However, by the early months of 1944 the Group's squadrons were also becoming increasingly involved in the SOE operations and became especially engaged in dropping small units of SAS (Special Air Service) men into occupied territories.

It was largely as a result of the harsh winter of 1944/5 that Shepherd's Grove first began to be used by No 38 Group. The heavy frosts that were experienced during this winter had resulted in the break-up of the concrete runways at Wethersfield and the two squadrons based there – Nos 196 and 299 – were forced to use another airfield at Gosfield for their operations. However, it was decided that a larger airfield with better facilities was needed and, in January 1945, the two squadrons arrived at Shepherd's Grove on a permanent basis. No 196 had been first formed in November 1942 as a bomber squadron and ultimately served in No 3 Group before being transferred to No 38 Group in November 1943.

Despite the fact that by January 1945 the Allied armies were moving closer and closer to the German borders there were still plenty of special operations to mount as the resistance workers in Norway, Denmark and Holland were now ready to attack the German occupying forces more overtly. As weather conditions improved during February the Group's squadrons were quite active supporting the regular SOE squadrons. These missions were certainly not without danger as even at this late stage of the war the enemy's flak was still a potent force, although the Luftwaffe fighters were now mainly concentrated in Germany to try to counter the massive operations of both Bomber Command and the Eighth Air Force.

On the night of 25/26th February 196 squadron lost a Stirling over southern Norway and just five nights later (2/3rd March) two Stirlings from 299 squadron failed to return from another Norwegian mission. For some unaccountable reason No 38 Group was placed under the control of Fighter Command, which does seem a strange

226

parentage, although the change had very little effect on the operational life of the two squadrons at Shepherd's Grove, as they found themselves increasingly engaged in missions to Holland, Denmark and Norway. However, towards the end of the month both squadrons were engaged in Operation Varsity – the Allied armies' crossing of the Rhine. The Allied Air Chiefs had learnt much from the disastrous Arnhem operation of the previous September when there had been eight separate lifts with a very heavy loss of aircraft and gliders. For the Rhine crossing there would be just a single air operation. Thus on 24th March there was a massive paratroop and glider landing made by the Allied Airborne Divisions in the Weser – Emmerich areas, north-west of Essen. Both squadrons were involved in the airlift of the troops of the British 6th Airborne Division. This large combined Allied operation, involving over 1,100 aircraft and gliders, proved to be a most successful military operation with the RAF losing only four aircraft, although the USAAF suffered heavier losses. The Group's contribution was 319 Stirlings and Halifaxes towing Horsa and Hamilcar gliders.

Within a week the two squadrons were back on special operations and on the night of 30/31st March both sent out aircraft to separate dropping zones in Norway. Unfortunately these proved to be a little costly as each squadron lost two aircraft. A couple of nights later (2/3rd April) another two aircraft were shot down. One of the Stirlings from No 299 squadron was captained by Pilot Officer Dillon; it crashed on the north coast of Denmark after suffering severe flak damage. Dillon was the only survivor and managed to evade capture, then with the help of the Danish underground he made it back safely to England.

The rate of special operations did not abate, despite the fact that the war was obviously nearing conclusion. The night of 7/8th April was selected for a large SAS operation code-named Amhurst, which involved dropping supplies, SAS troops and jeeps into northern Holland, which then was still under German control. The aircraft were detailed to fly over the dropping zone at a height of 500 feet and at a speed of just 130 mph, which made them vulnerable to even small arms fire let alone flak. Of the 44 aircraft sent out by 38 Group only one aircraft was lost. However, four nights later both squadrons at Shepherd's Grove lost an aircraft on missions to Holland and Denmark. On the following day a badly damaged Mosquito attempted to make an emergency landing at the airfield but unfortunately it crashed killing two of the crew. Towards the end of

Short Stirlings were given a new role: glider towers. (Via H.R. Smith)

April the Group's involvement in these special operations finally came to an end.

It does seem rather unfortunate that these operations mounted by 38 Group and the other specialist SOE squadrons have received fairly scant recognition considering how dangerous they were and, at times, quite costly. However, the wartime work of the Group's squadrons was not yet completed. During May they were engaged in ferrying small parties of troops to Norway and Denmark, who would form the advanced groups of occupation forces. By now, of course, the two squadrons had the airfield to themselves. The Miles Martinets TT1s of No 1677 Target Towing Flight, which had been based there since the beginning of the year, had left in April. Thus ended the airfield's quite brief and perhaps rather mundane wartime existence. The two squadrons stayed and were mainly used in a transport role until the airfield passed to No 60 Group, which was involved in signals work. Before the airfield ceased being a RAF station in early 1950, a few Ansons and Lancasters were detached there from its parent station – Watton.

28

STRADISHALL

Considering its prestige as a pre-war RAF airfield, Stradishall is perhaps the most disappointing of all Suffolk airfields to revisit, especially when faced with the high and formidable security fences that surround HM Highpoint prison, which since 1977 has occupied the site. However, all has not been lost and if one cares to retrace one's steps past the old RAF gatehouse, which now only 'guards' the large visitors' car park, to the small village of Stradishall and its delightful parish church, there can be found a stained glass memorial window to RAF Stradishall; and also in the churchyard is a neat row of bright white and pristine headstones – the last resting place of just a few of the airmen who lost their lives whilst operating from Stradishall. Both provide fitting memorials to this famous RAF station that was active for over 30 years.

Work on the airfield was started in 1935 and when it opened in February 1938 Stradishall was one of the jewels in Bomber Command's crown. It was one of the first pre-war RAF airfields to be supplied with concrete runways and it became the home of Handley Page Heyfords – the last bi-plane bombers to serve with the RAF. By the time it opened its gates to the public on Empire Day in 1939, the Heyfords had disappeared, being replaced by the very new Vickers Wellingtons. Therefore it is most surprising to find that at the outbreak of the war Stradishall was not actually an operational base but had been placed under 'care and maintenance' and was housing the Wellingtons of No 75 squadron, which was acting as No 3 Group pool squadron. Within days these aircraft had moved to Harwell under the newly formed No 6 (Training) Group to act as an Operational Training Unit.

It was to be another two months before Stradishall became active again when two new fighter squadrons were formed there – Nos 236 and 254 – both equipped with Blenheim Ifs. By early December these aircraft had departed for fighter airfields and there was a space of some two months before a heavy bomber squadron arrived. This was No 214, which was destined to make the airfield its permanent home for over two and a half years. The squadron dated from the days of the Royal Flying Corps when, in July 1917, it had been formed as a heavy night bomber squadron and after the post-war cuts was reformed in 1935. During 1941 it became known as 'Federated Malay States' having been adopted by that Federation. The squadron was first supplied with Wellington Ias but by the summer had exchanged them for Mark Ics. Although the squadron did not start its operations until June, it then proceeded to serve without a break throughout the war and had the rather unenviable record of having the highest rate of losses in the whole of No 3 Group.

On the night of 14/15th June the squadron opened its long and bitter wartime operations with just two Wellingtons being sent on a 'fire raising' mission over southern Germany. This was one of several rather hare-brained schemes which were included in the pre-war Western Air Plans, when it was thought that starting fires in the Black Forest and making incendiary attacks on the German harvest would greatly affect the morale of the German people! Small fire-raising devices known as Deckers, which were impregnated pieces of cloth with a delayed ignition action, were also dropped. These raids are now recognised as a considerable waste of time and resources.

For the rest of the year the squadron settled into a fairly regular pattern of operations, which were mainly conducted to Germany with power stations, railway yards and airfields being the normal targets. This was at a time when Bomber Command had a virtual free hand in selecting their operations with little interference from the Air Ministry or the War Cabinet. Although mostly directed to the Ruhr, the squadron was also active over Berlin on 23/24th September and again two weeks later. The first raid lasted over three hours and it was the first time that Bomber Command had concentrated its main force on just one city. Although the ground mist and the number of searchlights made visible bombing a problem, both operations were thought to have been more than effective, especially as only four aircraft were lost in total.

Like most of the squadrons in No 3 Group, No 214 was involved in the operation which was coded Abigail Rachel – the large raid

Memorial window at St Margaret's church, Stradishall.

mounted on Mannheim on the night of 16/17th December; this was in retaliation for the German heavy raids on Coventry and Southampton. The Wellington squadrons would be the first over the target and the early leaders would drop solely incendiaries with the intention of setting off fires to guide the main force onto the target. Of the 134 aircraft taking part almost 80% claimed to have bombed but unfortunately the leading crews had not been very accurate, despite the fact that the visibility was good and there was a full moon, with the result that the bombing was very scattered. It was not a particularly successful operation but because the flak defences were relatively light all the Wellingtons returned safely with the loss of three aircraft from the Whitley squadrons.

At the beginning of 1941 Bomber Command was given nine oil targets as their priority, names that would crop up again and again in the coming years as essential targets for both the RAF and the Eighth Air Force – Leuna, Pölitz, Ruhland, Magdeburg, Lutzendorf and Bohlen. However, hardly had the oil offensive got under weigh than the priorities were changed as a result of the Battle of the Atlantic, which was then at a critical stage with the British merchant

231

fleet losing a high percentage of shipping to the U-boat packs, and as a result the U-boat yards and pens became the order of the day for Bomber Command. Some of the squadron's targets reflected this change in operations – Kiel, Brest, Wilhelmshaven, Hamburg and Bremen all received special attention. On the night of 29th January one Wellington had just become airborne when one of its engines failed and it crashed back on the runway, bursting into flames. The station padre – Rev Harrison – was the first on the scene and he managed to rescue the crew. For this act of heroism he was awarded the George Medal.

During 1941 the squadron lost 28 of their Wellingtons in action and another three in training; no less than five aircraft were lost over four separate missions to Berlin – it was a rather arduous year for the crews. On the night of 7/8th September one of the Wellingtons which was shot down by enemy flak was piloted by the squadron's Commanding Officer – W/Cdr Cruickshanks DFC. The next Berlin mission mounted on 20/21st September turned out to be a complete disaster. Over 70 Wellingtons and Whitleys were despatched but because of worsening weather, the force was recalled. However, ten Wellingtons did not receive the message and went on to bomb alternate targets. Over Münster two of the squadron's aircraft were badly damaged and both received further heavy damage when the pilots made emergency landings at Manston. In fact on the night 16 aircraft were lost (21%), another example of the immense sacrifice made by Bomber Command's crews during the early war years. On the last Berlin raid for over two years, the squadron lost just one aircraft on the night of 7/8th November; it was severely damaged and had to ditch in the English Channel on return. The crew finally came ashore in their dinghy at the Isle of Wight three days later! The pilot – P/O Ercolani (of the Ercol furniture family) – was awarded the DSO in January for his exploits on this night.

Whilst the squadron had been ploughing its lonely bombing furrow over Germany, a rather unusual unit arrived in October 1940 to share the airfield's facilities, although all of its operations were cloaked in great secrecy. It was No 419 Flight, which had been originally formed at North Weald in August as the operational air arm of the Special Operations Executive (SOE). It was largely the brainchild of Dr Hugh Dalton, the Minister of Economic Warfare, who intended that it be used as a 'Fourth Arm' or 'Secret Army' – under which name its exploits were made into a very successful television series. The Executive's intention was to undertake 'irregular warfare in all its

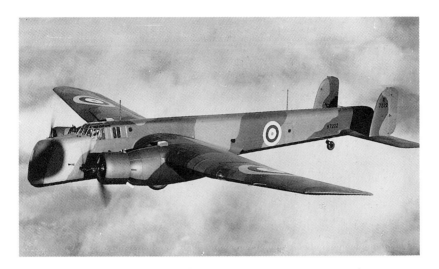

Armstrong-Whitworth Whitley: Mark Vs operated on special duties from Stradishall.

forms, which included industrial and military sabotage, propaganda, riots and strikes.' Winston Churchill thought that this Fourth Arm would 'Set Europe ablaze'!

The Flight, using Lysander IIIs and Whitley Vs, was responsible for dropping supplies and agents into occupied territory as well as picking up agents and other people. It had come to Stradishall mainly because that was the nearest available bomber station to London. However, many of the Lysander flights used Tangmere in Sussex as the final take-off airfield because of the range of the aircraft. Most of the secret agents were temporarily accommodated at Tangmere Cottage – a 'safe house' almost outside the airfield.

Of course all the operations were conducted in the utmost secrecy – in the early days even the Station Commanding Officer was kept in the dark about the nature of the operations. One of the continual problems the Flight faced was obtaining aircraft to carry out the vast number of operations they were asked to undertake. Bomber Command was very loath to release any of their precious aircraft from operations and especially the Whitley Vs. So the Flight, which was renumbered No 1419 in March 1941 (to avoid confusion with Commonwealth squadrons that were being formed in the 400 series), had to struggle along with just a handful of aircraft.

The Armstrong-Whitworth Whitley was the first twin-engined

heavy bomber to be produced in quantity for the RAF, although it had first been developed as a result of a request, in 1934, from the Czech Government for a long-range bomber. The RAF was impressed with the original design and ordered some to operate as Bomber/transport, and it came into service in March 1937. It was spacious, sturdy and very reliable, although it was also known as the 'slab-sided lumbering giant'. Nevertheless it was the first RAF aircraft to fly over Berlin and was engaged in the first bombing attack on Germany in May 1940, followed by Italy in June. The first Mark Vs appeared in 1940, powered by Rolls Royce Merlin X engines and had become involved in the training of airborne forces, so they were particularly suited to such special duties. The Whitleys operated successfully with Coastal Command but were withdrawn from front-line bombing duties in May 1942.

In March 1941, Stradishall took over the control of Newmarket Heath and less than two months later the Flight moved there, although already two Whitleys had been lost whilst on training flights. By the time the Lysanders and Whitleys returned to Stradishall at the end of the year, it had acquired squadron status – No 138 – commanded by W/Cdr Farley, who had undertaken the first successful pick-up in August 1940. The squadron mounted over 50 missions from the airfield, and their operations extended as far as Poland and Czechoslovakia. They had managed to 'acquire' a couple of Halifaxes and some extra Whitleys to increase their force. All the operations were normally flown within one week of the full moon, for obvious reasons. They were not achieved without some losses. Just after Christmas when four operations were mounted to Denmark and Poland, two of the Whitleys crashed at the airfield and about a month later another Whitley had to ditch in the North Sea when returning from a successful drop. Two nights later (28th January) a Lysander failed to return from France.

1942 brought several major changes at Stradishall. In June it was allocated to the Eighth Air Force as a bomber base but just two months later the order was rescinded and the Americans never occupied the airfield. When No 138 squadron moved out in March, it was replaced by a flight of Wellingtons of 109 squadron. Since December 1940 this unit – the Wireless Intelligence Development Unit – had been greatly involved in testing various radio-counter measures, perhaps most notably 'window' and the blind bombing system Oboe. During its short stay at the airfield the squadron was reorganised into two flights operating with a variety of different

Wellington marks, including a couple of the rather rare VIs (only 20 were produced) for very high altitude use – up to 40,000 feet – with a special pressurised cabin mounted in the forward fuselage. In July an extra flight was formed equipped with Mosquito IVs with the specific intention of testing and trialling Oboe in operations. Another squadron – No 101 – made a brief appearance with its Wellington IIIs during the late summer but it had moved to Yorkshire by the end of September.

During the spring of 1942 No 214 squadron was in the process of changing its Wellingtons for Stirlings but before this happened, it was to suffer its heaviest loss of the war. This occurred on the night of 1/2nd April 1942 when rather unwisely, especially considering the Command's early operations, the Wellington crews were detailed to make a low-level attack on railway targets at Hanau and Lohr to the east of Frankfurt. Of the 35 Wellingtons involved in this operation only 22 aircraft bombed and twelve were shot down (34% loss rate!). No 214 squadron lost seven of its 14 aircraft, which must have been a shattering blow.

Perhaps the squadron's first major test with their Stirlings came on the famous 1,000 raid on Cologne at the end of May 1942, and it is interesting to note that the faithful Wellingtons still provided 60% of the force, although many of these came from operational training units. The squadrons of No 3 Group were scheduled to be in the vanguard of this large armada. It would be the first time that a new flying tactic would be used – the bomber stream. Hitherto bombers had attacked singly in spaced intervals, making them rather vulnerable to both flak and enemy fighters. On this operation the squadrons flew in a concentrated stream along the same route thus, in theory, saturating the German defences. It was estimated that every minute at least six aircraft would be bombing, and as 75% of the bombs were incendiaries the intention was to create a tremendous fire-storm. Out of the 1,047 aircraft taking part in this historic operation 39 were shot down (3.7%) and only two were involved in collisions – unfortunately one of these was a Stirling from No 214 squadron, which proved to be their only casualty.

When Chedburgh opened as a satellite airfield in September it was decided that No 214 squadron would operate from the new airfield – not a particularly popular move for the crews who were loath to exchange the comfortable accommodation at Stradishall for the basic facilities of a wartime airfield. However, it had been decided that Stradishall would be largely engaged with the training of aircrews within No 3 Group and on 1st October 1942 No 1657 Heavy Conversion Unit was formed. These units filled the gap between the training of aircrews at Operational Training Units, where all the aircraft were twin-engined, and the operational bomber squadrons now mostly equipped with the four-engined 'monsters'. Normally these HCUs had 32 aircraft in use with very experienced crews acting as trainers. Bomber Command had invested heavily in this advanced training, involving over 700 heavy bombers (mostly Stirlings and Halifaxes) and some 17,000 personnel. In May 1943 Stradishall had become known as No 31 Base and its sub-stations – Chedburgh and Wratting Common – shared this training responsibility. During this period Stradishall was also engaged in Blind Approach training, and for over two years it ceased being a strictly operational airfield. However, in November 1944, a new Group was formed in Bomber Command – No 7 – to co-ordinate and centralise all this advanced training, which released the Base for operational flying.

Just before Christmas 1944 the airfield echoed to the sound of Lancaster BIs and IIIs of No 186 squadron, which had been reformed as a heavy bomber unit at Tuddenham just a few months earlier. The squadron saw out the rest of the war at the airfield. Its last bombing mission took place on 24th April 1945 when just 13 Lancasters bombed railway yards at Bad Oldersloe. Over 100 Lancasters took

After Wellingtons, Whitleys and Stirlings, Lancasters finally came to Stradishall just before Christmas 1944.

part in almost the last wartime operation of Bomber Command and not a single aircraft was lost. The town, which is almost midway between Hamburg and Lübeck, had not expected a raid at such a late stage of the war and its air-raid precautions were said to be 'slack', with the result that over 1,000 people were either killed or injured in this operation. During its brief operational life with Lancasters the squadron mounted over 1,200 sorties losing just eight aircraft in action and another four in accidents.

Like so many other squadrons in Bomber Command, No 186 was active in both Operation Exodus and Manna during late April and early May. In total over 460 Exodus flights were made to Brussels and later to other airfields to collect British prisoners of war who had been recently liberated from their camps. Some 75,000 prisoners were brought back to England by this method. These missions were the most pleasurable for all who took part in them. 'Never had aircrew, returning weary and battered from a mission, made a more joyous landfall than these passengers, who came crowding into the navigator's and engineer's cockpit to peer with eager eyes for the first glimpse of the white cliffs of Dover.'

From 29th April until the German capitulation on 8th May Bomber Command was engaged on Operation Manna – the dropping of food in western Holland, which was still in German hands. On 7th May 15 Lancasters left Stradishall for the racecourse at The Hague, one of the agreed dropping points. Bomber Command made over 3,000 sorties, dropping some 6,670 tons of food until the area was liberated. However, most crew members realised this was their final mission of the war and as they returned to base there was time to recall all those friends and comrades who had not returned – it was also a very sad moment.

As the stained glass window at the parish church shows, the RAF retained Stradishall for another 25 years and during this time some of the most famous fighters of the post-war Service appeared at the airfield – Spitfires, Meteors, Vampires, Venoms, Javelins and Hunters. But perhaps rather appropriately, considering its considerable wartime training commitment, Stradishall's final years as an active RAF station were as a training establishment.

29
SUDBURY

One of the lasting and most enduring effects of the presence of the Eighth Air Force in East Anglia was the many close and friendly relationships that were built up with the local communities around and near their many airfields. Even 50 years later this affection still remains strong and constant and most of the combat groups have their own local people dedicated to keeping these historic links and fond memories very much alive. It might seem a little invidious to single out just one Group to exemplify this aspect of the Eighth's sojourn in England, but it does appear that the 486th Bomb Group, which was based at Sudbury from April 1944 to August 1945, was particularly successful in achieving strong bonds of friendship with the residents of this historic town and its neighbouring villages. They are remembered by two memorials – one near the entrance to the old airfield and another fine and imposing commemorative stone outside St Gregory's church, dedicated in July 1987. During their brief stay the young American airmen made quite an impact on the town!

It all started in August 1942 when a site between the villages of Acton and Great Waldingfield was selected for a USAAF airfield and work was started in the following year. Known for some time as 'Acton' the airfield was finally handed over to the Eighth Air Force on 23rd March 1944 as Station 174 although by now it had taken its name from Sudbury, which was about two miles to the south.

The first ground personnel of the 486th Bomb Group moved in early on 5th April 1944 after a long overnight train journey from Scotland, where they had only arrived the previous day. They were joined a week or so later when the aircrews arrived with their B-24Hs. The Group was one of the five B-24 Groups allocated to the Third

B-17s of 486th Bomb Group: note the group's mark 'W'. (486th BG Association via R. Andrews)

Division and was placed in the 92nd Combat Bomb Wing, which also proceeded to set up its headquarters at the airfield. The only other member of the Wing was the 487th Group stationed at nearby Lavenham.

All Bomb Groups comprised four Bomb squadrons. In the early days each squadron had a complement of twelve aircraft, but as supplies of aircraft improved this figure was increased to 15 and later to 18. The Group's squadrons were numbered from 832 to 835, and each had its own call sign, which were Trappist, Pebbly, Deepset and Nightdress respectively! Before the Group had left America, the Commanding Officer, Colonel Glendon Overing, had allowed the aircraft of No 834 squadron to be named after the signs of the Zodiac, and there was an ex-commercial artist serving with the Group – Corporal Brinkman – who vividly illustrated some of the signs of the Zodiac on the B-24s.

The two new Groups went into action on the same day – Sunday 7th May. Heavy clouds over the target – railway yards at Liège in Belgium – frustrated accurate bombing. A mission to the same target on 20th May resulted in two of the Group's aircraft crashing after take-off. A rather sorry aspect of these unfortunate incidents was that the mission was ultimately aborted by the Division because of the heavy cloud cover. Indeed, on this day the Eighth Air Force lost no less than eleven aircraft due to accidental causes.

The first loss due to enemy action occurred on 28th May when the three Divisions mounted a major offensive against German oil targets with over 1,300 aircraft engaged in the day's operations. The Third Division's B-24 Groups were bound for the Wintershall synthetic-oil refinery at Lutzendorf set in deep southern Germany. This was the Group's longest mission to date and it would be a very stern test for the inexperienced crews. Just three of the 106-strong B-24 force failed to return and two belonged to the 486th. By the end of the month 13 missions had been completed for the loss of just four aircraft. Certainly many Bomb Groups fared far worse during their first month of operations.

However, soon, like the other B-24 Groups in the Third Division, the crews would relinquish their rather inelegant aircraft for the sleek, streamlined and more comfortable B-17Es; this was despite the fact that they had only recently been supplied with the new model Js. Their last operation with the B-24s was to Düren, some 25 miles south-east of Cologne, and of the 34 aircraft sent out that day (21st July) just one failed to return. The change came in the last weeks of July and although the short break from operations no doubt came as a blessed relief, after all they had completed 46 missions in about twelve weeks, the crews, both on the ground and in the air, were busily engaged in a hectic familiarisation programme with their new aircraft. The change of aircraft also brought about different Group identity markings; in place of the 'Square O' the tail-fins carried a white W in a dark square. In just nine days the Group was ready for its first B-17 mission, which was mounted on 1st August and turned out to be no more exacting than a gentle trip across central France to Tours airfield. The following afternoon it was France once again, this time rail targets in the Pas de Calais area – each was conducted with the minimum of fuss and incident.

Hamburg and its oil refineries proved to be a vastly different matter – three aircraft failed to return, two of them had unfortunately collided over the target area. That was on Friday and on the following Sunday (6th) at the early morning briefing the crews knew the worst – the target was Berlin, which really was the ultimate test for any Bomb Group, be they experienced or not. The stories of the Eighth's early and costly raids to the German capital in the previous spring were only recent history and they must have been uppermost in most crews' minds as they prepared for this mission. However, on this occasion the crews of the 486th passed this severe test with flying colours, in that they managed to survive perhaps the heaviest flak defences in Germany without a single loss. The joy and relief of this successful mission must have been very real at Sudbury that evening, a great boost to the crews' morale.

During September and October the Group undertook 30 missions losing seven aircraft. Such an intensity of action ensured that there was a rapid turnover of crews, as some of the lucky ones reached the magical number of 35 missions and departed back home to the States, only to be replaced by yet more eager youngsters, all keen to get into the fight. The Group was moving inexorably towards its first major milestone – its 100th mission. However, before that was achieved the crews were involved in a rather rugged operation to the Leuna oil complex at Merseburg.

On 2nd November, 680 aircraft from the two B-17 Divisions made a combined strike and it proved to be a very harsh day indeed, with 46 B-17s lost and well over half the force returning with flak damage. Just two aircraft from the Group failed to return. One was called *Blue Streak*, which had received a direct hit on the main fuel tank and was quickly engulfed in flames leaving no possible hope of escape for the crew. The navigator – 2/Lt Beeson – was on his 32nd mission and so close to the end of his tour. Furthermore the aircraft belonged to No 834 squadron and this casualty brought the squadron's remarkable record to an end. Just five days later the 100th mission was mounted with an attack on Neumünster airfield, which was situated about halfway between Kiel and Hamburg; one crew were compelled to force-land their badly damaged B-17 near Ghent in Belgium.

Although the Eighth was a young Air Force in more senses than one and although the average age of its aircrews was 21 years, not all were young lads. The 486th had the oldest pilot on operations in the whole of the Eighth – Captain Dick Grace – who, when pressed, admitted to the ripe old age of 46 years! Grace had been a combat pilot in the First World War, a Hollywood stunt flyer, and a ferry pilot. Such was his fame that he almost became a living legend in the Eighth. On Boxing Day he was piloting the lead aircraft of the Group and whilst over Coblenz his aircraft was badly damaged by flak (later 156 holes were counted) and yet he still managed to bring the aircraft back to Sudbury on only two sound engines. He was injured by flak but after a short spell in hospital he was back on operations on 10th January 1945 – his 47th birthday! Grace completed his tour with the 486th but refused to go back to the United States. Somehow he managed to wangle a posting to 448th Group at Seething in Norfolk as an Assistant Group Operations Officer, and he even managed to

B-24s of 833 Squadron of 486th Bomb Group. (486th BG Association via R. Andrews)

fly some missions on their B-24s before finally being ordered back to the States in April 1945. He no doubt felt that as the war was virtually over, all the excitement had gone out of operations!

Whether they be old friends or newcomers to the Group the loss of crews was always keenly felt by other members of the Group, if for no other reason than each casualty was a sharp and painful reminder of their own mortality and that their luck could just as easily desert them. The nearer a crew approached the figure of 35 missions the more they carried the earnest good wishes of the rest of the Group. It was therefore a rather chastened and soulful group of airmen that returned to Sudbury on 3rd February 1945. The relief at having survived another visit to Berlin – Templehof marshalling yards – was tempered by witnessing one of their B-17s go down in flames as it reached the English coast. The aircraft was *Blue Grass Girl* and whilst it was over the North Sea the rear gunners had come forward to celebrate the end of their tour. Suddenly the aircraft burst into flames. Four parachutes were seen to open and the fifth crewman jumped too late as the aircraft crashed near Southwold. It was later discovered that the pilot and the co-pilot had given their parachutes to the gunners, who were unable to return to retrieve theirs – five men were killed. It seemed a cruel and bitter blow for the crew to survive a last mission to Berlin and yet to crash almost within sight of their own airfield.

Most Bomb Groups felt, quite rightly, that with the coming of April they were on the 'home run'! The harsh winter weather had passed, the Allied armies were making rapid strides into Germany and the targets that the Groups had incessantly bombed just a few weeks earlier were now being captured almost daily. And yet, for some unaccountable reason, April proved to be a particularly disastrous month for the 486th, their worst of the war. They lost nine aircraft in just four missions, which proved to be 27% of their total losses for the whole of the war, and this was at a time when the overall losses of the Eighth Air Force were minimal – barely 0.6%.

On the 7th of the month whilst in action over airfields in central Germany, two aircraft were lost – one, from No 835 squadron, was struck by fragmentation bombs from an aircraft above it. The following day Grafenwöhr, south of Bayreuth, and its munitions factories were the target and three crews failed to make it back to Sudbury. Two days later another two aircraft came to grief over Brandenburg, and then a week later (17th), whilst in the Dresden area, the only two aircraft to be lost out of a force of 410 B-17s both came from the Group. Perhaps the crews had become complacent as they were aware that the war was rapidly coming to a conclusion, and as a result their tight formation flying had suffered. However, it seems more likely that it was purely a matter of being in the wrong place at the wrong time – the Group's luck had suddenly taken a turn for the worse.

Their last operational mission was flown on Saturday 21st April and all the aircraft returned safely. Rather unfortunately six airmen were killed when two aircraft collided on a training flight in early May. One of the B-17s crashed, whilst the other managed to make it back to Sudbury. However, despite this rather unhappy conclusion to their operations, the 486th can be justifiably proud of their war record – 188 missions completed, with over 8,000 individual sorties flown, all for the loss of 33 aircraft through enemy action, another 24 due to accidental causes. Apart from these impressive sets of figures the young men of the 486th Bomb Group earned the respect and affection of the people of Sudbury and the surrounding villages, and that surely is their best memorial.

30

TUDDENHAM

When the airfield at Tuddenham was completed in the autumn of 1943, two things became virtually inevitable; that it would be placed under the control of Base 32 (Mildenhall), which was almost a stone's throw to the north-west, and that Short Stirlings would ultimately use the new airfield. There had been so many Stirling squadrons in No 3 Group that the manufacturers – Short Brothers – had set up a special depôt at Madingley near Cambridge, not only to undertake basic repair work if necessary but also to make modifications to their aircraft. However, when the Stirling IIIs of No 90 squadron arrived at Tuddenham during the middle of October, their existence as a front line bomber – certainly over German targets – was rapidly coming to a close. No 90 squadron had experienced a somewhat chequered and rather peripatetic wartime career thus far. However, the squadron's travels were now over and it would settle down at Tuddenham for the rest of the war.

Within a day or so of their arrival (13th October) at the airfield some of the crews found themselves engaged on mine laying at the French ports along the Bay of Biscay and this type of operation was proved to be the bread and butter work of the squadron for the next six months or so – Brest, Lorient, Frisian Islands, Biscay and Texel all figured large in their itinerary. During the major Bomber Command raids to Berlin and Leipzig during January and February 1944 the Stirling squadrons were out in strength mining the Dutch coast and Kiel Bay some hours in advance of the main bomber force with the intention of drawing the Luftwaffe night fighters. Often on these mining missions the crews dropped massive amounts of 'window' as they flew across the North Sea in order to simulate the approach of a large force. These metal anti-radar strips had been first used on the famous Hamburg operation of 24/25th July 1943 and had been designed by the boffins to affect the German Würzburg radar, which controlled the night fighters, flak batteries and searchlights.

It was in September 1943 that the Allied Chiefs of Staff were alerted about the threat of V-rockets: 'it is probable that the German Air Force has been developing a pilotless aircraft for long-range bombardment in competition with the rocket, and it is possible that the aircraft will arrive first.' Already the USAAF had attacked a large site at Watten near St Omer and subsequently seven of these sites were located; the task of bombing was laid to the Eighth Air Force and AEAF. It was not until the end of November that almost 80 'ski sites', as they were known, for launching V1 rockets were identified, and they were mainly sited in the Pas de Calais. Of these identified sites Bomber Command were allocated eight and although Air Chief Marshal Harris was reluctant to divert his forces he agreed, with the proviso that mainly Stirlings should be used for this task.

Operation Crossbow, as it was known in the RAF, commenced on 16/17th December when 47 aircraft – 26 of them Stirlings – attacked two sites near Abbeville and the mission was not particularly successful. Over the next month some 400 sorties were mounted with an astonishingly low loss rate, just one Stirling lost. However, Air Chief Marshal Harris had managed to persuade the Air Ministry that such attacks were more suited to the light and medium bombers of the 2nd Tactical Air Force and it was not until June when the V1 rockets were actually landing on south-east England that Bomber Command returned once again to the V1 rocket sites.

During the early months of 1944 as a build up to the invasion of Europe, the quantities of supplies being dropped to Resistance workers in France, Holland, Belgium and Germany was quite beyond the resources of No 38 Group, with the result that the Stirling squadrons of No 3 Group were brought in to assist on these special operations. No 90 squadron started on these clandestine missions on 3/4th March when nine Stirlings were operating over dropping zones in France. The following night one of the squadron's aircraft fell to enemy flak whilst over the Savoy region of France, this was followed by two more later in the month. In April the squadron was seconded to No 38 Group and it launched another six operations losing five aircraft in the process. The last sorties flown by the squadron took place on the night of 7/8th June.

Already the squadron was being equipped with Lancaster Is, the

Memorial to members of No 90 Squadron on the village green at Tuddenham.

crews being trained at the Lancaster Finishing School at Feltwell. The first Lancaster mission was sent out on 10/11th June when a variety of railway targets at Achères and Dreux were bombed; it proved to be a quite costly mission with 18 aircraft lost out of 432 despatched. Five nights later railway yards at Lens and Valenciennes were attacked with an even heavier cost – over 5%. On the night of 16/17th June Bomber Command returned to the rocket sites, and No 90's crews were in action over the Pas de Calais; these missions were marked by 'Oboe' Mosquitos. There was such an intense bombardment of these sites by the Allied Air Forces that they became so marked with craters that it was almost impossible to discover from photographs just how much damage was sustained on each bombing mission!

On the night of 17/18th June the squadron's Stirlings left on their last operational mission – mine laying off the Channel Islands. Whilst the squadron had been operating in No 3 Group it had mounted over 1,930 sorties, losing 58 Stirlings in action (3%) – another example of how the Group's Stirling squadrons had suffered compared with Bomber Command's other heavy bombers.

During June and July Bomber Command were called upon to operate in support of the Allied armies in Normandy. On 30th June came the first operation in daylight when 266 aircraft – Lancasters, Halifaxes and with a few Mosquitos leading – bombed a road junction at Villers-Bocage, where tanks of the two German Panzer divisions were moving forward to the frontline. The operation was controlled by a Master Bomber and it demanded a high standard of accuracy from the crews, with the pilots instructed to come down to 4,000 feet in order to be sure of seeing the markers in the smoke. Over 1,000 tons of bombs were dropped with quite amazing and devastating accuracy, which ensured that the planned advance of the German divisions did not take place. Just two aircraft were lost and all of the crews returned safely to Tuddenham.

On 7th July over 460 bombers attempted to break the deadlock between the armies north of Caen, but although once again the bombing was very accurate with just the loss of a single aircraft, the target area had been poorly selected. Much of the bomb damage occurred to the north of Caen and unfortunately had little effect on the German forces that were grimly defending the city. Eleven days later (18th) the Air Forces mounted a massive air offensive in support of the Allied armies' Operation Goodwood. Over 900 aircraft from Bomber Command bombed five fortified villages east of Caen – over 5,000 tons of bombs were dropped and this is now recognised as the most successful operation carried out by the Command in direct support of the Allied armies in Normandy. Such air power was devastating and it was repeated in September when the Command launched a series of heavy raids on enemy positions around Le Havre that were still holding out. Six daylight operations were made for the loss of just two aircraft.

On 5th October 'C' Flight of 90 squadron was transferred to form the nucleus of another Lancaster squadron – No 186. This squadron had originally been formed in April 1943 as an Army-support unit equipped with Hurricanes, then Typhoons and finally Spitfires, before being renumbered as 130 – a fighter squadron with the Air Defence of Great Britain. Few RAF squadrons could have claimed such a variety of commands during such a short space of time! The crews were ready to mount their first operation from Tuddenham on 18th October when 18 Lancasters joined a force of 110 Lancasters bombing Bonn in daylight.

This was the first completely independent operation mounted by No 3 Group and over one-third of the aircraft were fitted with G-H, the blind bombing device. These aircraft had their tail fins prominently marked in order that other aircraft without the

Stirling III of No 90 Squadron. (Via J. Adams)

advantage of G-H would follow the G-H leaders and bomb when they did. Bonn was not a strategic target, with no industry to speak of, in fact it was a fine old town, which had hardly been attacked during the war. It is probably for these very reasons that Bonn was selected because it would be easier to discover just how effective the G-H operation had been. It proved to be a most successful mission with the heart of old Bonn virtually destroyed; only one aircraft was lost.

This first and very satisfactory use of G-H Lancasters really set the pattern for No 3 Group's squadrons for the rest of the war. The Group proceeded to launch heavy and very effective operations to mainly oil targets in and around the Ruhr. It was perhaps only right and proper that this Group should have made such a resurgence at this late stage of the air offensive. It had largely led the Command's early bombing raids with its Wellingtons before going through a torrid and expensive time with its Stirling squadrons.

By December No 186 squadron had left for Stradishall and the 90th once again had the airfield for itself. Most of the missions to the Ruhr were undertaken by day with a heavy fighter escort. Although not all of the targets were oil or indeed in the Ruhr. On 2/3rd January 1945 over 500 Lancasters of four Groups went once again to Nuremberg, which of course had seen the heaviest defeat of the war for Bomber Command almost nine months previously. This could almost be likened to a revenge mission, it was a powerful demonstration of the might of Bomber Command with the centre of the city almost obliterated. The important industrial area containing the MAN and Siemens factories was severely damaged. Just four Lancasters were victims of enemy flak and two more crashed in France. However, Bomber Command would return again to this target in the next two months, most notably on 16/17th March when over 10% of the Lancasters were shot down by night fighters. The crews of Bomber Command were finding, like their colleagues in the Eighth Air Force, that the Luftwaffe was certainly not a spent force.

For the last two months of the war the squadron was joined by No 138 squadron, which had spent most of the war engaged on special operations. The crews arrived at Tuddenham on 9th March with their Lancaster BIs and by 29th March three crews joined 90 squadron on a G-H operation to the Hermann Goering Benzol oil plant at Salzgitter, south-east of Hanover. Unfortunately due to heavy cloud that obscured the target area, no results of the bombing could be seen, but no losses were suffered.

During April both squadrons were in action over the Leuna synthetic oil plants near Merseburg, and four nights were engaged at Kiel specifically attacking the Deutsche Werke U-boat yards, which proved to be a most accurate and damaging mission. Just three nights later Kiel was targeted again but without the same success, even Bomber Command rated it as 'a poor attack'! The following night the Command launched their last major offensive against a German city when 500 Lancasters bombed the Army barracks at Potsdam near Berlin – not a single aircraft was lost. A daylight operation to the railway yards at Munich took place on the 19th, followed by the Command's last operation against oil targets at Regensburg – a name etched on the hearts of the Eighth Air Force! The squadrons' last operations were mounted on 22nd April when 28 aircraft left Tuddenham for Bremen to attack the city in advance of an offensive to be made by the British XXXth Corps. Only about 200 of the 767 force actually bombed. Because of the heavy cloud and the smoke and dust caused by the early bombing the Master Bomber called a halt to the operation. Just three days later Bremen was captured; it was the first major German port to fall to the Allied Forces.

For the very short time that No 138 had acted as a pure bomber squadron, it had mounted nine raids for the loss of just one aircraft. However, it is fair to say that the squadron's fame was made prior to arriving at Tuddenham when at least 438 operations were carried out on Resistance work flying Halifaxes, Stirlings, Whitleys, Lysanders and Liberators of which almost 70 aircraft were lost. The *Official*

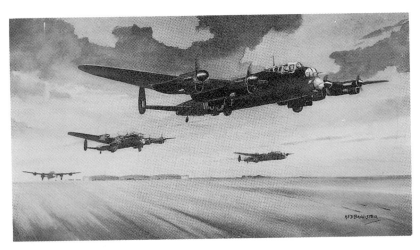

Lancaster Is: three squadrons of Lancasters operated from Tuddenham in the last stages of the war.

History of the Royal Air Force 1939-45 includes some statistics of these special duties operations: '. . . Between 1942 and 1945, in round figures, 6,700 persons of 18 nationalities were dropped or landed in Europe and 42,800 tons of supplies conveyed to their correct destinations in 22,000 sorties . . .' The squadron could take pride in the large part they played in this 'secret war'. In the post-war Service No 138 became one of the first RAF V Bomber squadrons.

No 90 squadron had a fine war record with 412 raids mounted for the loss of 86 aircraft (1.9%) and this has been proudly remembered by the village with a fine memorial sited in the centre of the village green. There is also a propellor from a Stirling of No 90 squadron in the village church at Beck Row, which is close to Mildenhall. This Stirling crashed on 9th November 1943 whilst on a fighter affiliation exercise with a Hurricane from Newmarket Heath; the nine crewmen were killed, only the fighter pilot survived.

31

WATTISHAM

This famous RAF station is now the home of 7th Battalion REME and 3rd Regiment of the Army Air Corps, with only helicopters using the airfield that once echoed to the sounds of generations of famous RAF aircraft from Blenheims right up to Phantoms. For over 50 years the RAF used this pre-war airfield and despite this long period of service, it could be argued that its real days of glory were during the first three years of the war when its Blenheim squadrons left on so many brave operations mounted by No 2 Group of Bomber Command. The losses sustained in these missions were quite staggering; indeed, at one period it was considered that a posting to the Group was close to a sentence of death! The sheer determination and bravery of the Blenheim crews were quite outstanding and they have written a glorious page into the history of the RAF.

The airfield first came into operational use in April 1939 under the aegis of No 2 Group and the two squadrons of Blenheim IVs – Nos 107 and 110 – that were based there at the outbreak of the war actually formed one third of the strength of that Group, less than 150 Blenheims in total – a somewhat meagre bomber force that would all too quickly be reduced in numbers when they went into action.

The motto of No 107 squadron was 'We shall be there' and it certainly lived up to that adage by being engaged in the very first bombing operation of the war. On the afternoon of 4th September 1939 15 Blenheims, five each from Nos 107, 110 and 139, set out to bomb a large German warship, which had been sighted near Wilhelmshaven. The Blenheims of No 139 could not find the target and so they returned to Wyton. The Wattisham squadrons were more successful in their quest, as Flt/Lt Ken Doran, who was leading

110 squadron described: '. . . Within a few minutes the cloud base lifted to 500 feet and we saw a large merchant ship; just behind it was the *Admiral Scheer* [the pocket battleship *Admiral von Scheer*] . . . We climbed as high as we could, which was about 500 feet and made one attack in a shallow dive . . .' Unfortunately the bombs that struck the German vessel just bounced off its armoured plating and the only damage that was inflicted in the raid, was by the Blenheim that crashed onto the cruiser *Emden*. Only five aircraft (one from 107 and four from 110) arrived safely back at Wattisham – a 50% loss on the station's first operation, which was an ominous sign of things to come.

Just over a week later one of the most famous airmen of the Second World War arrived at Wattisham – Wing Commander Basil Embry. He had been selected to take command of No 107 squadron and was quite determined that his squadron 'would carry the torch in No 2 Group'. His first Blenheim sortie took place on 25th September. It was a solo photo-reconnaissance flight over Münster and although his aircraft was attacked by two enemy fighters he managed to evade them and escape with just superficial damage. These flights were particularly lonely and dangerous missions for the crews as the Blenheim was certainly no match for the Luftwaffe fighters. Wing Commander I. Cameron, the CO of No 110 squadron crashed at Kiel on one of these flights and they became so costly that by November the Group called a halt to them.

After a spell of detached duty at Lossiemouth in Scotland, where both squadrons were engaged in bombing attacks and anti-shipping strikes off southern Norway, the crews arrived back at Wattisham at the beginning of May just in time to face their severest test over the old battlefields of the First World War. From 10th May, when the Germans launched their offensive in the west, until after the evacuation at Dunkirk, the Blenheims in conjunction with the ill-fated Battles of the Advanced Air Striking Force fought a most courageous, very unequal and bloody battle suffering grievous losses to enemy flak and fighters. They attacked bridges, enemy positions and troop movements, most of the time flying in very low, almost at ground level in the face of severe ground flak. Frequently two operations a day were flown and as Embry later wrote, 'By the law of averages our survival was impossible'. On no less than 15 occasions Embry brought home a badly damaged aircraft. On 14th May Embry led the two squadrons against the bridgeheads near Sedan. Although the Blenheims were on this occasion escorted by Hurricanes, nevertheless it was the terrific barrage of flak that caused the

Blenheim IV 'R3600' of No 110 Squadron at Wattisham. (Via J. Adams)

problem; at the end of the mission five aircraft had been shot down and another two had to force-land on their return. At one stage the squadrons had less than three serviceable aircraft and during this brief period of operations Embry was awarded two bars to his DSO.

On 26th May Embry was informed that he had been appointed to command West Raynham in Norfolk as acting Group Captain. So keen was he to stay with the squadron that he attempted to get the posting delayed but without success. However, the following day he was handing over command to his successor – Wing Commander L.R. Stokes – when an order came through for the squadrons to attack enemy columns which were approaching the BEF at Dunkirk. With Stokes going along for the experience, Embry commanded the squadron for the last time. His aircraft was shot down near St Omer, by a strange coincidence close to where another legendary airman, Douglas Bader, also came to grief about a year later. Embry managed to bale out but was captured, then he escaped and his subsequent amazing adventures are admirably recalled in his book *Mission Completed*. Three years later Embry returned to No 2 Group as its AOC. His name, along with Bader, Gibson, Cheshire et al, is writ large in the annals of the RAF during the Second World War.

At the beginning of June 1940, No 2 Group Headquarters issued an order: 'It is essential that the destructive effects of our night bombing operations over Germany should be continued throughout daylight by sporadic attacks on the same objectives. The intention is to make attacks only when cloud cover gives adequate security. These attacks will be made *regardless of cost.*' Each station in the Group was allocated separate targets, Wattisham was given the oil refineries at

Air Chief Marshal Sir Basil Embry GCB, KBE, DSO (3 bars), DFC, AFC. (RAF Museum)

Hamburg and Wanne-Eickel and the marshalling yards at Hamm and Osnabrück. The squadrons were also directed to raid airfields which were being used by the Luftwaffe to bomb Britain. On one such mission, to Amiens, No 107 squadron lost five out of six aircraft despatched. Towards the end of the year the Blenheims were also operating at night attacking airfields in northern France, Holland and Belgium in an attempt to prevent the returning Luftwaffe bombers from landing safely.

However, came a new year, came another new type of operation – Circus. These oddly named missions involved maybe a handful of Blenheims despatched with a very large escort of fighters to targets of no real consequence, because the main object of the exercise was to draw the Luftwaffe fighters into action. They proved not to be particularly successful operations and were, of course, limited by the operational range of the fighters. One thing to be said in their favour was that they were relatively light in casualties, mainly because the Luftwaffe did not often rise to the bait. During the whole of 1941 No 110 squadron lost only two aircraft on these missions and No 226, which had replaced No 107 in May, lost three Blenheims.

The same could not be said for another new operation – Channel Stop – which was introduced in the spring of 1941. This was an attempt to close the eastern approaches of the English Channel to enemy shipping by day. The Blenheims normally operated in pairs and were escorted by fighters. However, the attacks involved a slow dive from 5,000 feet through heavy flak and considering that their 250 pound bombs had only five-second delay fuses there was very little time to get clear. Many aircraft crashed either into the sea or directly onto the vessels. Each Blenheim squadron was expected to take their turn on these dangerous operations and they were normally detached to Manston in Kent. They proved to be very costly, some squadrons only managed to last about two weeks before being denuded of aircraft and crews. No 110 squadron was at Manston during May and June and survived very well, although one of their Blenheims lost early in May had completed 48 missions – a rare occurrence in No 2 Group as only seven Blenheims managed to survive 50 or more sorties.

In July and August the Blenheims of No 2 Group made two memorable attacks against the docks at Rotterdam. On 16th July, 36 aircraft made a low-level attack, which caused considerable damage, for the loss of four aircraft. Then on 28th August 18 Blenheims made a second attack in which at least two large merchant ships were badly damaged as well as several dock installations set on fire. However, seven of the 16 failed to return and also one had crashed on take-off – a 50% loss! It is not surprising that the average loss rate on the Blenheim daylight raids was double that of the night operations. Although deeply concerned by such horrifying losses Winston Churchill was full of admiration for the sheer determination and bravery displayed by the crews of No 2 Group. At the end of August he sent a message to the headquarters of the Group: 'The devotion of the attacks on Rotterdam and other objectives are beyond praise. The Charge of the Light Brigade at Balaclava is eclipsed in brightness by these almost daily deeds of fame.'

Just after Christmas 1942 No 110 squadron was detached to Lossiemouth in Scotland to support the first combined operation of the war against German-held territory – a Commando raid on the island of Vaagso off the Norwegian coast, which took place on 27th December. Just six Blenheims of the squadron made an attack on shipping in the area in order to draw the Luftwaffe fighters away from the Commando landing. Unfortunately four aircraft were lost – a harsh end to the year for the Wattisham squadron. However, three months later the squadron would leave for service in the Far East.

Wattisham was left with just a single Blenheim squadron – No 18 – although the days of the Blenheim as a bomber were now severely numbered. In the previous October three Douglas Boston IIIs had arrived at the airfield for trials and tests; the American Boston would make its first operation in No 2 Group in March 1942, to be followed by other American light/medium bombers – Mitchells and Venturas.

During March 1942 another aircraft appeared at Wattisham – Bristol Beaufighter Is of No 236 squadron. The squadron had recently been stood down from operations and most of its experienced crews sent out to the Middle East; the remainder formed the nucleus of a new squadron to operate with Coastal Command. These twin-engined aircraft had first been designed as a long-range fighter but with the heavy night raids of 1940 they were rushed into service as the best night-fighter available to Fighter Command. Immensely robust with an armament of four cannons, six machine guns, and with a top speed in excess of 300 mph it proved to be a most successful and versatile night-fighter, especially when equipped with the improved AI radar. However, the aircraft ultimately found its real forte as an anti-shipping strike aircraft able to carry a torpedo, rockets or bombs. The squadron made its very first anti-shipping sorties from

Wattisham on 15th March and by June the aircraft were adapted to carry two 250 pound bombs; the rest is history. In July the squadron left for Oulton but by the end of the year it made up part of the first Beaufighter Strike Wing at North Coates.

The writing was on the wall as far as Wattisham was concerned, its time as an RAF wartime base fast coming to a close. On 4th June 1942 it had been allocated to the Eighth Air Force. In a final flourish eight Blenheims of No 18 squadron went out on the night of 17/18th August to attack airfields at Rheine, Trente and Vechta and all returned safely. This proved to be the last operational flight by Blenheims in Bomber Command, and appropriately Wattisham had mounted the first and last Blenheim operation of the war. When No 18 squadron moved out to West Raynham on 24th August, it was a sad day for the station – the farewell to those truly historic aircraft of the Second World War.

The Americans moved in during September and there were plans to use the airfield as a heavy bomber base, which would necessitate the building of concrete runways, so the construction work was immediately put in hand. However, the Eighth Air Force also had a pressing need for an Advanced Air Depot and the airfield was selected for the use of 4th Bomb Wing, as there seemed no good reason why the ample facilities at the airfield should not also house a combat unit.

The first American aircraft to land did not in fact belong to the Eighth Air Force, but were P-39Ds of 68th Observation Group attached to the Twelfth Air Force and destined to serve overseas. These rather unorthodox aircraft were probably better known as Bell Airacobras and were quite distinctive in as much as their Allison engine was placed to the aft of the cockpit, which ultimately gave rise to servicing problems

By the end of November 1942 most of the P-39s had left for North Africa and the air depot was beginning to take shape due south of the airfield. On 14th December it was designated the 4th Strategic Air Depot and named Hitcham from a nearby village. Although there were already four hangars at the airfield, another four were built as well as more hardstandings. During June 1943 the construction of the runways was suddenly halted with only one completed and the other two barely started. Because of changed plans it had been decided that the airfield would no longer house heavy bombers but a Fighter Group instead. Thus the two partially completed runways were finished by using steel meshing. Furthermore it was proposed that the depot would now specialise in the repair and overhaul of fighters, mainly P-47s.

It would be almost another twelve months before the first operational aircraft arrived. During May 1944 the fairly rare P-38J Lightnings of 479th Group landed at Wattisham. This became only the fourth P-38 Group in the Eighth and it brought the Fighter Command up to its planned complement of 15 Groups, giving the Eighth some 900 fighters against an estimation of the Luftwaffe day force of maybe 1,500. However, the Ninth Air Force had about 1,000 fighters and with the RAF fighters, it would suggest that as the Allied forces had an overwhelming superiority in numbers the air battle was as good as won – it certainly did not prove to be quite that simple!

Lt Colonel Kyle Riddle, the Group's Commanding Officer, managed to get his pilots ready for operations within just eleven days of their arrival, and they owed their name to him – 'Riddle's Raiders'. No less than 58 aircraft set out on their first mission on 26th May, which proved to be a fighter sweep of the Dutch coast just to get the pilots familiar with the area and operational control procedures. It was quite amazing that the Group went almost a month before its pilots claimed their first victory in the air and by that time they had lost eleven aircraft. They did not shine in the first few months, only managing to chalk up 18 victories, and those for the loss of 42 aircraft either in action or in accidents. The inferior performance of the P-38, especially at high altitude, and its unreliability had decided the Eighth Fighter Command to exchange its P-38s for P-51s.

On 4th June the P-38s were painted with black and white stripes around the wings and tail booms, although with its rather distinctive and unique profile these recognition markings would seem superfluous. The pilots joked that the Naval gunners would shoot at anything that moved above them! The P-38s were given the task of escorting the Allied shipping armada across the English Channel on D-Day. Almost 4,500 ships were engaged in Operation Neptune and a rota system was devised so that at least two P-38 squadrons would be on Channel patrol from dawn to dusk. These tended to be rather tiresome exercises, especially as the Luftwaffe was conspicuous by its absence and the pilots felt that the action was elsewhere. They were more than delighted to hear that from 12th June this responsibility would be taken over by RAF and the Ninth Air Force's fighters.

During the next six weeks the Group suffered a steady trickle of losses with only two victories to balance the loss of 14 aircraft, mainly in accidents. On 28th July the Group went out on the longest trip to date – Merseburg. It was during their return from this operation that the first sightings were made of one of the Luftwaffe's new weapons – the rocket powered Me163. The following day the Group was over the same target and Captain Arthur Jeffrey chased a Me163. It was last seen going into a vertical dive and after aerial photographs had been examined Jeffrey was credited with the first victory of a jet fighter. However, after the war the German records did not show a fighter lost on that day.

Although the Group seemed to have problems finding enemy aircraft in the air, the pilots had become rather adept at ground strafing and it was on one such mission, on 10th August, that the Commanding Officer was shot down. Lt Colonel Riddle managed to bale out, evade capture and finally made it back to England. The command was offered to Lt Colonel David Schilling, the Group Executive of the 56th but he preferred to remain with the Group. However, his Commanding Officer, Colonel Hubert Zemke volunteered himself for the post. No doubt this was very popular with the Group's pilots as his fame had spread throughout the Eighth Air Force. Zemke arrived at Wattisham on 12th August and just six days later he led them on their most successful ground-strafing operation so far, with over 100 aircraft claimed destroyed, although this figure was later amended to 43 destroyed with another 28 damaged after close examination of the combat films. About three weeks later the Group had another excellent day, claiming 52 aircraft destroyed on the ground; it can certainly be said that Colonel Zemke was having a great effect on the pilots.

By September the Group was in the process of re-equipping with P-51s and on the 26th of the month the Group had their most successful day of the war so far whilst engaged in providing support for the Allied airborne landings in Holland – 27 Me109s were destroyed in a short but sharp air battle. It is interesting to note that the Group had 31 P-38s and twelve P-51s on this mission and Zemke claimed two victories, his first whilst flying P-51s. For this operation and their earlier ground-strafing mission the 479th was awarded its only Distinguished Unit Citation. It was not until 9th October that P-38s were finally phased out of the Eighth Air Force.

On 30th October there was a sad blow for not only the Group but also for the Eighth Air Force when Colonel Zemke, Lt/Col Herren (the Group Executive) and another pilot were lost when their P-51s broke up in a severe storm to the south-east of Hamburg. Herren was killed

P-51 of 479th Fighter Group. (USAF)

but Zemke managed to bale out and was taken prisoner of war. The Eighth could ill afford to lose such a brilliant pilot and leader as Zemke. At the time his victories totalled 19½ (mainly with the 56th Group) and he finally retired from the USAF in 1967. In the light of these tragic accidents it is interesting to note that by this time all fighter pilots were using the Berger pressure suits, which were designed to prevent pilots losing consciousness during aerial combat, steep dives and spins. These 'G Suits' as they became known, probably saved many lives and gave the American pilots a decided advantage over the Luftwaffe pilots who were not similarly suited.

The new Commanding Officer was none other than Lt Colonel Riddle, who had acted as Zemke's deputy since returning from his foreign escapades. Perhaps December could be considered the Group's most successful month and despite the unfavourable weather conditions it managed to mount 17 missions. From 23rd December until the New Year it was active every day and completed the month with 41 victories to add to its now growing total. Unfortunately four aircraft were lost on Christmas Day, one of which was shot down by American anti-aircraft guns in Belgium! In February whilst on an escort mission to Berlin one of the pilots returned to Wattisham claiming to have destroyed an 'enemy' B-17 on the ground at Steernizk airfield. Nobody seemed prepared to believe his story, least of all his fellow pilots, but when the combat film was developed, his very unlikely claim was confirmed!

The following month, along with two other Fighter Groups, the

479th went to Italy to add support for the Twelfth Air Force's bombing mission, but it was a short sojourn in the sun because they were back in time for Operation Varsity – the Allied armies' crossing of the Rhine. Like most Fighter Groups the 479th went out on escort for the last of the Eighth's bombing missions, directed at airfields and rail targets in southern Germany and Czechoslovakia. Only one enemy aircraft was shot down, the very last Luftwaffe fighter to fall to the Eighth's guns – the end of what had been a very long, hard and bitter battle of attrition. The aircraft was credited to the 479th and 1/Lt Hilton Thompson. It was his second jet – an Arado 234 – which was a very effective reconnaissance/bomber; few American fighter pilots could claim one jet destroyed, let alone two! In less than twelve months the Group managed to mount over 350 missions and accounted for almost 440 enemy aircraft in the air and on the ground. The airfield was returned to the RAF on 15th December 1945 and thence commenced its second RAF life as a fighter base par excellence with all the famous RAF fighters of the post-war era – Meteors, Hunters, Lightnings, Javelins and Phantoms – operating from there.

32

WESTLEY

This small airfield, which was situated to the west of Bury St Edmunds on the A45, has completely disappeared under a large housing estate. In 1938, it was a snug little airfield with two small hangars, serving the needs of the West Suffolk Aero Club purely for pleasure flying. Perhaps because Westley was close to a rather large Army camp – the Suffolk Regiment had its headquarters at Bury St Edmunds – the small airfield was earmarked for the use of the Army Co-operation Command, which had been formed in late 1940.

The first squadron to be formed at Westley came into being on 30th September 1940 and it was numbered 268. It was equipped with Westland Lysander IIs; these 'Lizzies' were ideally suited to Westley as they were specifically designed to land and take off from rather confined landing strips. The Lysander, of course, was also designed for Army Co-operation work and the squadron immediately became involved in mounting patrols along the east coast, keeping a watch for any invading forces as well as working closely with the Army's Eastern Command. Soon, however, it was recognised that the Lysanders were becoming rather obsolete and it was decided to re-equip the various Army squadrons with Curtiss Tomahawks. These American fighters had proved to have a poor performance at high altitude and were thus not really suited for escort duties so another role had to be found for them – low-level tactical reconnaissance missions appeared to be their forte. However, the Tomahawks needed a far longer runway than that found at Westley so, on 1st April 1941, it was decided to move the squadron to the newly constructed airfield at Snailwell, just over the county boundary in Cambridgeshire, which had just opened as a satellite to Duxford. The connection between the two airfields was retained with Westley being used for circuits and landing training by some of the aircraft from Snailwell well into 1942.

However, by 5th August 1942 Westley became fully recognised as an RAF station in its own right and soon another squadron was in residence – No 652 (AOP or Air Observation Post). This squadron was originally equipped with de Havilland Tiger Moths. The Moth had become a legend in the Service. It had been designed as a two-seater trainer, which had first come into service in November 1932. Before the war no less than 44 RAF flying training schools used them, then with the vast increase of the training commitment during the war this number had nearly doubled. The majority of RAF pilots, both pre-war and wartime, had completed their basic flying training on these aircraft and forever held a fond appreciation of the little aircraft. The Tiger Moths proved to be the last bi-plane trainers used by the RAF and were still being operated by some units of the Vounteer Reserve even as late as 1951. The aircraft had a small engine (130 hp), which gave it a top speed of a mere 109 mph, but it cruised at less than a ton! The Tiger Moth could hardly be said to be a potent war machine, but perhaps it could lay claim to have been one of the world's most famous training aircraft, and most certainly it served the Service very well.

By the end of the year the Moths were being phased out of Air Observation Post duties and they were replaced by Taylorcraft Austers. These aircraft were of an American design and produced by Taylorcraft Aeroplanes (England) Ltd under licence. They were the direct military version of their very popular civilian sports aircraft which, in 1938, had sold for £450! The aircraft was exceedingly light in construction, indeed it was the manufacturer's proud boast that

British Taylorcraft Auster I – the Austers were very familiar at Westley. (Via J. Adams)

the tail section could easily be lifted by 'a young lady'! They were also blessed with the ability to need a very short take off and landing run, and although they appeared to be very fragile they proved to be quite rugged and Austers saw service in North Africa, Italy and in Europe after the Normandy invasion. Nearly 1,600 in varying marks were produced during the war and they became indispensable for Army support duties.

On the very last day of 1942 the second and last squadron to be formed at Westley – No 656 – came into existence and it was also equipped with Taylorcraft Austers. The pilots had been trained at No I School of Army Co-operation, which was based at Old Sarum near Salisbury. However, the squadron was not destined to stay very long at Westley as early in 1943 the crews left for service in India. Although the Army Co-operation Command was disbanded on 1st June 1943 when the Second Tactical Air Force was formed, several Taylorcraft Auster squadrons still used Westley and were involved in the various Army exercises mounted during late 1943, especially the major exercise Link mounted by the Eastern Command during 13/19th September 1943. However, after the Normandy landings in June 1944, the operational need for the airfield ceased and no more flying from there took place. Westley's rather inconspicuous existence as a warfield airfield came to an abrupt end.

33
WOODBRIDGE

'Give me a heading for Woodbridge' was the crisp order given by many a bomber pilot to their navigators, with the reassurance that their chances of making a safe landing had been so greatly enhanced since Woodbridge had been opened in November 1943. Although the airfield was known officially as an Emergency Landing Ground – specifically constructed for helping aircraft in distress – it was known by all aircrews as the 'Prang or Crash-drome' or sometimes just plain 'Oz' from its pundit code (recognition letters). But by whatever name it was called, Woodbridge proved to be a veritable haven for several thousands of aircrews who were struggling back home in either badly damaged aircraft or desperately short of fuel or, as was more often the case, flying back in rather adverse weather conditions. No less than 4,115 aircraft made emergency landings at Woodbridge and the vast majority of their airmen survived to fly again even if many of their aircraft did not.

Woodbridge airfield was once likened to 'a large slab of concrete carved through a pine forest' and this rather unflattering description was probably fairly accurate, as its main feature was one massive concrete runway measuring 3,000 yards long and 250 yards wide, which was five times the width of a normal runway then in use; and in addition there were two grassed areas at either end of the runway, each 500 yards long, to take account of any under or over-shoot.

It was not until 1943 that specially designated emergency landing grounds were first developed when the long grassed runway, some 4,500 yards in length, at Wittering began to be used for such landings. However, it was quickly found that damaged aircraft blocked the runway, greatly effecting the station's normal operations and

This Junkers 88 landed at Woodbridge in July 1944.

furthermore that Wittering was really too far inland to be of much practical use. Other sites, as close as possible to the coast, were sought and three in eastern England seemed ripe for development – Manston, Carnaby and Woodbridge.

The airfield was situated in the rather exposed and open landscape of Sutton Heath some four miles south-east of the town, and it was often referred to as 'RAF Sutton Heath'. It was almost surrounded by a large Forestry Commission plantation, and could be a rather bleak place especially in the winter but it had one important climatic feature, it appeared to be virtually free of fog. These large emergency runways were all built east to west so that any disabled aircraft could make a dead straight approach from the sea and land downwind. Woodbridge's runway was completed in November 1943 but even before the station was formally opened several aircraft (mainly American B-17s) had already made use of the partially completed facilities, indeed the first emergency landing had been successfully accomplished on 18th July 1943.

Within 14 days of its opening no less than 54 landings had been made, ample evidence to show just how much such a 'prangdrome' was needed. About 30% of all the landings made at Woodbridge were brought about by bad weather conditions over the home stations, which was normally due to fog or low cloud base. A perfect example of this occurred on the night of 16/17th December 1943 when Bomber Command's heavies were engaged over Berlin. On their return most of the crews found that all of eastern England was covered by extremely low cloud. On this night no less than 32 Lancasters came to grief either by crashing or by being abandoned by their crews. It proved to be the worst night of the war as far as bad weather accidents were concerned and allied to the 25 aircraft lost on the raid, this Berlin mission turned out to be a very costly affair. It was a busy night for Woodbridge and a particularly unfortunate one for the Halifaxes of Nos 138 and 161 squadrons from Tempsford that had been despatched on SOE missions over France. Because of the low cloud over the dropping zones all the Halifax missions were aborted. Only one aircraft managed to make it safely back to Tempsford, the rest tried to land at Woodbridge. One made it safely down but another failed to locate the runway and hit a pylon, killing three of the crew and injuring three others. Another Halifax made too low an approach and crashed into the river Deben with one fatal casualty. Yet another aircraft had problems in making the right approach and crashed into trees near the airfield and two more plunged into the sea off the mouth of the river Orwell. The final Halifax was lost off the Lincolnshire coast. A very harsh night for the Special Duties squadrons and as a result of these tragic accidents the runway lighting at Woodbridge was improved.

During this same unfortunate night many Lancasters were diverted to Ludford Magna and Graveley airfields, which were then equipped with FIDO; this was short for Fog Investigation Dispersal Operation although the RAF later maintained that it should be more properly called 'Fog, Intensive, Dispersal Of'! Basically FIDO was a system by which large pipelines were laid along each side of the runway into which petrol was injected under pressure, which was then fired by burners set at certain intervals along the pipeline; the intense heat so created caused an updraught that dispersed the fog in the near vicinity of the runway. It was said that visibility could improve from 200 to 2,000 feet by using FIDO.

The first tests took place in February 1943 at Graveley and further experiments were made during the next six months or so, some at nearby Lakenheath. One flying test conducted early in November reported, 'FIDO is a practical emergency aid, provided the pilot is sufficiently competent in instrument flying and beam approach on the aircraft type.' The first operational use was on 19/20th November 1943 at Graveley and the decision was taken to install it at the three Emergency Landing Grounds as well as several selected airfields spread through eastern England, for instance locally at Foulsham in Norfolk and Tuddenham in Suffolk. Such landings were not for the faint-hearted and some pilots said it was like flying into 'the mouth of hell' or 'Dante's inferno', although another described it more

Lancaster taking off with 'FIDO' in action. (Via T. Murphy)

poetically as '. . . into a great glowing cathedral with a fire-framed nave . . .' FIDO was not only instrumental in saving the lives of many crews but it also enabled Bomber Command to maintain its operational schedule when weather conditions at the home stations would have dictated otherwise. The system became operational at Woodbridge in June 1944.

During March 1944 Woodbridge experienced a very busy month with 150 aircraft using the airfield. On 24/25th March when the last operation of the Battle of Berlin was mounted, no less than nine badly damaged aircraft landed there in just half an hour. This operation has gone down in RAF folklore as 'The Night of the Strong Winds' when winds of over 130 mph were experienced over the target area and the North Sea. These were the indirect cause of a very poor and scattered bombing and the heavy loss of aircraft to enemy action – 72 missing or over 9% of the total force.

The number of support units to cope with all these emergency landings was considerable. A detachment of No 54 Maintenance Unit based at Newmarket Heath arrived to deal with the damaged aircraft and had at their command a full range of cranes, bulldozers and other heavy lifting equipment; later USAAF personnel were detached to Woodbridge to deal with the numerous American aircraft that were forced to use the airfield. The medical staff were on a 24 hour alert to attend to the many injured crews and the catering facilities had to be very flexible as it was never known from day to day just how many airmen would need to be fed.

On 13th July 1944 there was a most surprising landing – a Junkers Ju88GI – a twin-engined night fighter from Volkel in Holland. The pilot had become completely lost due to the malfunctioning of his wireless and radar equipment and he was quite convinced that he had landed on an airfield near the Danish/German border! The aircraft was completely intact and moreover was fitted with the latest FUG220 Lichtenstein interceptor radar, as well as a Flensburg homing device, which was designed to counter the effects of Bomber Command's 'window'.

From 19th to 24th March the airfield was closed to landings because it was involved in the build-up for the massive airborne operation code-named Varsity – the Allied armies' crossing of the Rhine, in which over 1,500 aircraft and 1,300 gliders took part. Woodbridge's large runway was literally crammed with 48 Hamilcars and twelve Horsa gliders along with 60 Halifaxes from Nos 298 and 644 squadrons to act as their towers. After five days of hectic loading with tanks and armoured vehicles the force took off at 6 am on the 24th and was said to be completely airborne within 40 minutes.

During the last three months of the war 230 aircraft had used the airfield for emergency landings but by the end of July the figures fell off sharply. Nevertheless, Woodbridge had made an immense contribution during its short wartime existence and thousands of Allied airmen owed their lives to the welcoming lights of the airfield, returning after long and harrowing operations. After the war the RAF retained the airfield, mainly for experimental work, until March 1948, when Woodbridge was placed under 'care and maintenance' for over four years. Then during June 1952 the airfield received a new lease of life as the first American jet fighters arrived and from then on it was developed into a major USAF base. The Americans have now departed and like so many RAF airfields throughout the country, Woodbridge's future has yet to be decided.

34

CIVILIANS
AT WAR

On the evening of 8th May 1945 Winston Churchill addressed the large and jubilant crowds that had gathered in Trafalgar Square to celebrate VE Day with the following words: 'God bless you all. This is *your* victory – the victory of the cause of freedom in every land. In all our long history we have never seen a greater day than this.' Thus ended what has been described as 'the people's war', and for all those who lived through the war years, whatever their age, it would be an experience that they would never forget!

The changes wrought by the Second World War were probably more apparent in East Anglia than elsewhere and they inevitably had a great effect on those living in the area. Like the other counties in East Anglia, Suffolk was predominantly rural with over half the population living in the countryside rather than in the three main towns – Ipswich, Bury St Edmunds and Lowestoft. Suffolk people had always been known for their independent manner; they tended to be self-contained and very slow to accept change. It is a county of churches, manor houses, country pubs, thatched cottages and winding lanes, where in 1939 cars were something of a rarity, with horses still in regular use on the farms and on the roads. Most of the country areas were then devoid of electricity, mains water and sewerage and little seemed to have changed since the days of the last Great War.

However, this 'rural paradise' was in the throes of a deep agricultural depression with many of the farms left untenanted and thousands of acres of farmland uncultivated and derelict, with thousands of people having left the land. In February 1939 over 2,000 agricultural workers from Suffolk had marched to London to protest about the low prices for agricultural produce. If nothing else the war, with its insatiable demand for food and the large financial incentives to increase its production, would force dramatic changes on the agriculture in the county and bring forth modernisation in farming methods, which perhaps otherwise would have taken many decades. Nevertheless it was the presence of almost 30 operational airfields in the county that brought the biggest changes for the local people, and more especially after 1942 when there was a vast influx of American airmen, who by D-Day numbered over 70,000!

Unlike August 1914 when the declaration of war had brought about a frenzy of euphoria throughout the country, Neville Chamberlain's broadcast on 3rd September 1939 was greeted with an equanimity almost bordering on a tired resignation, with a very real fear of the anticipated aerial bombardment that would surely follow fairly imminently.

From the beginning of the year the country had been placed on a war footing. In January the National Services Committees, under the Air Raid Precautions Act passed in December 1937, were established and the first Civil Defence volunteers – wardens, firemen, first aid helpers, ambulance drivers, demolition and rescue workers – were recruited. Soon Suffolk, except for Ipswich, had far more volunteers than established posts – especially in the case of air raid wardens. One of the Government's deep concerns was the threat of poison gas attacks and ultimately some 38 million gas masks were distributed to the civilian population with instructions that in the event of war, they should be carried at all times. Anyone who was compelled to wear one of these gas masks, if only in the regular practice drills, has never forgotten the chilling experience, or indeed the very distinctive and unpleasant smell of the rubber!

During the early part of the year air raid sirens began to appear in towns and many of the important public buildings assumed a strange appearance as they were surrounded with sandbags. The provision of public shelters was rushed ahead, although they would never accommodate more than 10% of the population, trenches were dug and buildings were requisitioned for Civil Defence purposes. The Government debated long on the question of private shelters, and ultimately it was decided to offer air raid shelters to all households. They were of a corrugated sheet design, intended to be sunk several feet into the ground and then covered with earth or sandbags. They

WAAFs hauling up a barrage balloon. (Daily Telegraph)

became known as Anderson shelters from Sir John Anderson, who in 1938 had taken charge of the nation's Civil Defence. These shelters, which were free to all households with an income of less than £250 per annum, became a feature of so many suburban gardens and a lasting image of the war days.

On 24th August the Emergency Powers (Defence) Bill was passed because of 'the imminent peril of war', and people rushed home from their holidays on the coast to await the dread news. The Bill gave the authorities very wide and almost draconian powers. This was just the beginning of countless and seemingly endless restrictions placed on civilians. Houses could be entered and searched without reason or warning, property and land could be requisitioned for war use at will, people could be moved from certain areas, the ports and railways were taken over by the Government and bus and train services greatly curtailed.

The evacuation of children from London began on 1st September and the first trains pulled into Suffolk towns, with other parties arriving by paddle steamers at Lowestoft and Felixstowe. Many eye-witnesses considered this 'the most heart-rending consequences of the beginning of the war'. The images of young children labelled like parcels, their boxed gas masks around their necks and clutching their few prized possessions, were one of the most poignant sights of the war. The operation also brought to light the depth of poverty and hardship suffered in many areas of London and other big cities. Some of the evacuated children later recalled the peace and quiet of the Suffolk countryside, as if 'the war had gone away'; though most remembered best the food, '. . . fresh eggs, rabbit pies, fruit tarts . . .' However, the decision to billet the children, and sometimes the mothers, in private houses became a quite controversial issue, especially when refusal could lead to a £50 fine! In the event many children returned home by the end of 1939, only for thousands to move back again during the latter months of 1940.

Perhaps the most immediate signs of the war were the strict imposition of blackout regulations, the daily wail of the air raid sirens, which seemed to be activated for the slightest reason, and the appearance in the skies of the barrage balloons. As far as the blackout was concerned, heavy and dark material had to be placed at all windows, car headlights were hooded, traffic lights deflected down, and, of course, street lighting became a thing of the past. At first the blackout did give rise to some annoyance and there was a very marked increase in the number of road accidents and minor injuries. However, somewhat grudgingly the public adapted to the change, without really ever accepting it, and indeed it was considered by the majority of the public to be the greatest inconvenience of the war – rationing and bombs included! The restrictions stayed firmly in place until September 1944 when the all-out blackout was replaced by 'half-lighting', though not in coastal regions.

The barrage balloons soon became the most familiar sight in the British skies, and were somewhat aptly called 'pigs'; although people living close to a site often gave them personal names. They did however provide the public with a certain feeling of security and satisfaction that they were being defended, although it could be said that their defensive qualities were somewhat over-rated. In fact it is thought that they were the cause of the downfall of more friendly aircraft than the enemy! When inflated with hydrogen, which cost about £30 a time, they measured some 66 feet long and 30 feet high and could reach a height of 10,000 feet.

The so-called Phoney War, which really lasted from September to April 1940, was rather remarkable for the lack of enemy activity over

273

England. The dire and frightening heavy bombing that had been predicted by the Government since early 1939 had not materialised. Furthermore the public were becoming rather blasé about the sirens, the blackout and other petty restrictions, and indeed greatly resented the rather officious manner of many of the volunteer defence workers, especially air raid wardens, who in any case were often regarded as 'draft dodgers' and were not the most popular members of the community. The issue of identity cards and the requirement that these should be produced on demand to anybody 'in authority' caused considerable animosity, so much so that the armed forces and the police were ordered to only request their production 'for extreme reasons'! It was a far from easy time for civilians; petrol rationing had been introduced in September followed two months later by the first food rationing – bacon and butter – and in the New Year by sugar, ham, cheese and meat. Also the winter of 1939/40 proved to be the coldest since 1881 with severe frosts and heavy snowfalls, which were not made easier to bear by the acute shortage of fuel.

This unreal world was rudely shattered on 30th April when a Heinkel bomber crashed into a house at Clacton and its mines exploded, killing two civilians with another 132 injured – the first civilian casualties of the war in England. The German invasion of Holland and Belgium suddenly marked a difference in the war

Old Pill Box looking very forlorn in a field near Euston.

situation and the mood of the country reflected this change. The formation of an all-party coalition government headed by Winston Churchill only emphasised the perilous state of the country and most of the population were convinced that invasion was imminent. In June, *Rules for Civilians in case of Invasion* was issued to all households, which instructed people to stay put in their houses, hide maps, petrol, food and bicycles and await other directions! Churchill's now famous speech at the end of May, which promised the country '. . . nothing but blood, toil, tears and sweat . . .' only illustrated the gravity of the situation.

The whole of the East Anglian coast was designated a Defence Area with the children from towns such as Southwold, Aldeburgh and Felixstowe being evacuated. Later only essential workers would be allowed to remain in this area, and severe restrictions were placed on movements in and out of a ten mile distance from the coast. Strange constructions began to appear throughout the county – anti-tank traps, concrete emplacements, rolls upon rolls of barbed wire, and the very familiar pill-boxes, many of which have survived to this day; indeed it has been suggested that they should now be preserved as historical buildings! At the end of May all the road signs disappeared, as did the names on railway stations and maps were taken out of shops. The carrying of cameras led to grave suspicion and there were several spy scares in the county, foreigners were rounded up, and posters exhorting people to 'Be like Dad, keep mum!' appeared in public places. 'Careless talk costs lives' was treated very seriously indeed. Later, censorship of letters was brought in for those people who lived close to airfields.

On 14th May Anthony Eden made a radio appeal for men between the ages of 17 and 65 years to join a new force – the Local Defence Volunteers – and the response was instant; within a week over a quarter of a million had enrolled for what became known, at Winston Churchill's suggestion, as 'The Home Guard'. Almost every village had its own platoon and soon the Home Guard began to make their presence felt throughout Suffolk. Their primary function was to deal with any parachute invaders and they took their duty very seriously. They manned road blocks, patrolled their territory and inspected the identity cards of anyone moving during the hours of darkness. By mid 1942 they numbered almost 1.6 million but by that time the real threat of invasion had long passed. Despite the images created by *Dad's Army* it eventually developed into a well-trained force that was used as a reserve army, releasing regular units for other military

'Land Army girls were in great demand for the local dances' – an American Red Cross club in Suffolk.

duties. On the night of 18/19th June 1940 a member of a LDV platoon near Newmarket was credited with capturing the first Luftwaffe airman shot down from a Heinkel III, whilst it was engaged in attacking RAF Mildenhall.

One of the features of the early war years was the number of women taking on voluntary war-work. The contribution of the Women's Voluntary Service – WVS – was quite prodigious. It had been first formed in 1938 to assist the ARP and ultimately the Service had over one million members. Their duties were quite varied, from operating reception and rest centres, and mobile canteens at airfields, to dealing with evacuated children, distributing clothes and other items to bombed-out people, and manning telephones during air raids and emergencies. The first WAAFs, too, began to appear at the RAF airfields at Mildenhall, Wattisham, Honington, Stradishall and Martlesham Heath. The Women's Auxiliary Air Force was formed in June 1939 and ultimately they would serve at all the airfields in

Suffolk, including the American bases, as well as operating many of the barrage balloons.

But perhaps the most obvious sign of these changes could be observed in rural Suffolk with the welcome appearance of the Land Army girls in their green jumpers, khaki corduroy breeches and wide brimmed hats. They were drawn from all walks of life and soon became an essential part of the Suffolk countryside. After a month's training they were sent to the farms and quickly proved to be excellent workers, gaining rather grudging praise from the suspicious farmers. Great concern was expressed about their 'moral welfare', especially after the arrival of the Americans when the Land Girls found themselves to be in great demand at the Saturday dances at the many Suffolk airfields!

It was on 22nd May 1940 that the first bombs fell on Suffolk. Some dropped harmlessly off Felixstowe and one at Butley landed very close to Bentwaters airfield. However, during June the RAF airfields attracted attention from the Luftwaffe with Mildenhall appearing to be a special target, although later in the year Martlesham Heath, Honington, Stradishall and Wattisham would all come under attack. During June both Ipswich and Lowestoft suffered their first air raids and these two towns would bear the brunt of enemy raids on civilian targets, although neither suffered as much damage as Norwich and Great Yarmouth. On 3rd July both Ipswich and Lowestoft sustained daylight 'terror attacks'. By the end of the war Ipswich had been bombed on 50 separate occasions, causing over 480 deaths and serious injuries, but Lowestoft fared worse with some 80 raids, which resulted in 266 killed and almost 700 persons seriously injured. The heaviest and most destructive raid occurred on the afternoon of 13th January 1942 when much of the heart of the town was destroyed with 69 fatalities and another 104 seriously injured. The town of Newmarket sustained particularly heavy damage in October 1941. Besides the airfields being obvious targets, the several Chain Home radar stations along the coast – Hopton, Dunwich, High Street and Bawdsey – attracted enemy attacks. In fact all the towns along the coast, and Southwold in particular, were prey to enemy intruder raids as well as to being strafed by machine guns. The almost continuous alerts as enemy aircraft entered the region's airspace and the almost continual threat from the skies proved to be particularly stressful despite the fact that Churchill maintained that, 'Everyone should learn to accept air raids and air raid alarms as if they were no more than thunderstorms'!

The local Home Guard on the march at Stratton. (Mrs Ellen Barber)

Everybody, especially schoolchildren, was exhorted to support the various National Savings campaigns, in fact 'save' was the watchword of the war, and 'Make-do and Mend' seemed to be the slogan of the day. Old metal, rags, bones, rubber, pots and pans, and waste paper were religiously collected, nothing but nothing was thrown away. There is a delightful piece of wartime film showing a crowd of young Suffolk lads collecting tins and pots and pans in a battered old pram. Perhaps the most famous phrase of the war years was 'Dig for Victory'! Allotments appeared in the most odd and unlikely places and the production of home produce was considered one of the most important civilian tasks of the war. Despite the influx of Land Girls, everybody was exhorted to spend their week's holiday working on the land. These 'harvest helpers' came in fairly large numbers to Suffolk and were housed in special centres to lend a hand with the harvest or potato picking; most admitted that it had been a very exhausting but wonderful experience! Another feature of life in the county was the several 'jam making centres' that were set up by the Women's Institutes and local children found a ready way to earn some pocket money by collecting jam jars for these centres.

Without doubt the greatest inconvenience and upheaval suffered by the local people during the whole of the war was the construction of the numerous airfields in the county. In 1940 there were just seven active RAF stations and four years later another 23 had been built. No corner of Suffolk was free from this massive construction programme, which reached its peak during 1943. It brought in its wake utter chaos with the narrow roads and lanes being choked with heavy machinery and lorries and deep in mud. Hordes of construction workers (mainly Irishmen) arrived and camped in tents around the villages until they moved on to, literally, fresh fields. The whole landscape of the area, which had hardly altered since the days of the enclosures, suddenly changed almost beyond recognition under the tons of concrete and airfield buildings and accommodation sites. It must have been a painful experience for those villagers that had lived in the area for all their lives.

It was during 1942 that the first American servicemen arrived in the county and these belonged to the Engineer Battalions of USAAF. Most villagers remember the day when 'the Yanks arrived'! It was quite a surprise for them to find that many of them were 'black skinned', the first time many Suffolk people had seen a coloured person. They found them polite and courteous, and many local people recall that they were not aware of any 'colour bar' until the white American servicemen arrived!

By the end of the year the first American airmen would begin to arrive in Suffolk and in the middle of 1944 they occupied no less than 19 airfields, well outnumbering RAF stations. It was said that by D-Day there were over 71,000 US servicemen in the county, more than were based in either Norfolk or Essex. It would be stating the obvious to say that their presence had a terrific impact on the local people. For most of the small villages that were close to the American air bases it was the biggest event for centuries. As one Suffolk lady remarked, 'I still remember the Yanks almost more than I do the war', and another commented, 'To go to one of their bases was absolutely fantastic because there were no shortages of anything. Each base was a little America, plenty of food and drink . . .' Soon Ipswich, Bury St Edmunds, Stowmarket, Sudbury and Lavenham echoed to the sounds of American accents as the streets were crowded with these young airmen. The roads too became crammed with their lorries and those omnipresent jeeps.

It could be said that there was a certain resentment at first. Their brashness, confidence, and at times arrogance were difficult to bear. The fact that they were very well paid and had ready access to all manner of goods that had long since disappeared from English shops made for bitterness and envy. However, their friendly and generous nature soon broke down the local reserve, and generally a very good relationship was established with the local communities; indeed, many of these friendships have lasted down the years. Most of the airbases became greatly involved with local charities, children's wards in hospitals as well as orphanages. The local pubs, of which there was no equivalent in the United States, became the favourite places of recreation for the Americans, and although at first they complained about 'the warm, flat and weak' British beer, they soon acquired a taste for it, which in itself caused certain problems. For the majority of the war beer was strictly rationed and when the 'No Beer' signs went up, the Americans just moved to another pub, much to the annoyance of the 'genuine locals'! Very many of the servicemen were 'adopted' by local families, and their laundry was undertaken in return for some welcome extra money to the family income. Many American airmen maintained that this entry into family life greatly helped them cope with the stress of operational flying and long-standing friendships were made.

By 1944 when 29 airfields were fully operational, the skies above Suffolk were rarely, if ever, empty and quiet. At night the RAF bombers left for their missions, returning in the early hours of the morning. Then barely a few hours later the American heavies took to the air for their daylight raids and would return mostly in the late afternoon, and so it would go on day after day and night after night. Although as one local resident recalled, 'The American aircraft would take off in the early hours of the morning, and after a time we got used to the noise and it didn't even wake us'!

Perhaps now the greatest danger from the air for the local people was the threat of Allied aircraft crashing either from accidents or on returning to their home bases badly damaged. Those living in close proximity to the airfields could be said to be under a constant threat. Fortunately there were few tragic accidents that resulted in the deaths of civilians.

During 1944 there were an increasing number of night intruder raids over Suffolk. These were conducted by Me410s, which were quite difficult to prevent due to the speed of the aircraft, as it almost matched that of RAF Mosquitos. However, by the middle of June 1944 the Luftwaffe attacks on Suffolk had virtually ceased, except for the odd and sporadic raid on mainly airfields. Since the invasion of Europe most civilians felt, with some justification, that the long trial

A party of Land Army girls at Risby. (Mrs Diana Abrey)

was nearing an end and at last there was some light at the end of the tunnel. However, just after midnight on 16th July the residents of Peasenhall, north of Saxmundham, were awoken by a terrific explosion overhead; this announced the arrival of the first V1 rockets over Suffolk. These flying bombs or doodlebugs, so dreaded for their noise and indiscriminate nature, would proceed to fall on the county until the following January. One Suffolk man described them as 'very noisy beasts with flames coming out of their backsides'! The two worst months proved to be September and October when, because the rocket bases in northern France had been overrun by the Allied armies, the Germans took to launching them from Heinkel IIIs from over the North Sea. During September Ipswich suffered from two attacks in which five civilians were killed and considerable damage was caused to over 1,000 buildings. In the same month buildings and houses in Southwold sustained severe blast damage from one of the rockets.

On 25th September the more deadly V2 rocket arrived in Suffolk at Hoxne. These 45 foot rocket projectiles, which flew faster than the speed of sound and carried one ton of explosives, unlike the V1s, gave no warning of their approach and caused considerable damage. Fortunately of the 13 rockets that were directed at Suffolk most landed in open countryside and two exploded in the air, so they did not cause quite as much damage as the earlier V1s. The final one landed on 20th January 1945 near Earl Soham.

Surely now victory was near? Life on the Home Front was just beginning to improve. There had been a slight increase in the food rations, beer had become more plentiful, ice cream suddenly appeared again, the strict blackout restrictions were lifted, the Home Guard had paraded for the last time, coastal resorts could again be visited, gas masks had been put away into lofts and forgotten. With the coming of spring, after yet another harsh winter, life appeared to be getting back to some semblance of normality. There was a rising tide of belief that perhaps the long and hard fight had not just been against Hitler and the Nazis, but also for a better and fairer Britain. One historian has suggested that 'The Luftwaffe was a powerful missionary for the Welfare State'!

The regular BBC news bulletins, which had become such an established and essential feature of wartime Britain, were followed with even greater interest as they chronicled the Allied armies' steady advance into Germany. Then on 2nd May came the announcement that the British people had been waiting to hear – 'Hitler died yesterday in Berlin'. Six days later the country was celebrating VE Day with victory parades, thanksgivings services, street and village parties, fireworks and rockets – a day of great rejoicing, only tempered by the fact that many loved ones were still engaged in the war in India, Burma and the Far East. One newspaper wrote that the VE celebrations were more 'a conscious sense of relief from strain, rather than triumphant exultation.'

The demise of the airfields after D-Day was really quite amazing, at least as far as the American bases were concerned. Within a matter of months most of the American airmen had left. As one Suffolk resident recalled, '. . . Everything became silent. The Yanks had come and now they were gone . . . one moment it was all noise and then dead silence and everything deserted . . .' These airfields remained empty and deserted, their runways and forlorn buildings providing a poignant reminder of the great void left by the departing servicemen. One perceptive resident recalled, '. . . it was if everybody was asleep.'

The 'people's war' had changed many things. Suffolk people had always been rather a close-knit society where they 'kept themselves to themselves', but the communal spirit engendered by the hardships and perils of the war had changed that for the better. Perhaps the wartime years had been, as A.J.P. Taylor believed, 'a brief period, in which the English people felt that they belonged to a truly democratic society.' The influx of so many Americans into the county did have an effect. They had challenged the British way of life and had brought fresh ideas and new concepts. Over the last 50 years many of the American servicemen that served at all these East Anglian airfields have returned again and again to revisit the area where 'their youth was lost', despite the fact that most of those airfields have, to all intents and purposes, disappeared almost as if they had never existed.

The civilian population had paid a heavy price for their victory – more than 60,000 killed (over one fifth of the total British casualties in the war) with another 86,000 seriously injured and countless thousands made homeless, even without the loss of so many fathers, husbands, brothers and sons. As King George VI expressed in his victory broadcast: '. . . the years of darkness and danger in which the children of our country have grown up are over, and please God, for ever. We shall have failed, and the blood of our dearest will have flowed in vain, if the victory which they died to win does not lead to a lasting peace . . .'

BIBLIOGRAPHY

During my research I consulted various books. I list them below with my grateful thanks to the authors, especially Roger A. Freeman – an aviation historian par excellence.

Andrews, Roland A., *The Threads of Yesterday: 486th Bomb Group*, R. Andrews, 1984.

Appleby, John T., *Suffolk Summer*, East Anglian Magazine, Reprint 1977.

Ashworth, Chris, *RAF Coastal Command, 1936-1969*, Patrick Stephens, 1992.

Bowyer, Michael J.F., *Action Stations: 1. Military Airfields of East Anglia*, Patrick Stephens, 1990.

Cooper, Alan, *Air Battle of the Ruhr*, Airlife, 1992.

Cross, Graham, *Raydon Airfield: Fighter Station to Farmland*, G. Cross.

Embry, Sir Basil, *Mission Completed*, Methuen, 1957.

Freeman, Roger A., *The Mighty Eighth*, Arms & Armour, 1989.

Freeman, Roger A., *The Mighty Eighth War Manual*, Janes Publishing Co, 1984.

Hamlin, John F., *The RAF at Newmarket*, J. Hamlin, 1989.

Holmes, Malcolm R., *RAF Beccles at War*, M. Holmes, 1994.

Kinsey, Gordon, *Aviation: Flight over the Eastern Counties since 1937*, T. Dalton, 1977.

Merrick, K.A., *Flights of the Forgotten: Special Duties Ops in WWII*, Arms and Armour, 1989.

Middlebrook, Martin, *The Battle of Hamburg*, Allen Lane, 1980.

Middlebrook, Martin, *The Berlin Raids*, Viking, 1988.

Middlebrook, Martin & Everitt, Charles, *The Bomber Command War Diaries*, Viking, 1988.

Moyes, Philip J.R., *Bomber Squadrons of the RAF*, Hutchinson, 1981.

Rawlings, John, *Fighter Squadrons of the RAF*, Crecy Books, 1993.

Richards, Denis, *The Hardest Victory: RAF Bomber Command in the Second World War*, Hodder & Stoughton, 1994.

Richards, Denis, *The Royal Air Force, 1939-45*, HMSO, 1953.

Smith, David J., *Britain's Military Airfields, 1939-45*, PSL, 1989.

RAF SQUADRONS

2	48
7	209
9	14, 120-5
15	198-202
17	173-4
18	256-7
22	91
25	173
46	175
64	49-50
71	176
75	197, 208-210, 229
85	173
90	139, 244-250
99	203-6
105	42
107	139, 206, 251-5
109	234
110	138-9, 251
115	194, 197
118	49
126	49
129	49
130	247
138	207-8, 234, 249-50, 267
139	7-8, 42, 251
149	151-6, 193-6
151	172
161	207, 267
165	49-50
182	176-7
186	236-7, 247-8
190	203
192	203
196	226-8
199	155-6
209	89-90
214	71-4, 230-5
218	74-5
226	139-40, 255
234	48-9
236	230, 256-7
242	175-6
249	175
254	230
280	43-5
298	269
299	226-8
310	122, 180
312	180
313	180
320	90
340	140
419	196
504	171
604	171
618	42
620	73-4
622	198-202
644	269
652	263-4
656	264
810 (FAA)	45
1419 Flt.	206-7, 232-4
20 OTU	151

USAAF GROUPS

25th Bomb Group	57
31st Fighter Group	28
34th Bomb Group	84, 181-5
44th Bomb Group	114
47th Bomb Group	59, 129-30
55th Fighter Group	167
56th Fighter Group	109-113, 116-7, 133, 222, 224
92nd Bomb Group	106
93rd Bomb Group	52-4
94th Bomb Group	59, 61-8
95th Bomb Group	41, 47, 92, 97, 129-137, 189
96th Bomb Group	145
97th Bomb Group	28
100th Bomb Group	133
310th Bomb Group	51
322nd Bomb Group	59-61
345th Bomb Group	165
351st Fighter Group	141
353rd Fighter Group	186-9, 220-4
356th Fighter Group	177-9
357th Fighter Group	88, 163-9, 219-20
359th Fighter Group	47, 189
361st Fighter Group	167, 189
364th Fighter Group	88, 126-8
385th Bomb Group	101-8, 143
388th Bomb Group	102, 142-9
390th Bomb Group	92-100
446th Bomb Group	51, 53-8
447th Bomb Group	211-8
448th Bomb Group	54
452nd Bomb Group	145, 184, 258-61
486th Bomb Group	238-43
487th Bomb Group	157-162
489th Bomb Group	113-5
491st Bomb Group	189-191
493rd Bomb Group	77-82
1st Strategic Air Depot	125
4th Strategic Air Depot	257
3rd Emergency Rescue Squadron	116-8

INDEX